WORK, FAMILY, and PERSONALITY:

Transition to Adulthood

Jeylan T. Mortimer
University of Minnesota

Jon Lorence
University of Houston

Donald S. Kumka
State University of New York at Buffalo

A Volume in the Series
Modern Sociology
Gerald M. Platt, Editor

ABLEX PUBLISHING CORPORATION
NORWOOD, NEW JERSEY

Printed in the United States of America.

Library of Congress Cataloging in Publication Data
Mortimer, Jeylan T., 1943-
　Work, family, and personality.

　Bibliography: p.
　Includes index.
　1. Work and family—Michigan—Longitudinal studies.
2. Personality and occupation—Michigan—Longitudinal
studies. 3. Adulthood—Michigan—Psychological aspects
—Longitudinal studies. I. Lorence, Jon P.
II. Kumka, Donald S. III. Title.
HD4904.25.M67 1986　　　306'.36'09774　　　85-20951
ISBN 0-89391-293-X

Ablex Publishing Corporation
355 Chestnut Street
Norwood, New Jersey 07648

Contents

Preface and Acknowledgements

This monograph represents the culmination of work extending over two decades. We explore the interrelations of work, the family, and personality as men make the transition from adolescence to adult work and family roles. Based on a panel study of 512 men, we examine the implications of experiences in the family of origin for subsequent occupational attainment, the effects of early adult work experiences on change in psychological orientations over time, and the linkages of work and men's own families of procreation.

Because the project has had such a long history, there have been many supporters and contributors. The study was initiated in 1962 as an assessment of the impacts of college on attitude change. The original investigators, Gerald Gurin and Theodore Newcomb, obtained data from entering freshmen at the University of Michigan. Their questionnaire assessed attitudes and values, as well as information concerning relations with parents and college experiences. This project, "The Michigan Student Study," extended through the respondents' senior year in college (1966–67). Shortly thereafter, Jeylan Mortimer, then a doctoral candidate at the University of Michigan, utilized these data for her dissertation on the process of career decision-making. This work focussed on the effects of family background characteristics and the college experience on the development of work values and occupational choice (Mortimer, 1972, 1974). She was supported by a National Science Foundation Graduate Fellowship (1968–1970) and a Rackham Dissertation grant (1969–70).

Further analyses of the Michigan Student Study data were undertaken in 1974–75, supported by a small grant from the National Institute of Mental Health (MH 26180), to examine the implications of relationships in the family for occupational value development and career choice. These analyses pointed to the importance of parental support as a mediator of the influence of the father's occupation on the son's values (Mortimer, 1975, 1976).

As these analyses proceeded, the value of an additional follow-up of the graduates became increasingly apparent. For only further data would allow assessment of the persistence of psychological orientations over time. Are work-related attitudes and values, formed in the context of the family of origin, and of such importance in the career decision-making process, fixed from the time of entry to the work force? Or do they continue to change over time, in response to important work experiences?

In 1976, a follow-up study was initiated to assess the psychological impacts of occupational experiences. It was jointly funded by the National Science Foundation (SOC 75-21098, 1976–78) and the Center for Studies of Metropolitan Problems of the National Institute of Mental Health (MH 26421, 1976–78). By repeating the same psychological measures that were obtained earlier, and including information on work experiences over the decade since college graduation, inferences could be made concerning the stability of earlier psychological attributes, and the effects of work experience on change in them over time. Jon Lorence, then a graduate student at the University of Minnesota, joined the study at this point. He began as field coordinator for the data collection effort and as data analyst and quickly became a full collaborator in the work. This research demonstrated the pervasive significance of work autonomy for psychological change (Lorence and Mortimer, 1981; Mortimer and Lorence, 1979a, 1979b).

As these analyses moved toward completion, our attention turned back to some of the earlier issues with which the research began. That is, how did the men's earlier work-related attitudes and values, nurtured in the family setting, influence their early occupational attainments? Moreover, we realized that a more comprehensive assessment of the linkages of work and family life was now possible, including the family of procreation for the men who married. Whereas the 1976 follow-up questionnaire concentrated on work experiences, enough information was obtained about the families of the respondents to permit this expanded scope. Therefore, the earlier more restricted focus on work and psychological change was extended to a more complex and multifaceted life course analysis of the transition to adulthood. This phase of the research, which led, most directly, to the development of this monograph, was supported by a two-year competing renewal grant from the National Institute of Mental Health (MH 26421, 1979–81). Donald Kumka, also a graduate student at Minnesota at that time, joined the study during this period, initially as data analyst, and subsequently as third collaborator. We turned to an examination of the effects of the family of origin and the family of procreation on psychological development and achievement during the early adult life course (Mortimer and Lorence, 1981; Mortimer and Kumka, 1982; Mortimer, Lorence, and Kumka, 1982). A comprehensive causal analysis of the development of five psychological dimensions, in response to experiences in both work and family, was undertaken. This analysis constitutes the foundation of

Chapters 2 and 3 of this volume. During this period, the first author was granted a sabbatical from the University of Minnesota (1979–80). A second leave from the university, during the 1983-84 academic year, enabled the completion of the monograph. The work was also supported by grants from the Graduate School and the University of Minnesota Computer Center.

The first chapter of this book introduces the conceptual framework, describes the panel, the questionnaire, and the data analytic procedures. It also sets forth the three closely related but analytically separable questions, which guided the research. A pervasive issue is the degree of psychological stability over time. Are individual psychological attributes mainly formed by the end of adolescence, or do they continue to change over time in response to major life experiences encountered in adulthood? A second, closely related concern is the effect of social structure, particularly occupational location, on the personality. A third issue involves the linkages of work and family life. How do these different spheres of life experience come to interpenetrate and mutually affect one another as they influence the developing personality?

The second chapter focuses on the family of origin as a source of development of psychological orientations that are conducive to early adult occupational attainment. A central concern is to examine the mechanisms through which parents enhance the attainments of their children. The third chapter assesses the implications of later life experiences, including educational attainment, the career pattern, and work experiences, for psychological change. The findings demonstrate the broad scope of attitude and value change that can be attributed to work experience.

Chapter 4 explores the interrelations of work and the family of procreation, considering the implications of marriage for occupational attainment; whether the family acts as a "buffer," modifying the impacts of work on the individual; and the effects of work experiences (including occupational attainments, involvements, and time demands) on the family. The final chapter summarizes the major findings and presents our conclusions. There are two appendices. The first presents information about the processes of locating the respondents and collecting the data; the second gives the questionnaire measures that are utilized in these analyses.

Because a series of publications has resulted from the study, it is important to note their relation to the contents of this volume. The conceptualization of psychological stability and change in Chapters 1 and 2, and the analytic model which forms the basis of Chapters 2 and 3 build on our earlier work on self-concept stability (Mortimer, Finch, and Kumka, 1982; Mortimer and Lorence, 1981). Chapters 1 and 4 incorporate material from a previously published literature review (Mortimer and London, 1984). All data analyses presented in the second and third chapters are new. However, they build on the findings of our earlier analyses of the effects of work on psychological change (Lorence and Mortimer, 1981; Mortimer and Lorence, 1979a, 1979b). Chapter 4 incorporates previously published analyses (Mortimer, 1980; Mortimer, Lorence, and Kumka, 1982) and presents new work as well. We thank the following publishers for permission to include prior work: Academic Press, JAI Press, Mayfield Publishing Company, Sage Publications, the University of Chicago Press, and the *Western Sociological Review*.

Given the duration of this project, there are many people who deserve our gratitude. Many of our colleagues have already been thanked for reading and evaluating our papers in previously published articles. We wish to acknowledge here those whose support and assistance have been sustained over a long period of time and those who have been especially influential in the development of the volume. At the University of Michigan, Gerald Gurin provided access to the 1962–1967 data, and with Zelda Gamson, also on the staff of the Michigan Student Study, gave much-appreciated help and support. Edward Laumann, as Jeylan Mortimer's doctoral advisor, guided the early explorations of the data and has continued to provide excellent advice and encouragement over the years. Max Heirich served on her dissertation committee, and was particularly helpful in the early development of the study.

The work of Melvin Kohn and Carmi Schooler and their colleagues at the Laboratory of Socio-Environmental Studies, National Institutes of Health, has been a most potent influence. Melvin Kohn's many readings and thoughtful critiques of our articles have been of tremendous benefit, contributing to the conceptual and methodological framework for the study over many years. We are indebted to Karen Miller and Joanne Miller for their support and suggestions at various stages of the study, and to Ronald Schoenberg for adapting the LISREL program for our use and for assistance and advice regarding statistical problems. Morris Rosenberg, previously also at the Laboratory, provided important suggestions which we have built upon, especially in Chapter 3. Others who have contributed helpful comments and suggestions include Orville Brim and Viktor Gecas.

Our present and past colleagues at the University of Minnesota have been most supportive of the study. Geoffrey Maruyama introduced us to confirmatory factor analysis and structural equation modelling with LISREL, and assisted us often as the analyses proceeded. Theodore Anderson and Robert Leik have also offered valuable suggestions related to the data analysis. Roberta Simmons gave us numerous critiques and encouragement. Richard Hall, while at the University of Minnesota and since that time, has read many of our papers and has contributed valuable suggestions. Irving Tallman gave us much support and useful criticism. Michael Finch collaborated with us in the analysis of self-concept stability and change (Mortimer, Finch, and Kumka, 1982), and provided much appreciated technical advice and assistance.

The research has also benefited from the careful work of student assistants, Mark Grey and Carmen Johnson, Linda Grohoski, and Joan Dreyer. Lisa Thornquist cheerfully and painstakingly typed and re-typed the many chapter drafts and corrections.

Finally, we are most indebted to the 512 respondents who participated in the study during their years in college, and carefully completed a 28-page questionnaire a decade thereafter. It is their contribution of time and effort, in spite of demanding careers and family lives, that ultimately made this study possible.

CHAPTER 1.

*Introduction**

In modern society, work and the family are the two most central institutions impinging on the life of a person. The family of origin is the main social context for personality development in the very early years of life. Even in adolescence, when teachers and peers share this socializing influence, the family is still central to the formation of the most basic, and enduring, psychological orientations. Morever, the socio-economic status of the family—determined mainly by its linkage to the world of work—sets important constraints on the educational and occupational achievements of the next generation. When individuals reach early adulthood, they form their own families. In this phase of life, the family of procreation takes on a crucial set of functions for the individual. It becomes the primary source of intimacy, companionship, and social support. At the same time, an important new role is added in the occupational sphere. The work role provides the person with economic resources, social status and identity, interpersonal relationships, and connection to the wider community. Work also determines the major experiences, challenges, and problems that people cope with on a daily basis. Social scientists are just beginning to recognize, and to systematically investigate, the impacts of work experiences on the personality, along with the effects of work on family life.

These important sources of influence on the person's development and well-being, in the family and in work, are generally studied quite independently of one another. Socialization, taking place in the family of origin, is investigated by family sociologists and child and adolescent

* This chapter builds on ideas presented in the following publications: "Persistence and Change in Development: The Multidimensional Self-Concept," in *Life-Span Development and Behavior* (Mortimer, Finch, and Kumka, 1982); "Self-Concept Stability and Change from Late Adolescence to Early Adulthood," in *Research in Community and Mental Health* (Mortimer and Lorence, 1981); and "The Varying Linkages of Work and Family", in *Work and Family: Changing Roles of Men and Women* (Mortimer and London, 1984).

1

psychologists. The effects of work experiences on the individual is the domain of occupational sociologists and social and vocational psychologists. It is our contention that work, family, and personality are linked, and mutually dependent on one another, throughout the life cycle. As a result, they should be studied simultaneously. This research attempts to draw together the diverse processes which link these phenomena by studying a panel of male college graduates, including their family relationships and their work experiences, from the senior year of college to a decade following graduation. During this 10-year period, spanning late adolescence to early adulthood, we investigate the impacts of the family (of origin and of destination) on the men's psychological development and attainment, the effects of work experiences on psychological change, and the mutual interrelations of work and family life.

Let us first consider the central theoretic concerns that have guided the research. We will then describe our methodology—the composition of the panel, the questionnaire, and the data analytic procedures.

CENTRAL CONCEPTS AND ISSUES

Because the effects of the family and of work on individual development are generally studied separately, by different investigators drawing on quite different conceptual frameworks, each chapter of this book has its foundation in a somewhat distinct theoretical and empirical literature. Chapter 2, focusing on the implications of the family of origin for psychological development and occupational attainment, is conceptually based in the literature of social stratification and status attainment. Chapter 3, considering the impacts of work experience on the personality, has its origins in occupational social psychology—extending from the classic works of Marx and Durkheim to the contemporary investigations of Blauner and Kohn. Chapter 4, assessing the interrelations of work, personality, and the family of procreation, draws insights from the literatures on status attainment, occupational sociology, social psychology, and work and family linkages. Instead of examining them here, we discuss these particular precursors of the research as they become most relevant, in the initial sections of each of these empirical chapters. In this introductory chapter we wish to address some more general, overarching issues, which encompass all of these more specific concerns.

This study is grounded most basically in the central problems that arise whenever the problem of change and development through the life course, in its social context, is seriously considered, whether by psychologists, social psychologists, sociologists, or other social scientists. Three closely interrelated questions guided the research.

A most central and pervasive issue is the degree of psychological stability versus change over time. Are individual psychological attributes mainly formed by the end of adolescence, or do they continue to change over time in response to major life experiences encountered in adulthood? Do experiences in the family during adolescence have lasting impacts on the personality? Or does personality development occur subsequently in response to experiences in adulthood—in work and in the family of procreation?

A second, strongly related but analytically separable, concern is the effect of social structure on the personality. That is, how does position in the social structure influence personal development and change? In studying change over the life course, it is not sufficient to study the individual alone. Nor can one expect to obtain an adequate understanding of psychological development by examining only the contexts in which socialization takes place. A direct examination of the interrelations of social structure and personality is necessary. We use the term "personality" to refer to wide range of prominent and enduring psychological attributes, including attitudes, values, and life involvements (see House, 1981:527). The elements of social structure with which we are most concerned are the institutions of work and the family. We view the experiences persons encounter, as a result of their incumbency of work and family roles, as important sources of developmental change.

The third major issue to be considered involves the linkages of work and family. How do the different spheres of life experience, in work and in the family, come to interpenetrate and mutually affect one another as they influence the developing personality? How does position in the occupational structure affect the character of family life? With respect to the men's families of origin, we examine whether an important dimension of the socialization process varies with the father's socio-economic status. Further, we assess the implications of achievement, work pressure, and involvement for the men's families of procreation. We also examine the family's influence on the occupational attainments of its members, including the effects of the family of origin on the occupational achievements of children, and the influence of marriage on attainment in adulthood.

Each of these issues is of great importance in understanding individual development through the life span. Let us now consider each one more closely.

PERSONAL STABILITY VS. CHANGE

Social scientists have long debated the degree of stability of personality as the individual moves through the life course. The extent to which individual attributes remain the same or change through the process of human development is of critical importance in life-span research. According to Haan and Day (1974): "The fundamental question for developmental research is the nature of the dialectical interplay between change and preservation of sameness over a lifespan" (p. 11). The volume, *Constancy and Change in Human Development* (Brim and Kagan, 1980) testifies to the continuing centrality of this issue.

It was customary in an earlier period to view the experiences of early childhood as crucial determinants of the course of individual development, after which the personality was considered to remain quite stable (Baltes et al., 1980:94; Gergen, 1977; Neugarten, 1977). Social scientists' earlier preoccupation with the study of childhood and adolescence resulted from the conviction that "the child is father to the man," that early experiences, especially in the context of the family, form the crucible for subsequent personality development. Psychoanalysts, ego psychologists, and learning theorists alike heralded the primacy of earlier over later socialization experiences, and looked for the source of adult adaptation in the intense parent-child relationships of early life (Lidz, 1968; Luborsky and Schimek, 1964). Social structural influences and change were believed to influence the personality through their effects on the developing child, as they are filtered through family child rearing practices, roles, and relationships (House, 1981).

Increasingly, however, this view has been challenged by social scientists espousing "life-span" perspectives. The life-span approach views development "as a life-long process" (Baltes et al., 1980:70) and indicates the potential for change and redirection even in later phases of life (Brim, 1980a,b; Brim and Kagan, 1980; Brim and Ryff, 1980). In fact, "a general antagonism toward the stability orientation" (Gergen, 1977:141) has been noticed in the life-span literature (Costa and McCrae, 1980b). The "stability model" has been further eroded by the claims and experimental findings of some psychologists who emphasize the contingent character and situational determination of attitudes and behavior.

Some have attempted to resolve this issue by taking an intermediate stance; according to this perspective, basic predispositions, constituting the "core" of personality, are formed rather early in life, while specific or more "peripheral" changes occur later in response to new environmental circumstances (Bloom, 1964; Cottrell, 1969; Yarrow and Yarrow, 1964:500). Whereas this position is plausible, the extent to which personality attributes are stable or unstable can only be determined empirically, through systematic longitudinal research that assesses the same persons through different phases of the life cycle.

Unfortunately, the time and resources necessary to conduct longitudinal studies have limited the accumulation of findings that address the degree of personality consistency through time. There have been relatively few studies across broad phases of the life course, beginning in infancy, early childhood, or adolescence, and continuing through the adult years. Highly notable instances of such long-term research are the Berkeley and Oakland studies (Block and Haan, 1971; Elder, 1974; Jones et al., 1971; Peskin and Livson, 1972; Siegelman et al., 1970), the Fels study (Kagan and Moss, 1962; Moss and Kagan, 1972), the Terman study of the gifted (Oden, 1968), and the Grant study of Harvard men (Vaillant, 1977). Other research covers more limited time periods, such as the years in college (Feldman and Newcomb, 1969; Heath, 1968; Katz, 1968; King, 1973), or those spanning the teens to the twenties (Bachman et al., 1978; Golden et al., 1962; Offer and Offer, 1975; Symonds, 1961).

These studies, taken together, have emphasized the persistence of individual characteristics from childhood and adolescence to adulthood. This persistence is manifest when personality is defined behaviorally, such as by dependency, spontaneity, or aggressiveness (Crandall, 1972; Kagan and Moss, 1962; Tuddenham, 1971); intellectually, by grades in school or by performance on intelligence and achievement tests (Bloom, 1964; Kagan and Moss, 1962; Oden, 1968); motivationally, by level of task involvement and perseverance (Block and Haan, 1971; Kagan and Moss, 1962; Oden, 1968; Vaillant, 1974); interpersonally, by strength of "object relations" (King, 1973); or in terms of subconscious processes, such as defense mechanisms (Vaillant, 1974) or fantasy projections (Buben, 1975; Symonds, 1961). Research on early and middle adulthood also indicates considerable stability in intelligence, vocational interests, racial attitudes, self-confidence, and values (see Kelly, 1955; Kuhlen, 1964; Sears, 1981). The work of Costa and his colleagues (Costa and McCrae, 1977–1978, 1980b; Costa et al., 1980) provides persuasive evidence for the continuity of personality in adulthood. They highlight the stability of extroversion and neuroticism (which approaches the reliability of their instruments), and, to a lesser extent, openness to new experience. Leon et al. (1979) also provide evidence for stability in personality from middle to old age.

Some investigators, instead of studying trait continuity, have focused on overall life adjustment, as gauged by clinical assessment of mental health, personality test performance, the acquisition of normal adult roles, or occupational achievement. Some have begun their research by purposely selecting a sample (or sub-sample drawn from a larger study) on the basis of evidence of adequate functioning (Cox, 1970; Golden et al., 1962; Vaillant, 1977; Vaillant and McArthur, 1972). These persons are then followed through life, and their adjustment monitored in succeeding periods. Other investigators have divided their samples at the last period of data collection into better and more poorly adjusted groups, and then have examined the attributes of each in earlier periods (Grinker et al., 1962; Oden, 1968; Siegelman et al., 1970). What is again most pervasive in this research is the emphasis on the stability of adjustment and mental health, in spite of the diversity of operational measurements and methods employed (see also Block and Haan, 1971; Fischer et al., 1979; Offer and Offer, 1975).

Stability of personality is generally defined normatively. Normative stability (Kagan, 1980:32; Moss and Susman, 1980) refers to the persistence of individual ranks or differences on an attribute of interest. Does the ordering of individuals, with respect to a given personality trait or characteristic, persist across age periods or through distinct life phases? Normative stability is usually measured by the correlation between measures of an attribute across time in a group of individuals. Strong positive correlations would indicate that individuals who score high or low at the first period, in relation to others in the group, retain the same relative positions in the second.

With respect to such normative stability,[1] social scientists have generally been impressed with the constancy shown by their panels from adolescence to adulthood, or between phases of the adult life course (Moss and Susman, 1980, comprehensively review this research). Still, the growing body of longitudinal findings does not fully resolve the issue of stability versus change, even when data have been collected over long periods. When stability is defined normatively, differences in interpretation arise from the fact that there is no agreed-upon baseline, or accepted standard of comparison. Whether stability coefficients are "high" or "low" seems to depend, to a large extent, on the judgment of the investigator. If a researcher expects to find considerable change over a period of time, or when there is high unreliability of instruments, moderate correlations may be viewed as quite large. Still, it must be remembered that even when correlations are as high as .7, half the variance is unexplained. Correlations of .5, quite typical in research of this kind, leave 75% of the variance unaccounted for. Though high unexplained variance may be attributable to measurement error, it could also indicate a potential for change and responsiveness to external influence. The fact that there is often only moderate correlational stability may therefore indicate support for the claims of the life-span theorists, who emphasize the potential for personality redirection throughout life.

---

[1] Elsewhere (Mortimer, Finch, and Kumka, 1982) we have contrasted normative stability with three other conceptualizations of stability: structural invariance, level stability and ipsative stability. These definitions were applied to semantic differential data on the self-concept, using all three waves of data (freshman year, senior year, and 10 years following college graduation) from the Michigan Panel Study. The analyses show that these four definitions of stability are empirically, as well as conceptually, distinct.

Some investigators have approached this issue somewhat differently, focusing on differences in rates of personal change over the life cycle. Instead of describing the level of stability between two points in time in a panel of persons of about the same age, they examine differences in psychological stability over a period of time between persons of different age. These investigations have been guided by "the aging stability thesis"—that "attitudes, values, and beliefs tend to stabilize and to become less likely to change as persons grow older" (Glenn, 1980:602). Though there is disagreement in the literature as to the particular timing of the decline in "change-proneness," it is generally accepted that late adolescence and early adulthood, the particular age periods that we are studying, are times of high susceptibility to change.

Sears (1981) proffers two relevant hypotheses. According to the "impressionable years" hypothesis, "people are unusually vulnerable in late adolescence and early adulthood to changes of any attitudes, given strong enough pressure to change." The complementary "persistence hypothesis" states that "residues of early preadult socialization are relatively immune from change in later years" (p. 184). Sears cites a considerable amount of research, though restricted largely to the domain of political and social attitudes, that is consistent with these hypotheses, showing more instability over time in younger than in older cohorts (for example, Jennings and Niemi, 1978; see also Glenn, 1980). Moreover, there are substantial generational differences in political attitudes, which well account for cross-sectional patterns by age (Sears, 1981). Persistent generational effects are fully in accord with the aging stability model.

Though accurate description of stability across life phases is very important, the ability to explain and predict the degree of constancy and change through the life course has been recognized as the central problem of developmental analysis (Baltes et al., 1980:95; Brim and Ryff 1980; Costa and McCrae, 1980b; Dannefer, 1984; Moss and Susman, 1980:544). The dominent explanation of the "aging stability" pattern emphasizes the declining rate of change in the person's environment over the life cycle. The degree of psychological stability is seen as a function of the constancy of environmental circumstances surrounding the individual (Baltes and Nesselroade, 1973:237–238; Kagan, 1980:62). Moss and Susman (1980) represent this environmental approach very well:

> Longitudinal findings on stability or change are occasionally discussed as if they represent a discovery of an invariant and irrevocable developmental truth . . . if a study demonstrates stability for individual differences on "aggressive behavior" it is tempting to proclaim that aggression is stable (as an absolute phenomenon) without considering the relative nature of

this finding and all the contingent and contextual factors that might alter or dilute it. Longitudinal findings such as these should be viewed not as conclusive facts but as information that, when interpreted . . . in the context of the life events and prevailing conditions for the subjects being studied, could enhance a developmental theory of personality. Much of the stability that is observed is probably a function of the individual's living in a stable environment while maintaining a psychological equilibrium. However, a crisis or major change in environment . . . could dramatically alter a personality. (p. 543, © 1980, Harvard University Press; reprinted by permission)

Thus, psychological stability or change should not be attributed to an unalterable internal dynamic, or to temporally distant determining forces (such as early parent-child relations) operating through a person's life, but may be explicable in terms of ever-present continuities or discontinuities in environmental circumstances (Kagan, 1980:68). Clausen (1972) has observed that personality stability is anchored in stable role positions and in the interpersonal commitments accompanying incumbency of stable social roles.

Moreover, it is clear that the period from late adolescence to early adulthood is a time of environmental changes. Glenn (1980) speaks of the "dense spacing" of life events in early adulthood, including status changes, new role behaviors, and shifts in social relationships. Sears (1981) notes the importance of primary groups for attitude maintenance and observes that they are very likely to change in composition in late adolescence and early adulthood. Thus, some psychological orientations may become more stable after early adulthood because the social environment also stabilizes following this period.

We are studying the period following college graduation. It is characterized by many age-graded, normative events (Baltes et al., 1980) or expected role changes, such as the completion of formal education, the entrance into full-time employment, marriage, and parenthood. These experiences may be important sources of psychological change. Nonnormative events (Baltes et al., 1980:74–76), such as career change, unemployment, divorce or other crisis-like circumstances, may also be more likely to occur during this period than subsequently. These events, disrupting earlier environmental stability, could lead to a redirection of the course of psychological development.

Adolescence has been viewed as a period of "identity diffusion" (Erikson, 1968), a time when individuals are seeking values and ideas to anchor themselves as persons. The crystallization of identity around certain attitudes, values, and roles may make the latter quite resistant to change (Sears, 1981). Glenn (1980) hypothesizes that attitudes function to help the individual adjust to life circumstances: "once the person arrives at a constellation of attitudes and beliefs that gives a sense of understanding and being able to deal with reality, the person tends to resist influences that would change those attitudes and beliefs and perhaps lead to feelings of dissonance" (pp. 603–604).This "sense of coherence" and predictability may protect the individual from stress and its harmful consequences for health (Antonovsky, 1979). Presumably such attitude change, fostering adjustment, would be most pronounced at times of major role change, such as late adolescence and early adulthood.

If attitudes are viewed as the product of accumulated experience, resistance to change will vary with the amount of such experience (Glenn, 1980), the "affective mass," or "cumulative total of affectively toned information to which a person has been exposed in his or her lifetime" (Sears, 1981:191). With time, there is also more opportunity to express one's views and bring them into practice, increasing commitment to them, and reducing the propensity to change. There may be declining exposure to new, change-inducing information (Sears, 1981).

If the "aging stability hypothesis" is correct, there is considerable reason to study the early adult years, for psychological changes occurring during this time are likely to be enduring. But in spite of the formative potential of this period, researchers have concentrated their attention on other life phases: childhood, adolescence, and, more recently, the mid-life "crisis" and old age. Relatively little study has been given to sources of change in the early adult years.

However, the individual should not be considered merely as a passive recipient of external forces, but as an active selector and molder of the situational context. According to Cottrell (1969), "Much of our activity and striving, perhaps most of it, is directed toward establishing and maintaining social contexts supportive of desired identities, or toward changing contexts that impose unwanted identities" (p. 550; see also Rosenberg, 1979, Ch. 11). The preservation of a consistent and stable sense of self has been postulated as a major motivational goal (Epstein, 1973; Korman, 1970; Lecky, 1945; Rosenberg, 1979). Experimental evidence (Snyder, 1981a,b) supports the proposition that individual consistencies are a result of consistency in the actor's constructed social worlds. The active creation of consonant and reinforcing environmental contexts could thus be an important mechanism through which personal stability is attained (see Costa and McCrae, 1980b; Mischel, 1973; Wachtel, 1973).

We assume that the person is a significant determinant of those life experiences and events that will come to influence the personality in subsequent life phases. If certain personality orientations and values are found to foster different adult experiences, and if these experiences, in turn, reinforce the same psychological attributes at a later period, an underlying dynamic of the "aging stability" pattern may be revealed. Thus we posit a kind of "dynamic stability" (Morris Rosenberg, personal communication), a process by which early psychological orientations produce subsequent external events. These, in turn, "feed back" on the personality, promoting psychological stability over time.

Given this conceptualization, it is insufficient simply to measure and describe the degree of stability over time. It is necessary to explain that stability by viewing it as an outcome of a continuing, dynamic interaction between the person and the environment. Like many other investigators, we too find evidence that there is considerable psychological stability, but we examine whether this stability is at least partially dependent on the individual's own prior self-perceptions, values, and orientations. The latter may serve to construct subsequent life experiences which support the earlier personality. For example, we examine the implications of work-related psychological orientations, formed within the family of origin, for subsequent career attainment and occupational experiences. The men tended to select occupations that provided rewards which were consonant with their prior values. We then investigate whether these later occupational experiences are determinants of the future course of psychological development, whether work experiences, linked to earlier occupational values, reinforce the same values over time. Marriage, likewise, is seen as a possible outcome of prior individual development, and as defining an adult role with important psychological implications.

SOCIAL STRUCTURE AND PERSONALTY

Interest in the effects of social structure on the personality has a long history in social science, extending back to the time of Adam Smith. Durkheim's writings on social structure and anomie, Weber's treatise on the "Protestant Ethic" and entrepreneurial development, and Marx's work on capitalism and worker alienation are major precursors of contemporary work. House (1981) has recently provided an excellent review of the development of this field. Empirical research initially had a holistic emphasis, pointing to global societal influences on molar personality configurations. Adorno's (Adorno et al., 1950) study of the authoritarian personality, and Mead's anthropological studies (1928, 1935), exemplify this approach. With Inkeles' work on the psychological concomitants of modernization, researchers shifted to more analytic investigations of the implications of specific aspects of society for particular dimensions of personality.

According to House (1981), a strong cultural paradigm dominated early work. Behavior was seen to result from shared attitudes and values, transmitted, during the early years of life, from parents, teachers, and other socializing agents to children. In contrast, the central distinguishing feature of current work is its structural emphasis. Attention is directed to the immediate constraints, demands, and opportunities facing the individual as a result of the specific location in the social structure. These immediate situational features are viewed as the major determinants of behavior. But attitudes and values are seen as outcomes of structural forces as well: psychological orientations are "internalized as a consequence of engaging in a pattern of behavior in response to external contingencies" (House, 1981:543) Emphasis on the immediate, continuing realities as determinants of adult behavior and attitudes leaves open the possibility that personality continues to change, well beyond childhood. This potential openness or malleability, in response to important adult life experiences, is a crucial starting point for the present research.

Contemporary work in the area of social structure and personality has thus given major attention to psychological variation within societies. Researchers ask, how does the individual's social location within a complex modern society—as determined by sex, age, race, ethnicity, social class, and other attributes—influence important attitudes, values, personality orientations, and beliefs? But House notes, and we concur, that much of the work in this field merely describes the relations of structural and psychological variables, showing consistent covariation but paying scant attention to its explanation. Social scientists must go beyond these descriptive accounts, working toward the development of comprehensive, explanatory models.

House proposes three principles to enhance the theoretical development and integration of future research in the area of social structure and personality. The first is the components principle; the researcher should identify the aspects or dimensions of social structure that are important in producing change in personality. The second is the proximity principle; the researcher should explicate how larger structures impinge on the person, affecting the more proximal social experiences and stimuli facing the individual. The third is the psychological principle: to obtain a full comprehension of the mechanisms underlying the associations of social structure and personality, investigators must understand the psychological processes through which people respond to the various stimuli and interactions encountered in their social environments.

Three continuing, monumental studies of the effects of social structure on the personality may be viewed as illustrative of these three principles. They have also provided continual inspiration for our own study.

The questions and issues they have raised have guided the research in all its phases. Melvin Kohn, Carmi Schooler, and their colleagues' work on occupational experience and psychological functioning, Glen Elder's studies of the developmental impacts of the Great Depression, and Morris Rosenberg's conceptualizations and findings regarding the self-concept have each had a profound influence on our work. It is noteworthy that all three of these studies have a central focus on social stratification: Kohn and Schooler examine the psychological implications of occupational conditions at different social class levels; Elder studies the effects of economic loss in childhood and adolescence on the further course of individual development; and Rosenberg investigates the linkages of socio-economic status and self-esteem in children and adults. Social-psychological investigations of status attainment have also made a substantial contribution to the conceptual framework for our study. The substantive convergence on social class in all of this research testifies to the centrality of the person's position in the socio-economic order for psychological development in modern societies.

Kohn and Schooler initially examined the relationships between social class and psychological orientations and values, using cross-sectional data obtained from a representative sample of 3100 employed men. *Class and Conformity* (Kohn, 1969) showed clear differences, by social class position, in men's values for both themselves and their children, and in their orientations to work, self, and society. A basic distinction between self-direction and conformity appeared to underlie these differences:

> Self-direction is a central value for men of higher class position who see themselves as competent members of an essentially benign society. Conformity is a central value for men of lower class position who see themselves as less competent members of an essentially indifferent or threatening society. Self-direction, in short, is consonant with an orientational system premised on the possibilities of accomplishing what one sets out to do; conformity, with an orientational system premised on the dangers of stepping out of line. (Kohn and Schooler, 1969:676)

While documenting this trend was an important contribution, the major thrust of Kohn and Schooler's work has been toward explaining it, determining the components of social class position that have such pervasive impacts on psychological functioning. Kohn and Schooler identified two central components. The first is education, which "provides the intellectual flexibility and breadth of perspective that are essential for self-directed values and orientation" (Kohn and Schooler, 1969:676). The second, which receives much greater emphasis in their work, is occupational self-direction, as indexed by closeness of supervision, the substantive complexity of work with data, things, and people, and the complexity of the organization of work as a whole. According to Kohn (1977:xlviii), "people thrive on meeting occupational challenges." Education exerts its effects on psychological functioning both directly and indirectly, for it "is a prime determinant of the substantive complexity of work" (Kohn, 1981). These two conditions of life, education and occupational self-direction, are quite different for persons of different social class position. They were found to substantially mediate the effects of social class on values and orientation.

Kohn and Schooler's cross-sectional analyses thus provided considerable initial evidence that work attributes have significant impacts on the adult personality (Kohn, 1969, 1977; Kohn and Schooler, 1969, 1973). But cross-sectional data cannot resolve the problem of causality; as these investigators are well aware, men may choose more self-directed work, mold their jobs in accord with their prior abilities and dispositions, or be selected for positions by employers on the basis of earlier attributes. If these psychological characteristics remain stable over time, such selection effects could fully account for the cross-sectional variations.

A follow-up of a sample of the men, 10 years later, provided the longitudinal data necessary to test more definitive causal models of the manner in which work experiences influence psychological functioning. These further analyses have provided much more convincing evidence that work experiences, particularly occupational self-direction, are of crucial causal importance for psychological development. Using this panel data, Kohn and Schooler (1978) first demonstrated that substantive complexity has significant positive effects on intellectual flexibility, even with the earlier psychological variable controlled. The fact that 1964 intellectual flexibility had lagged (but not contemporaneous) effects on 1974 substantive complexity indicated a truly reciprocal process by which job affects man, and man affects job. Since then, the effects of occupational self-direction on a wide range of psychological constructs, including parental values, standards of morality, trustfulness, idea conformity, self-deprecation, and anxiety, have been clearly demonstrated by similar longitudinal test (Slomczynski et al., 1981).

Kohn and Schooler's (1981, 1983) more recent research has moved beyond occupational self-direction to explore a wide range of "structural imperatives of the job". These analyses consistently show that diverse conditions of work which promote occupational self-direction have positive psychological implications, increasing intellectual flexibility. In contrast, factors restricting self-direction and those generating pressure and uncertainty, such as closeness of supervision, being responsible for things that are beyond one's control, and the heaviness of work, have negative psychological consequences.

The work of Kohn and his colleagues has thus fully addressed the

two issues featured in House's (1981) components and proximity principles. Education and occupational experience, especially occupational
self-direction, are the components, or "conditions of life" which are
importantly determined by social class position. These phenomena are
also highly proximal to the person, impinging directly on individual
behaviors and psychological functioning.

The psychological principle designated by Kohn to explain the effects
of occupational conditions is a simple process of generalization, "a direct
translation of the lessons of the job to outside the job realities" (Kohn,
1981:290). According to this "learning-generalization model," attitudes,
values, and ways of thinking are abstracted and generalized from the
modes of successful adaptation to daily life pressures and situations
(Kohn, 1977; Kohn and Schooler, 1973; Schooler, 1972). Psychological
attributes that are adaptive to the problems encountered in everyday life
will generalize, to affect the most basic attitudes toward the self, values,
orientations to other people, self-directedness, and intellectual flexibility.
In contrast to other prominent approaches to socialization, such as the
"cultural perspective" described by House (1981), role theory, identification theory, and symbolic interactionism,[2] the generalization model
does not presume that psychological orientations, found to be related
to work experience, are necessarily transmitted or taught by other persons in the work situation. Instead of positing a need for mediation by
significant others or groups, socialization is seen as occurring more directly, through the resolution of daily problems and the adequate adjustment to important life activities, demands, and situations (Kohn,
1976:100–101; Kohn and Schooler, 1973:105; Schooler, 1972).[3] Recently, this formulation has been extended beyond the occupational
sphere. Research has been undertaken to examine the psychological
implications of housework for both men and women (Schooler et al.,
1983) and the schoolwork of children (Miller et al., 1982). The reader
will find frequent reference to the work of Kohn and his colleagues
throughout this volume, testifying to the critical influence of that study
on our own work.

Morris Rosenberg's writings on the self-concept further exemplify the
structural approach to personality and social location. He views the enduring self-concept as a product of experience throughout the life span,
resulting from particular social roles that are occupied by the person,
social identities, and achievements. His early work (1965) drew attention

---

[2] Mortimer and Simmons (1978) contrast the generalization model with several other
approaches to adult socialization: role theory, identification theory, symbolic interactionism, exchange and expectancy theories, and developmental perspectives.

[3] This approach is also evident in the work of Kanter (1977a) and Spaeth (1976a).

to the parent–child relationship as a source of adolescent self-esteem. This research stimulated our own interest in the implications of the quality of the father–son bond for the formation of attitudes toward self as well as work. Rosenberg further showed the relevance of the self-image (1965) and values (1957) for vocational choice. Thus, for Rosenberg, the self is both "social product," reflecting prior experiences, and "social force," influencing the person's future social environment (1981). Like Kohn and Schooler and their colleagues, he views the relationship between social structure and personality as highly dynamic and reciprocal.

Rosenberg's psychological principle of attribution (1979) may be considered illustrative of the kind of psychological process subsumed under Kohn and Schooler's "learning-generalization" model. According to this principle, people view their behavior and its outcomes (their educational attainments, occupational statuses, work performances, and income) and attribute these outcomes to themselves: "it is not the individual's behavior but his interpretation of the behavior that has consequences for self-esteem" (1981:605). Achievements or performances will be seen as reflecting the self when they are viewed as internally motivated, determined by the individual's own volition, not the result of external forces. Rosenberg and Pearlin (1978) use this principle of attribution in their explanation of the positive relationship between social class and self-esteem for adults, and the lack of such relationship for children. For the child, socio-economic status is an ascribed, not an achieved characteristic, reflecting the parent's accommplishments, not the child's own acts. What does affect the child's self-image, particularly the academic self-concept, is individual achievement relative to peers, as indicated by school grades.

Like Kohn and Schooler, Rosenberg expects attitudes and behaviors formed in the context of one role to be carried over, or to generalize, to others, and to influence one's basic conception of self. This is especially likely to occur when the role in question is highly salient to the individual: "such social identity elements as race, religion, or gender . . . are arranged in a hierarchy of salience. Some elements are at the center of the individual's concerns, whereas others are more peripheral" (1981:606).

Given Rosenberg's principles of attribution and identity salience,[4] we may expect to find particularly strong effects of occupational experiences and attainments on the self-concept in a panel of professional and managerial men. It is probable that highly educated people, especially when

---

[4] Rosenberg's psychological principles of "reflected appraisals" and "social comparison" further enhance our understanding of the manner in which social structure affects the personality (House, 1981). These principles, however, are less relevant to the central concerns of the present study.

employmment conditions are favorable, perceive that they have a high level of control over their occupational destinations. Thus, the type of work they do is seen as largely determined by their own volition. Moreover, given the prominence of work as a determinant of social status and identity, that is, its high salience, occupational experiences and outcomes may be especially important for the development of the self in this highly advantaged social stratum.

Studies of the process of status attainment are generally not subsumed under the rubric of "social structure and personality." But the study of social structure and personality may include "the relationship between any macrosocial phenomena and any individual psychological attribute" (House, 1981:527). Social class origin has been found to influence a host of psychological orientations that can facilitate occupational attainment: achievement motivations and values, educational and occupational aspirations, and plans for the future. The work of Sewell, Hauser, Featherman, and their colleagues has accorded psychological orientations primary importance as mediators in the status attainment process (Featherman, 1980; Sewell and Hauser, 1976; Spenner and Featherman, 1978). Psychological variables have thus become quite prominent in explanations of the manner in which social class origin influences individual attainment. A central emphasis of the status attainment researchers is on social transmission—parental encouragement, tuition, and guidance as determinants of the higher aspirations and more ambitious plans of students from the more advantaged backgrounds.

But the status attainment researchers have recognized that the positive relationship between socio-economic origin and destination can be interpreted in other ways. One alternative approach stresses the direct allocation of role positions. Parents from higher socio-economic backgrounds are able to provide their children with advantages—they can support them through college and post-graduate education, provide them with economic resources, occupational inheritance, business and professional contacts, and the like, all of which make a high level of attainment more probable. In this study, we give considerable attention to the manner in which differences in socio-economic background influence adult occupational achievements—the extent to which their influence is direct or mediated by psychological transmission.

Another approach to the status attainment process features the ways relationships in the family are patterned in different social class locations (Gecas, 1981). Gecas's (1979) extensive review of the literature, highlighting Kohn and Schooler's work on parental values and socialization, shows that middle class families, when compared to those of the lower class, make use of different disciplinary practices. To control their children, middle class families make greater use of reasoning, as opposed to physical punishment, and use punishment in different circumstances, emphasizing the intent rather than the consequences of their children's acts. They are also more supportive and affectionate, more egalitarian, and have more open and flexible role definitions. Such experiences might be expected to stimulate the development of self-directed orientations and other psychological attributes enhancing achievement, without the need for the direct parental teaching of these values and orientations.

In this monograph, we give particular attention to the quality of the father–son relationship, both as a factor mediating the effects of social class on sons' psychological development, and as a variable that is important for the process of attainment in its own right. In Chapter 2 we investigate whether a close and supportive father–son relationship, more characteristic of families of higher socio-economic level, fosters the psychological orientations in sons that promote occupational achievement. We also examine whether paternal support fosters attainment in other ways.

Glen Elder's studies of the developmental outcomes of growing up during the Great Depression (Elder, 1974; Elder and Rockwell, 1979b) clearly demonstrate the importance of family relationships and activities in mediating the psychological effects of economic hardship. He compares two cohorts, the Berkeley cohort, who were born in 1928–29 and experienced the depression from their pre-school years, and the Oakland cohort, born in 1920–21, who experienced the depression in late childhood through adolescence. According to Elder, economic loss did not have direct impacts, constant for children of all ages, nor was its effects on children primarily mediated through change in the values and attitudes of parents. Instead, the changing structure of family relations, as it impinged on children of different age, receives primary emphasis.

While there are many complexities in Elder's anlysis, one pattern of findings is especially worthy of note: the older children were drawn into family activities, and actively contributed to their families' economic welfare. When their families suffered severe economic loss, boys were prematurely drawn into the labor market. And in spite of the tensions and strains surrounding the father's unemployment, this very process of contributing to the family's resolution of its economic crisis fostered a sense of personal efficacy and positive orientation to achievement. Thus, the adolescent children learned to directly confront and actively cope with life's problems and losses.

In contrast, the younger children were neither able to understand or participate in family activities, nor to contribute in this way. Adults were, to them, "unpredictable, sullen, and perhaps even hostile" (Elder and Rockwell, 1979b:252), discipline was inconsistent, and household routines disorganized. Faced with the emotional and economic distress on the part of their parents, and unable to deal with it in an efficacious manner, these children manifested much more evidence of psychological maladjustment and disturbance at the time of adolescence. Though the economically deprived in both cohorts were able to overcome their early disadvantages with respect to occupational achievement, continuing psychological distress and impairment were manifest at midlife even among the most successful of the younger, Berkeley men.

Elder's study clearly addresses House's components, proximity, and psychological principles. The historical experience of the Great Depression had its effects on families through severe income loss. This component was not present in all families, and clearly distinguishes families in terms of their immediate adjustments and the later life outcomes of children. The issue of proximity is addressed through careful elaboration of the changes in the family—its role structure, activities, disciplinary patterns, stress, tension, and division of labor—that had pervasive impacts on the development of children. Like Kohn and Schooler's research on occupational conditions and psychological functioning, and Rosenberg's study of the self-concept, Elder's work emphasizes that psychological growth and development arise from successful resolution of demanding life situations.

Both the status attainment research and Elder's study, though differing in their relative emphases, develop a similar explanatory logic. For both, the implications of position in the socio-economic order are heavily mediated by family processes. Socio-economic location influences the family (structure and pattern of functions, for Elder; parental encouragement of high aspirations, for the status attainment school), which in turn, fosters psychological change in children. Finally, adolescent psychological orientations are seen as having important implications for adult outcomes. But while the status attainment researchers are primarily concerned with adult occupational attainments, Elder is more interested in lasting psychological outcomes, and the implications of adult occupational achievement for subsequent psychological development. Elder and Rockwell recognize the open-ended character of life-span development: "longitudinal research has begun to document the varied developmental paths in which childhood promise is not matched by well-being or accomplishments in the adult years, and dismal life prospects among youth are at least partially repaired by growth-inducing experiences later on in life" (1979b:253). Thus, they emphasize the adaptive potential and beneficent outcomes of effective coping with problems and strains in adolescence, and of surmounting educational and occupational challenges later in life.

Our model parallels this explanatory paradigm. We, too, are interested in the family's position in the socio-economic hierarchy as a determinant of the character of parent–child relationships; in the effects of these relations on adolescent psychological development; in the implications of adolescent attitudes and values for subsequent worklife achievement; and the consequences of this achievement, in turn, for the further course of psychological development. Elder's comparison of adolescent and younger children also alerts us to the possiblity that similar life events and circumstances may have different implications for development, depending on the life stage of the person. We will see this clearly when comparing the implications of the quality of the father–son relationship for sons' psychological development in adolescence and early adulthood.

Consideration of the effects of social structure on the personality is inseparable from our initial concern, the stability of personality through the life course. For if personality is subject to the influence of adult experience—in work, as demonstrated by Kohn, Rosenberg, and Elder, and in the family, as we will show—then it cannot be stable through the period of early and mid-adulthood, but must change over time.

THE LINKAGES OF WORK AND FAMILY LIFE

Finally, a continuous concern with the interrelations of work and family life permeates this study, and underlies many of its most basic substantive questions. Though the structural differentiation of the institutions of work and family at the time of the industrial revolution (Smelser, 1959) severed their spatial connection, they are effectively linked together, and dependent on one another, in many ways. Occupational and family sociologists have tended to view these domains as quite separate fields of study, but research is increasingly demonstrating the "myth of separate worlds" (Kanter, 1977a; Moen, 1982). Work and the family are intricately tied together.

The structural linkages between work and the family may be conceptualized, most simply, in terms of a functional model of mutual interdependence. In their classic work, *Ecomony and Society*, Parsons and Smelser (1956) described the basic interchanges between the family and the economy. The economy provides income or wages for the family household, determines the family's social prestige in the community (traditionally, through the occupation of the male wage earner), and sets limits on the consumer goods and services which can be acquired. In return, the family socializes each new generation of workers for the economy, instilling the most basic attitudes and values concerning work and achievement. The family gives the adult wage earner one motivation to find a job, and to exert effort and achieve in the marketplace, which contributes to productivity and ultimately benefits the employing organization. Another major function of the family, according to Parsons and Smelser's analysis, is to help maintain the psychological equilibrium of the worker in the face of the impersonality, competition, and pressures of the workplace. Through the family's contribution to "tension management," stress is effectively dealt with and resolved (see also Parsons, 1955). Moreover, through its consumer spending, the family provides the demand for the economy's products.

This conceptualization of the interchanges of family and economy has been subject to great criticism, particularly because of its grounding in the highly traditional sex-typed division of labor of Parsons' time. Feminist scholars have objected to the assumption that the husband's specialization in instrumental functions (economic provision) and the wife's specialization in expressive tasks (socialization, personality maintenance) is functionally necessary or beneficial for either the family or the economy (Lipman-Blumen and Tickamyer, 1975; Oppenheimer, 1977). They have questioned whether the functionalist depiction of even the traditional situation is accurate, given the extensive overlap of instrumental and expressive functions in both work and family roles (Kanter, 1977a; Piotrkowski, 1978:215–216). But while these objections are justified, the functionalist conceptualization has recognized important linkages of work and family life, and has provided a point of departure for many highly productive debates, theoretical developments, and empirical studies.

A life course perspective further sensitizes us to the continuing linkages of the family and work as individuals move through their lives. For just as the individual can be thought of as having several life careers—in education, work, community life, and so on—so does the family have a career, or staged developmental sequence (Aldous, 1978; Hill and Mattessich, 1979). It begins with marriage and early parenthood, followed by family expansion and the rearing of children. Later in its career, the family faces the "empty nest" and a contraction in size. Elder's work (1974, 1978; Elder and Rockwell, 1976, 1977, 1979b) has greatly contributed to our conceptualization and understanding of life careers, and the interrelations of work and family career sequences. In both individual and family careers, the timing of events can vary, being on time, early, or late with respect to normative guidelines. And the sequencing of events in either of these careers will likely have important consequences for success and adjustment in the other. For example, because of the normatively structured reciprocity of husband and wife roles, men who marry "on time," shortly before or after completing school, may be more successful in their early occupational careers than men who remain single. Hogan (1980), in studying married men, found that those with normative transition sequences (i.e., educational completion, marriage, and work entry) had greater occupational and income returns to their educational investments. Analytically separating such career lines furthers recognition that the demands of each role may be incompatible. For example, heavy, time-consuming career involvement may prohibit close and companionate marital relations. Furthermore, the meaning of an experience in one sphere may be altered depending on its context in another. Thus, a promotion at work, or unemployment, may have different implications depending on whether the individual is married or single, a parent or childless. In Chapter 4, we investigate whether work experiences have different psychological implications for married and single men. Elder's research has further alerted us to the possibility of complex, lagged effects through time and across life careers, as he found that experiences during the Great Depression had repercussions much later in life in the family, in work, in mental and physical health, and in satisfaction (1974; Elder and Rockwell, 1979b). We attend to this possibility throughout the analyses to follow.

Recognition that the wage earner occupies a boundary role—at the intersection of work and family careers—gives rise to extremely important questions. To what extent is an individual's position and functioning in each sphere dependent on what is happening in the other? How does the individual's participation in work influence behavior in the family? According to a popular "segmentation model" (Brim, 1970; see Piotrkowski, 1978, for cogent discussion), there is little or no connection; persons adjust their attitudes and behaviors according to immediate situational demands. There is little carryover—participation in each sphere is quite distinct. (Kanter, 1977a, considers this a basic assumption of "role theory.") According to a second line of thought, work and family spheres are linked by processes of compensation—workers seek satisfaction or activities in one area that are lacking in the other (Parker and Smith, 1976; Piotrkowski, 1978).

Yet the evidence seems to fall most heavily in favor of still a third hypothesis. As we have seen in our discussion of the relationship between social structure and personality, according to the generalization model (Kohn and Schooler, 1973, 1978, 1982), attitudes formed in the work setting spillover or generalize to affect the most basic orientations toward self, others, and children; overarching values; intellectual flexibility; and other psychological attributes. Experiences in the workplace thus have powerful effects on the personality. Through these effects, they may also influence marriage, the parent–child relationship, and the socialization process.

Consideration of the connections of work and family life has generated a lively research tradition on work experience and child rearing values (Aberle and Naegele, 1952; Gecas, 1979; Kohn, 1969; Miller and Swanson, 1958). A persistent theme in research on fathering is that men attempt to inculcate attitudes and values in their children, especially in their sons, which are useful to them in their own occupations. Kohn's (1969) findings relating to social class and parental values are highly consistent with this position. According to Kohn, when work is routine and closely supervised, and lacks substantive complexity, men will place a high value on their children's comformity and obedience to authority, as these behaviors are quite necessary in their work settings. Following preordained rules, and showing respect and deference to the supervisor, may be at a premium in the blue collar work environment (Bowles and Gintis, 1976). Alternatively, when independent and complex thought is required, as in professional and managerial work, men will come to value self-direction in their children. Class differences in child rearing values, in accord with these expectations, have been found in many studies, including several replications in different national contexts (Kohn, 1977).

There is some, albeit more limited, evidence that the father's work situation affects his parental behavior, as well as his values (Kohn, 1977; Rubin, 1976). In comparison with men of higher social class position, blue collar men have been found to be more directive (rather than supportive) in their parenting styles and rely more on physical punishment than appeals to reasoning or guilt (Gecas, 1979). McKinley (1964) believed that lower class men more severely discipline and punish their children because of their frustration, due to low job satisfaction and the absence of work autonomy.

Piotrkowski (1978) reports that, when workers are stressed and upset at work, due to role conflict and overload, they come home fatigued, irritable, and worried. They then attempt to create "personal space" between themselves and other family members, blocking out their wives and children. The wives try to help their husbands by keeping the children "out of their hair," allowing time for rest and recuperation. The children, too, learn to distance themselves from the working parent. When they do not, the fathers become angry and irritable. Piotrkowski called this pattern of linkage between work and family life "negative carryover." A second pattern, fostered by boredom at work and the underutilization of skills, was called "energy depletion," there was simply little energy left to become involved with wives and children. The workers consequently withdrew from their families. But when fathers felt satisfied and challenged by their jobs a very different pattern emerged—one of "positive carryover." The worker, upon returning home, actively initiated contact with family members. The ensuing interactions were characterized by interest, concern, closeness, and warmth. Piotrkowski thus emphasizes the emotional linkages of work and family life.

As we have seen, men of higher social class position generally have closer and more supportive relationships with their children (Gecas, 1979). This pattern, replicated in many studies, is consistent with Kohn's interpretation of the relationships between social class, work experiences, and parental values. For if men of higher socio-economic status have self-directed occupational activities, one would expect them to have greater concern about the internal psychological development of their children. Fathers may recognize that self-direction depends on the acquisition of relevant abilities and character traits (such as a sense of responsibility, purposefulness, persistence in the pursuit of goals, self-reliance, personal efficacy, and so on). Concern on the part of the father with developing such self-directed attributes would likely promote close and warm father–child relationships.

In the next chapter of this book, we give central attention to the implication of family socio-economic level for the quality of father–son relations, and the effects of these relationships, in turn, on sons' psychological development. Moreover, we examine the chain of causation one step further, by assessing the implications of psychological attributes, promoted by supportive parent-child relations, for son's early adult occupational attainment. Kohn (1981) has declared that distinctive class-linked parental values, if implemented in parent–child relations and child rearing practices more generally, could be an important explanatory link, contributing to the persistence of social class membership across the generations. But few studies have pursued this suggestion empirically, by tracing the effects of class-linked styles of parent–child relations to children's self-concepts, values, and orientations to work, and the effects of these psychological attributes, in turn, on the process of attainment.

But this is just one example of the manner in which work experience can affect the family—through the specific attitudes and values, fostered by work, which influence parental behaviors and socialization processes. There are many other ways in which work affects patterns of relationship and behavior in the family. They have been studied in both traditional single provider families (Fowlkes, 1980; Scanzoni, 1970) and in nontraditional, dual career family contexts (Holmstrom, 1973; Rapoport and Rapoport, 1971; Rice, 1979). Generally, in accord with an exchange model of family dynamics (Scanzoni, 1970, 1972, 1979), as the husband's income and occupational prestige increase, marital satisfaction and stability also rise. But high occupational achievement may also have costs for the family (see Aldous et al.'s "success constraint' theory of marital dynamics, 1979). At high occupational levels, work may be so involving and demanding that the worker has little energy left over to become involved with the family. In professional and managerial families, wives often complain that their husbands are so highly involved or "absorbed" (Kanter, 1977b) in their careers, that they are psychologically unavailable, inaccessible to family members even when they are at home (see also Fowlkes, 1980; Maccoby, 1976; Machlovitz, 1980). Thus there may be optimal levels of work involvement for the family. When it is too low, under conditions of under-utilization and routinization, "energy depletion" (Piotrkowski, 1978) and withdrawal from the family may occur. But excessively involving and demanding occupations may have similar effects.

While, in this book, we give primary attention to these social psychological linkages of work and family, there are other, more structural interconnections. As Parsons and Smelser recognized, work provides social status for the family and economic resources for consumption, thereby setting upper limits on the family's standard of living. It can also give substantial opportunity for social mobility, as when the occupation is structured as a career. Alternatively, it may represent threats to economic security, as in some blue collar and service jobs where layoffs are frequent. Perceived opportunities and threats to economic well-being strongly influence family decision-making regarding employment of its members (Ghez and Becker, 1975) and may also influence the level of support which each spouse provides to the other. Work also sets external constraints on family organization and activities through the amount of time that is spent working and the scheduling of work. The particular patterning of work time may unduly interfere with, and disrupt, family functioning. Further constraints on the family are set by requirements for travel and geographic mobility. We will investigate some of these opportunities and pressures, and their implications for the family, in Chapter 4.

It appears that much more attention has been given by scholars to the effects of work on the family and socialization processes than the implications of the family for adult work behavior and occupational attainment. However, given the importance of the family in people's lives, one might expect that experiences in this sphere would have major implications for individual psychological orientations and behaviors in the workplace as well. The connection of work motivation to family responsibilities has often been recognized (Piotrkowski, 1978; Rubin, 1976; Sennett and Cobb, 1972). The "personality maintenance" functions of the family, provided, as Parsons and Smelser (1956) noted, in service of the individual's continued economic productivity, have been documented in single provider (Fowlkes, 1980) and dual career (Rice,

1979) families. Social psychologists have provided evidence that the family plays an important part in neutralizing the stresses of the workplace (Cobb and Kasl, 1977; Turner and Noh, 1982). Some have inferred that participation in family life, through its influence on individual well-being and coping behavior, creates interpersonal resources which foster productivity and socio-economic achievement (Voydanoff, 1980).

Others point to more direct forms of assistance that wives provide for their husbands. Although individualistic achievement is part of the mythology of success (Kanter, 1977a,b), it is increasingly recognized that wives make quite tangible contributions to their husbands' careers. Given the importance of work as a source of economic resources for the family, there are powerful incentives for wives to do so (Greiff and Munter, 1980).

But in recent years, scholars have expressed increasing criticism of the manner in which work and family ties have been studied by social scientists. Bronfenbrenner and Crouter (1981), in their review of research in this area, have outlined the very disparate assumptions underlying early work on this subject. Investigators focused their attention on the negative consequences of unemployment for men's families, and the deleterious implications of employment for women's families. Thus, for men, work was considered normal; a disruption in work was expected to disrupt the family. In contrast, when women were studied, investigators searched for evidence of maladjustment in children (Nye and Hoffman, 1963).

Such divergent assumptions, in accord with highly traditional sex role norms, persist in more recent work. Feldberg and Glenn (1979) have identified a "work model" for men and a "gender model" for women. When men are the subject of study, attention focuses on the variations in their occupational experiences, and the manner in which these experiences influence their lives off the job. But when women are studied, the mere fact of working assumes predominant importance. Their family characteristics, not their work experiences, assume the status of independent variables, and their implications for women's occupational attainment, role conflict, and job satisfaction are addressed.

Because ours is a study of men, we can do nothing to correct the imbalanced treatment with respect to women. But we do make several assumptions which lead to a somewhat broader perspective than has been manifest in the literature with respect to the work and family linkages of men. First, consistent with the generalization model of adult socialization and psychological functioning, we assume that men's employment will have broad repercussions in their family lives. That is, the character of work experiences will have important implications for the structure of family roles and the quality of family life. In Chapter 2 we ask, how does the father's position in the social structure of work influence parent–child relationships, and the transmission of attitudes and values to sons? We investigate the process by which work-related psychological orientations are formed in adolescence in the context of the family of origin, and then demonstrate how these orientations influence the attainment of different kinds of early adult work experiences and rewards. Thus, the first work and family linkage to be investigated focuses on the family of origin—its connection to the occupational structure through the father's occupational position, and its contribution to the vocational development and occupational attainments of sons.

We next investigate, in Chapter 3, the manner in which work experiences—including the career pattern, work autonomy, income, and the social content of work—affect change in psychological orientations over time. We show that as the individual moves into the labor force, work experiences take precedence over family relations in influencing the further course of adult psychological development. The psychological impacts of work experiences, though of interest and importance in their own right, are extremely important for the understanding of the linkages of work and family. For the psychological changes induced by work come to influence the worker's relationships and orientations with respect to the family he creates through marriage.

This brings us to the second major work and family linkage under consideration—between adult work experiences and the person's family of procreation. We examine the reciprocal interrelations of work and family in this context—whether, through the dynamics of the "two-person career," married men have significant advantages over single men in the process of attainment (or whether the apparent advantages of the married are due solely to processes of self-selection); whether marriage acts as a "buffer" sheltering men from the full psychological impacts of their work experiences; and finally, the implications of work experiences and orientation for strain in the family, husband–wife reciprocity and support, and marital satisfaction. In investigating these reciprocal relationships, we assume that, as in the case of women, men's success in the occupational structure, and adaptation to it, may be contingent upon their family lives, though the character of the effects for men and women may be quite different. Thus, in Chapter 4, family status becomes the independent variable in investigating the process of men's occupational attainment and their subjective evaluations of success. Men's socio-economic achievement, the temporal requirements and pressures of their work, and their work involvement are then viewed as forces having significant implications for their families.

The expectation that there are continuous, reciprocal interrelations between work and family life has thus guided the analyses to follow.

Men's work not only influences their families, but their families may also influence their behaviors in the workplace. Some of these mutual influences are contemporaneous; that is, events in the workplace have immediate impact on the family. Families must constantly adjust to changes in economic resources, the time scheduling of work, and psychological changes induced in their working members. Other influences may be lagged over long periods of time. For example, men's occupations may lead them to transmit different occupational values to their sons, which have important implications for the work experiences and occupational destinations of the next generation (Mortimer and Kumka, 1982).

The three central issues under consideration, the stability of personality through time, the relationships between social structure and personality, and the linkages of work and family life, can be viewed as analytically distinct. However, in studying the actual course of people's lives, they are inseparable. As work and family are the most central institutions in the social structure, impinging on individual lives, it is difficult to speak of the effects of social structure on personality without referring to the features of these two spheres. Moreover, persons will remain stable, or change, largely as a function of the experiences they encounter in work and family domains.

THE PANEL

This research has its origins in a 1960's study of college students, "The Michigan Student Study." This extensive research project was initiated in 1962 by Theodore Newcomb and Gerald Gurin, social psychologists at the University of Michigan, to investigate the impacts of college life. Since the investigators were interested in the development of friendship patterns, three-quarters of the 650 freshmen chosen for the original study, who entered the university in 1962 and 1963, resided in the same dormitories; the others were chosen randomly. Four years later (in 1966 and 1967), 150 additional seniors were randomly chosen to compensate for freshman sample attrition. (Gurin, 1971, gives a complete description of the study design.) While the initial selection of students from the total freshman body was not entirely random, the college panel was not chosen in a manner that would be selective on the basis of differences in social origins, psychological attributes, occupational values or aspirations, or other variables that are of interest to us here.

The earlier study was conducted by a series of interviews and self-administered questionnaires over the 4 years of college. The data from this earlier study that are used in this book were obtained by questionnaire during the senior year, close to the time of college graduation.

The measures were largely Likert-type items, concerning a broad range of experiences and attitudes, including relationships with parents, occupational values, orientations toward work, and other life activities. A semantic differential self-concept scale was also included. (Other analyses, focusing on the issue of stability over time, include the freshman year questionnaire data as well; see Mortimer and Lorence, 1981, and Mortimer et al., 1982.)

In 1976, approximately 10 years following the panel members' graduation from college, the authors successfully located 610 members of the senior sample. These constituted 88 percent of the 694 men from whom data had been obtained in the senior year of college. Eighty-four percent of those who were found were persuaded to return a mailed questionnaire that assessed the same psychological attributes that were measured earlier, including measures of the self-concept, work involvement, and occupational values, post-graduate educational and work histories, current occupational experiences, and information about marriage and family relationships. Thus, 512 respondents, or 74 percent of the senior target group, were successfully retrieved for the follow-up. (Further information about the location and survey procedures is given in Appendix A. Appendix B reports all questionnaire measures, from both the earlier study and the follow-up, that are utilized in the research.)

To assess the degree of sampling bias, comparisons were made between the 1976 respondents and the nonrespondents (including those who could not be located and those who refused to respond to the questionnaire), using data collected during the senior year. The two groups were almost identical in family background (incuding the father's occupational prestige, parents' education, ethnicity, religion, and urban vs. rural residence), college grade point average, senior year career choice, senior occupational values, and self-concept reports. Thus, there is little reason to believe that those who participated in the follow-up study are markedly different, in earlier background or attitudes, from the other students. Still, selection bias on the basis of subsequent attainments cannot be ruled out. Moreover, in their senior year of college, the respondents indicated a slightly higher level of work involvement (the estimated importance of work in the future) than did the nonrespondents. This attitude may have heightened their motivation to respond to a lengthy questionnaire that focused on occupational experiences and work-related concerns.

This panel is highly advantaged, both with respect to its social origins (Mortimer and Lorence, 1981) and its destinations. Fifty-one percent of the fathers, and 35 percent of the mothers, were college graduates. In 1966 and 1967, the respondents' senior years in college, 32 percent reported family incomes above $20,000. By the time of the 1976 survey, about 10 years following graduation, more than half the panel (52 percent) had obtained the highest academic and professional degrees (including the Ph.D., medical, law, dental, and divinity) and an additional 26 percent had received master's degrees. As shown in Table 1-1, the occupations of the graduates are concentrated at the higher professional and managerial levels. Thus, as indicated by their educational, occupational and income attainments (shown in Table 1-2), the graduates represent a highly advantaged sector of the work force. This panel is

Table 1-1.   Percent Distribution of Occupations

Occupation	Percent
Doctor	17.6
Dentist	3.3
Lawyer	18.2
Physical and biological scientist	6.6
Social scientist	7.0
Elementary or secondary teacher	4.7
Artist, writer	4.3
Managerial or other person-oriented occupation	22.7
Other technical occupation	11.7
Skilled worker	1.8
Other	1.0
No response or inapplicable	1.2
Total	100.1*
	N = 512

*Total percent does not equal 100.0 because of rounding.

Table 1-2.   Percent Distribution of Income

	Income	Percent
1	Under $3,000	1.2
2	$3,000–4,999	1.8
3	$5,000–9,999	4.1
4	$10,000–14,999	13.7
5	$15,000–19,999	22.5
6	$20,000–24,999	18.4
7	$25,000–29,999	14.5
8	$30,000–34,999	6.3
9	$35,000–39,999	4.9
10	$40,000+	10.4
	No response	2.5
Total		100.3*
		N = 512

*Total percent does not equal 100.0 because of rounding.

probably not unlike persons of the same cohort who attended other highly selective colleges and universities. King's (1973:11) random sample of 600 entrants of Harvard College in 1961 and 1962 is quite similar in terms of fathers' occupations, parental education, family income, birth position and intactness of family of origin. Moreover, Korn (1968:217) reports that, of men who entered Stanford in 1961 and subsequently graduated, 65 percent were in graduate school by 1966, a figure not too distant from the 78 percent of our panel that received advanced educational degrees. The distinctive character of this group must be kept in mind in interpreting the findings of the study. These persons have graduated from a prestigious public university, and have succeeded in entering what are generally the most rewarding occupational positions. They have, in the aggregate, experienced a quite favorable life course.

The restrictions on the panel—by sex, social origins, educational experiences, and socio-economic attainments—certainly limit the generalization of the findings to the broader population of young adults. They also restrict the variance in the central independent variables under consideration—in parent–child relationships, psychological attributes, and work experiences. This reduction in variance could attenuate the relationships under scrutiny, making our tests more conservative. Moreover, it might reasonably be argued that if hypothesized effects are found to be significant, for example, if work autonomy is found to influence psychological development in a panel of this kind, in spite of the relative invariance in the central predictors and dependent variables, it is possible that the relationships would even be strengthened in a more representative panel of the workforce. But surely to obtain evidence for the generalizability of the findings reported here, further study is necessary—including women and minorities, and persons of different socio-economic background and level of attainment.[5] We give considerable attention to the liabilities of this panel in interpreting the findings.

Nevertheless, the features of this panel may be considered advantageous in several respects. By studying a very restricted panel of this kind, numerous confounding factors and complications are avoided. For example, the exclusion of women, though unfortunate in other respects, makes it unnecessary to introduce controls for sex differences in the processes under consideration,[6] and to examine the interrelationships among fertility, work history, and attainment that mark the life careers

---

[5] A further study, supported by the National Institute on Aging, was undertaken to assess the generalizability of the findings to be reported in this monograph (Lorence and Mortimer, in press; Mortimer and Finch, in press; Mortimer, et. al., 1985).

[6] Tangri (1974) followed up the women in the Michigan Student Study 3 years following their college graduation. Her analysis focuses on the determinants of the women's postgraduate aspirations and experiences relating to education and work.

of women (Card et al., 1980; Moen, 1985; Polachek, 1975). The use of a single school graduating cohort permits us to ignore between-college differences; these men went to the same college, at about the same time, and experienced whatever advantages graduation from such a selective public university would offer in the labor market of the middle sixties. They faced the same labor market conditions at the time of graduation which were, in general, quite favorable. The Michigan panel were at the edge of the "baby boom," seeking entry positions just before the labor market became glutted with college graduates. Financial aid for post-graduate education was still quite plentiful. They faced the same military service obligations, graduating from college at the time of a major military buildup for the Vietnam War. Thus, the graduates experienced many of the same conditions—having similar college backgrounds, economic opportunities, and other formative experiences that often differ markedly between cohorts.[7]

This is a study of the implications of work and family life for psychological change in the early life course, a period encompassing the transition from adolescence to adulthood. Our substantive emphasis was dictated by our overriding interests in work and family, and our belief that experiences in these domains are central for the formation of personality at this time of life. But by this emphasis we do not mean to suggest that other experiences, in different institutional contexts, are unimportant or without lasting impact. Thus, we might have focused on educational experiences and attainments. Even within a single university, there may be vast differences between students in different colleges (engineering, liberal arts, business, etc.), between major groups, or between students with different subcultural orientation (social, academic, political, etc., see Clark and Trow, 1966). Post-graduate educational experiences may also have great significance for subsequent development. But this is not a study of the effects of education.

Alternatively, we might have focused on the impacts of military service. Surely, the obligation to serve in the military could entail considerable sacrifice, life disruption, and perhaps also, for some young people, maturation and growth. Twenty-three percent of the panel did spend some time in the military. But this is clearly not the type of study which would yield understanding of the disadvantage entailed by interruption of education or delayed labor force entry. Those who served were disproportionately doctors and dentists (constituting 37.5 percent of all servers but only 21 percent of the study participants.) These men entered the military after completing their professional education, and were able to

---

[7] The authors are indebted to an anonymous reviewer whose comments on an earlier manuscript emphasized these advantages.

practice their profession in this setting. Of all those who spent time in the military, more than half (54 percent) appeared to have had experiences or training that were relevant to their subsequent occupational careers. When we compared those who served with those having no military experience, there were no differences in educational attainment; experiences of underemployment, unemployment, or involuntary part-time employment since college graduation; in job satisfaction; or in perceived career progress. Those who served in the military, however, had significantly lower mean incomes. (When examined by occupational subgroup, this difference was significant only for doctors and lawyers.) This income disadvantage is probably attributable to the shorter career tenures of the military men (years in the civilian work force).

We present this information for those who might wonder why, given that these men entered adulthood at the time of a major war, this important historical event is given so little attention. Clearly, military service can be a profound and even life-threatening experience, with strong and lasting impacts. But less than one-fourth of this panel even served in the military. And we cannot discern any major advantages or disadvantages for those who did. Given the extent and outcome of military involvement in this panel, our choice of emphasis lies elsewhere.

THE ANALYTIC STRATEGY: A BROAD OVERVIEW

In describing our analytic strategy, some history of the development of this work is in order. This monograph synthesizes and extends a series of earlier, more limited analyses, which were focused on the effects of work experiences on psychological change, considering selected individual dimensions, one at a time. Several published articles have presented this work—on occupational values (Mortimer and Lorence, 1979a), the self-concept (Mortimer and Lorence, 1979b), work involvement (Lorence and Mortimer, 1981), well-being (Mortimer and Lorence, 1981), and political orientation (Lorence and Mortimer, 1979). These early analyses highlighted the importance of work experiences, and particularly work autonomy, for psychological change over time.

It became clear as the analyses proceeded, however, that this work, while yielding findings of major importance, was overly restricted. For the psychological variables of interest are influenced not only by work experiences, but are also formed through experiences in the context of the family. Work experiences and attainments, likewise, are known to have important antecedents in the family. Therefore, an extension of the analyses to include variables reflecting family background and relationships was deemed highly fruitful. We would thus consider work and psychological development in terms of a more broadly encompassing process. Investigating psychological development within the context of the family, and examining the implications of this development for early adult attainments, led to several major extensions of the earlier work: a consideration of work and family linkages in the family of orientation; the effects of social class and, by implication, fathers' work experiences for parent–child relationships and psychological outcomes, and processes of intergenerational attainment. The first author's prior studies of fathers' work experiences as sources of values that are transmitted to sons (Mortimer, 1974, 1975, 1976) alerted us to the importance of paternal support in mediating occupational value transmission. More recent analyses (Mortimer and Kumka, 1982) showed that the process of value socialization in the family affected sons' occupational destinations as well.

In this monograph, we examine the processes of attainment and psychological development by estimating a complex causal model. This model permits estimation of the effects of the family on psychological development, the implications of early psychological attributes for subsequent occupational experiences and attainments, and finally, the effects of work experiences on psychological change in early adulthood. To obtain more precise estimates of the causal parameters, we develop latent constructs with multiple indicators, using confirmatory factor analytic procedures, and utilize structural equation modelling techniques with maximum likelihood estimation (Joreskog and Sorbom, 1979). More specific information about the statistical procedures is given in Chapter 2. The causal model which is the basis of Chapters 2 and 3 portrays the development of five psychological constructs—competence, a dimension of the self-concept; work involvment; and three occupational value dimensions, intrinsic, extrinsic, and people-oriented—both prior to, and following, labor force entry. To simplify the presentation, we discuss the model in two parts: Chapter 2 examines the processes by which the family influences psychological development and attainment; Chapter 3 considers the effects of work experiences on psychological change.

This broad analytic framework certainly entails much additional complexity over our prior, simpler models of work experience and psychological change. But this more comprehensive approach has several significant advantages. First, including both family and occupational influences in a single model permits investigation of the entire causal process of psychological development at once, enabling observation of the interrelated, and often reciprocal, effects of family, work experiences, and psychological change over the period encompassing the transition to adulthood. Second, examining the effects of family and work experiences together, along with other factors known to influence the processes of occupational attainment and psychological development, permits more accurate estimation of the causal paths. Thus, in Chapter 3, we can examine the effects of work experiences on psychological development within the broader contexts of socio-economic origin, parental support, educational attainment, and psychological stability over time. In doing so, this research clarifies a changing pattern of developmental influences as individuals move through the early life course. Before graduation from college, the degree of support from the father is found to be important for development of all psychological attributes under consideration. Because of its impact on adolescent occupational socialization, the family of origin influences adult occupational experiences and attainments. But a decade following college graduation, we will see that the supportiveness of the father–son bond is no longer a significant determinant of these attitudes and values. After entering the workforce, work experiences appear to take precedence in determining the further course of psychological development.

Furthermore, the linkages of work and the family differ, depending on whether the family of origin or of destination is the point of reference. Adolescents are affected by the work experiences (and socio-economic positions) of their parents, largely via differences in the quality of parent–child relations and the psychological attitudes and orientations that are fostered through these relationships. But when individuals form their own families, or families of destination, a different set of issues becomes pertinent. Now the focus shifts to the manner in which marriage influences early socio-economic attainment, to the "buffering" effects of marriage, and to strains in the family resulting from work experiences. The respondents are, for the most part, in the early phases of family building. It is not possible to study the impacts of their work experiences on their own relations with adolescent children, and the occupational socialization processes that might ensue from these relations. If we were able to perform such analyses, our work would have come full circle.

Because of the different nature of the processes under investigation, and the somewhat less developed "state of the field" in the problem areas to be considered, the analyses of Chapter 4 are less unified and have a more tentative and exploratory character than those presented in Chapters 2 and 3. In investigating the effects of marriage on attainment, we include both objective and subjective criteria of success. We also incorporate prior variables, found to be important for attainment in the earlier model, as controls. But given the generally exploratory character of our analysis, we use more conventional path analytic techniques with ordinary least squares regression. Investigating the "buffering" effects of marriage and the wife's support necessitates the inclusion of interaction terms (reflecting the joint effects of marriage and work experiences) in multiple regression analyses of psychological change. In constructing these models, we again make use of the findings presented earlier. Chapter 4 concludes with the estimation of another path model focused on the effects of work experiences on family dynamics and marital satisfaction. It contains several new variables that had not been previously considered: constructs reflecting strain in the family, the wife's support of the husband's occupation, and marital satisfaction.

THE CHAPTERS TO FOLLOW

Our discussion of the central issues to be considered and our analytic strategy has already indicated to the reader the major themes and organization of the monograph. We close this chapter with a brief synopsis. In Chapter 2, we examine work, family, and personality from the perspective of the family of orientation. We examine the implications of the family's socio-economic status for the quality of the parent–child relationship, a linkage of work and family life that, as we have seen, has been given major attention in the sociological literature. We find that the closeness of the father–son relationship is an important mediator of the effects of social class on psychological development and attainment. But our main focus in Chapter 2 is the family's influence on the development of psychological orientations, regarding the self, work, and occupational rewards, and the relevance of these attitudes and values for future career achievement. The data analyses show quite clearly that psychological development in adolescence, within the context of the family of origin, has important consequences for subsequent occupational experiences and attainments.

In Chapter 3, we draw on the information gathered on the men's work histories and occupations to assess the implications of work experience for change in psychological orientations over time. The major dimensions of work to be considered are work autonomy, income attainment, and the social content of work activities. We demonstrate that psychological change continues to occur following adolescence—persons change in response to significant occupational experiences encountered in the work environment. From the findings of Chapters 2 and 3 we conclude that human development during this phase of life is a highly dynamic and reciprocal process. Earlier psychological orientations, formed in the context of the family of origin, influence later experiences and attainments, which, in turn, affect subsequent personality development.

In Chapter 4, the focus shifts to work, personality, and the family of

procreation. We examine the effects of marriage on occupational attainment and well-being, attempting to separate the effects of selection
to marriage from the influences of marriage. We assess the family's
function as a "buffer," shielding men from the full psychological consequences of their work experiences. Finally, we investigate the implications of occupational achievement, pressure, and involvement for
family life. We find clear mutual interrelations of work, family, and
personality in this early stage of adulthood: marriage fosters occupational attainment and well-being, while, at the same time, work experiences have important repercussions in the family.

Now that we have discussed the central conceptual issues guiding the
development of this work, described the panel, and presented our overall
analytic framework, the stage is set for consideration of the first substantive question: how does the family of origin influence work-related
psychological development and early adult occupational attainment?

CHAPTER 2

Work–Family Linkage I: The Family of Origin and the Process of Occupational Attainment*

Sociologists of diverse theoretical persuasion recognize that parents have a crucial influence on their children's placement in the social class structure (Bowles and Gintis, 1976; Parsons, 1951; see Aldous et al., 1979). A good deal of controversy, however, has surrounded the manner in which the family exerts this effect. As a result, much empirical research in the social sciences has been directed toward understanding the causal processes underlying the intergenerational similarities in socio-economic position. At least since Rogoff's (1953) classic study of intergenerational occupational mobility, investigators have continued to examine the association between fathers' and sons' occupational positions. Following the lead of her research, numerous studies have confirmed that when fathers' and sons' occupations are cross-classified, cases tend to cluster along the diagonal, indicating a high propensity toward occupational inheritance. When occupations are arranged in order of their prestige, this pattern is the most pronounced at the upper and lower extremes, while a reduction in cell frequencies occurs from the diagonal to the

---

* While the analyses presented in Chapters 2 and 3 are entirely new, they integrate and extend prior, simpler causal models described in four previously published works: "Work Experience and Occupational Value Socialization: A Longitudinal Study," in the *American Journal of Sociology* (Mortimer and Lorence, 1979a); "Occupational Experience and the Self-Concept: A Longitudinal Study," in *Social Psychology Quarterly* (Mortimer and Lorence, 1979b); "Work Experience and Work Involvement," in *Sociology of Work and Occupations* (Lorence and Mortimer, 1981); and "Self-Concept Stability and Change from Late Adolescence to Early Adulthood," in *Research in Community and Mental Health* (Mortimer and Lorence, 1981). They also build on ideas presented in "Persistence and Change in Development: The Multidimensional Self-Concept," in *Life-Span Development and Behavior* (Mortimer, Finch, and Kumka, 1982).

corners of the matrix (see Pullum, 1975). Analyses of mobility tables thus demonstrate the status similarity of fathers' and sons' occupations, but give few clues as to the mechanisms producing this association.

Blau and Duncan's (1967) landmark study of *The American Occupational Structure* initiated what was to become a dominant paradigm for the study of intergenerational mobility. A major innovation of their approach was to examine the continuous variable of occupationnal prestige rather than the occupational categories of origin and destination. The application of path analytic techniques to the study of mobility, made possible by this shift of focus, permitted considerable advancement in the understanding of causal processes. Blau and Duncan's model of attainment allowed examination of the variables intervening between the father's education and occupational prestige and the son's occupational status, and demonstrated the importance of education in mediating the effects of socio-economic origins on destinations (Duncan et al., 1972:42). Since then, Blau and Duncan have been joined by numerous other investigators in elaborating and refining this basic model—to include income as well as the socio-economic status of the job; demographic variables such as race, ethnicity, size of community, and sex; features of the family—its intactness, the number of siblings, and birth order; and historical developments engendering change in the process of attainment over time. In the continuing quest for an understanding of the causal dynamics underlying socio-economic achievement, Sewell and Hauser (1976; Hauser, 1971) added achievement-related social-psychological variables to the model. Academic ability and performance, educational and occupational plans and aspirations, and significant others' encouragement, including the adolescent's parents, teachers, and friends, have been found to be important intervening variables mediating the effects of earlier experiences on subsequent outcomes (see Duncan et al., 1972; Gordon, 1972; Kerckhoff, 1974; Turner, 1962).

The timing and character of familial influence has become a critical issue in the study of status attainment. Does the family of origin exert its effects on the socio-economic success of the next generation mainly because of its influence as a socializing agent in childhood and adolescence, before the children's completion of formal education? Or does the family continue to influence the children's life chances in adulthood, following their entry to the labor force? This question is intricately tied to the mechanisms of parental influence: Do parents affect their children's chances for achievement mainly by fostering the acquisition of aspirations, attitudes, and knowledge which facilitate academic and occupational performance, or, alternatively, do parents continue, beyond this early stage of their children's lives, to enhance their opportunities by providing further advantages, such as specific job information, access to contacts, and economic resources?

It is generally believed that the predominate influence of the family occurs in childhood and adolescence. Education is seen as the crucial intervening variable, mediating the influence of social origins on destinations. The socio-economic standing of the family of orientation is viewed as having only a marginal direct effect on attainments after the children complete their formal education. Parents influence the educational achievement of their children largely through their encouragement of high aspirations and plans. Educational attainment, in turn, is the major variable directly affecting the children's occupational attainment. Duncan et al. (1972:43) summarize this perspective:

> Substantively, we are led to the conclusion that family background matters most for attainments that are close in time to the period of residence in the family of orientation and has a progressively attenuated influence on achievements coming later and later in the life cycle.

But in spite of the empirical support for this position (Kelley, 1973; Ornstein, 1976:63; Sewell and Hauser, 1976:13; Sewell et al., 1977), there is also evidence that the socio-economic level of the family of origin continues to influence children's occupational attainments following their entrance to the labor force. Girod et al. (1973), for example, examined the white collar versus blue collar status of men's fathers' occupations, and their own first and current jobs. He found a tendency for persons to return to their origin level if their first jobs differed from their fathers' job status. But they remained in the status of the first job if it corresponded to the father's occupational position. He called this pattern "countermobility." Perrucci (1974) similarly showed that the father's occupation influences advancement in the engineering profession after the individual acquires this occupational role.

Evidence from tabular studies such as these is quite weak, however, given their failure to control relevant individual differences, such as educational attainments, abilities, and aspirations, that might account for these patterns of mobility. But Sewell and Hauser (1976:23–24), on the basis of their longitudinal study of Wisconsin high school seniors, reported that, even 7 years after high school graduation, paternal occupational prestige still had direct effects on sons' prestige. Paternal income similarly influenced sons' income. These effects were observed after a host of intervening variables, including educational attainment, academic ability and performance, significant others' influence, and aspirations, were controlled. The most recent follow-up of this panel, occurring 18 years after high school graduation when the men were in their mid-thirties, showed that the direct effects of the father's occupational prestige were virtually identical for the sons' first and current jobs (Sewell et al., 1977). Similarly, Schooler (1980), using data from Kohn and Schooler's longitudinal study of a large representative sample of adult male workers, has reported direct effects of fathers' occupational prestige on sons' first, 1964, and 1974 job statuses, as well as sons' 1964 and 1974 incomes. In this study, the father's occupation continued to influence the son's attainment in 1974, when the sons were well into their careers, even after the statuses of their prior jobs and a wide range of individual and family background characteristics were taken into account. The respondents had been in the labor force at least 10 years.

Though they are rather small in absolute magnitude, the presence of these significant direct influences gives rise to questions regarding the processes through which they occur. Do these direct effects of family background on sons' occupational status and income attainments, years after their initial entry to the labor force, occur because some important intervening variable, representing a process occurring much earlier in life, has been left out of the causal model? For example, though aspirations for achievement are taken into account, there may be other psychological orientations, subject to the influence of socio-economic background or other features of the family of origin, that have significant implications for future attainment. Sons of higher socio-economic origin may be more confident of their abilities or more committed to work, and these psychological orientations could enhance subsequent occupational performance. Or, alternatively, fathers may help their sons directly as they move from one occupational position to another, by providing information, contacts, and even, in the case of professional or business inheritance, job opportunities themselves.

The present work builds on this tradition of research on the process of occupational attainment by investigating the *continuing* effects of the family of origin in the early work career. We elaborate the basic model of status attainment by examining *three* dimensions of occupational achievement: income, an important extrinsic reward and measure of occupational success; work autonomy, a major reward that is intrinsic to the work itself; and the social content of work, reflecting the interpersonal experiences and gratifications to be found at the workplace. (Given the relative invariance in occupational prestige in a sample of college graduates, status attainment cannot be a central outcome variable in a study of this kind.) We give central attention to the following questions:

1. Do socio-economic origins affect sons' most basic psychological orientations, concerning the self, work, and occupational rewards? Are

these relationships mediated by the character of the father–son relationship?

2. How do work-related attitudes and values influence the process of attainment? Do the sense of self-competence, commitment to work, and occupational reward values, measured in the senior year of college, predict educational and occupational achievements ten years following college graduation?

3. Are achievement-related behavioral variables following college responsive—either directly or indirectly—to social class background and paternal influence? What implications do post-graduate educational attainment, the pattern of the early work career, and the respondents' modes of job search have for the process of attainment?

Examining these questions will help us to understand the family's role in the process of intergenerational attainment, whether the family influences sons' occupational achievements via processes of socialization and attitude formation occurring prior to college graduation, or via subsequent more direct forms of influence. We investigate these questions within the framework of a causal model that is summarized in Figure 2-1. This simplified figure describes the causal ordering of the variables, without specifying particular causal paths. In the next section of this chapter, we review prior studies relating to these questions, and justify our specification of the causal model.

This study diverges from most other research in the status attainment literature in its focus on a rather select group of individuals: a panel of male college graduates who were about 30 years old at the time of the last data collection. This panel presents both disadvantages and advantages for an examination of the issues at hand. Most obviously, it limits the range of both socio-economic background and attainments. This truncation of the major independent and dependent variables, as well as those conceptualized as intervening, likely reduces the magnitude of associations among variables, and certainly precludes generalization of the findings to the broader population.

But more important in our judgment, this longitudinal data set presents a rare opportunity to assess the implications of differences in socio-economic origins, family relationships, and work-related psychological orientations, measured prior to labor force entry, for occupational attainments, measured a decade following. It permits analysis of the direct effects of these factors on attainments, as well as their indirect effects, mediated by later achievement-related behaviors. It is hypothesized that within the range of occupational prestige that is represented in the occupations of the men in this panel, these variables will influence the character of attainment, including both its vertical and nonvertical di-

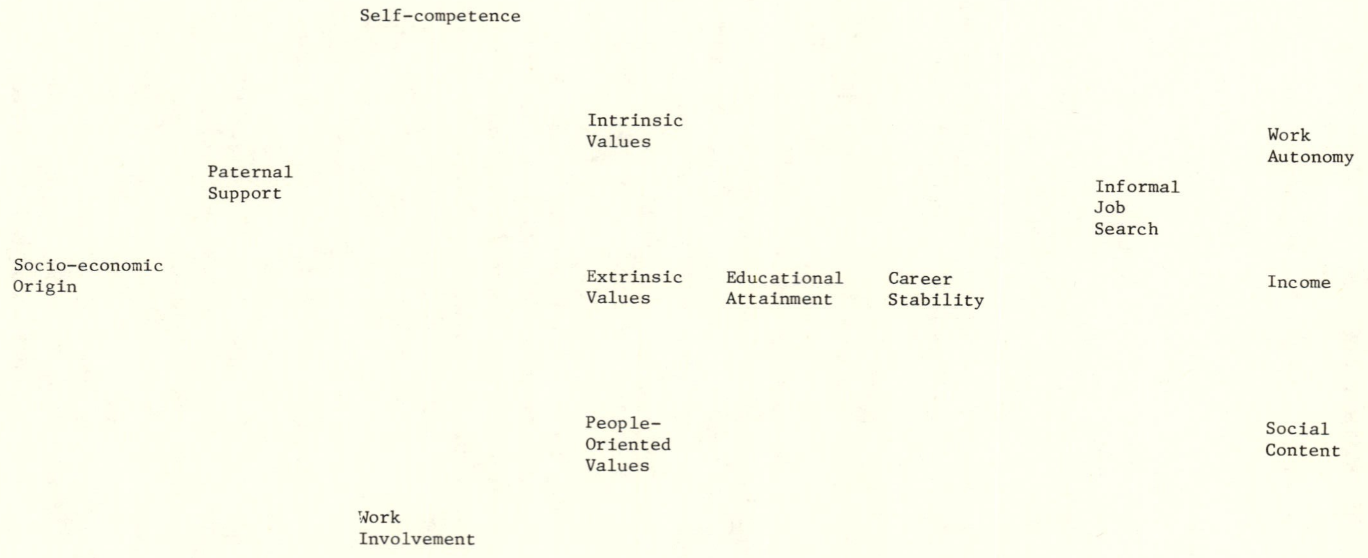

Self-competence

Paternal
Support

Socio-economic
Origin

Intrinsic
Values

Extrinsic
Values

People-
Oriented
Values

Work
Involvement

Educational
Attainment

Career
Stability

Informal
Job
Search

Work
Autonomy

Income

Social
Content

Figure 2-1. Variables in the Causal Model of Occupational Attainment

mensions. Though the findings are specific to young males in the early stages of professional and managerial careers, they will hopefully indicate basic processes of occupational attainment, generating hypotheses to be tested in future studies of more representative groups.

BACKGROUND

Socio-economic Origin, Father-son Relations, and Work-related Orientations

A positive relationship between socio-economic origin and adolescents' educational and occupational aspirations has repeatedly been observed (Gordon, 1972; Kerckhoff, 1974; Sewell and Hauser, 1976:17). Perhaps contributing to this pattern for men, there is evidence that fathers transmit their work attitudes to sons (Crites, 1962; Heilbrun, 1969). It has been reported that fathers' and sons' vocational interests are more similar than the interests of random pairs of men of the same age differential (Strong, 1957), and that interest similarity increases when there is evidence of adequate parental identification (Kahn, 1968). Other research has uncovered parallels between fathers' occupational prestige, functions, and other attributes, and sons' orientations to work and achievement (Berdie, 1943; Kahn, 1968; Lueptow, 1975; Turner, 1970).

But the *processes* facilitating this transmission of work-related orientations from parents to children have been subject to less systematic attention. The literature emphasizes parental behaviors which foster achievement motivation, the training for independence, and other practices which encourage the child to strive for high standards of excellence (Rosen, 1956; Winterbottom, 1958). Little is known about the manner in which parents influence other work-related orientations of their children that may affect achievement—the child's sense of competence, the interest in and commitment to work, and occupational reward values. These attitudes pertain not so much to a general need for achievement, but to the feelings of competence and commitment that would encourage vocational striving, and to the specific occupational targets toward which such an achievement motive might be directed.

Moreover, the implications of parental socio-economic position and occupational characterics for behaviors that could influence the transmission of their work-related orientations to children are far from clear. According to Aldous (1979:240), "Few research studies provide any helpful analyses of specific ways in which intrafamiliar factors associated with occupational status operate in the transmission of educational and occupational values."

The research of Melvin Kohn and his colleagues represents the most sustained effort to address this issue. Kohn's theoretical approach establishes three causal paths linking parental location in the social class structure with socialization outcomes: first, from parental occupational experiences of self-direction to parental values; second, from parental values to parental behaviors; and, finally, from parental values and behaviors to the values and behaviors of children. This theoretical model, sometimes called the "occupational linkage hypothesis" (Lueptow et al., 1979), has stimulated a great deal of research (see Kohn, 1977, 1981, for summaries of Kohn and Schooler's work and related studies), but has never been adequately tested in its entirety.

Kohn and Schooler (1973; Kohn, 1969) have devoted most attention to the first linkage in the causal chain—from parental occupational experiences to parental values. Their 1964 survey of 1500 employed fathers showed that differences in self-direction at work largely account for social class variations in parental values. At higher social class levels, parents valued self-directed qualities relating to the inner psychological development of children. At lower levels, there was greater emphasis on obedience or conformity to external standards of behavior. This pattern has since been confirmed by numerous investigators in a number of different societal contexts (Kohn, 1977). Kohn's interpretation of the finding places major emphasis upon the generalizing effects of work experience: those traits which are important for the father's own occupational success come to influence values concerning the most desirable qualities for children (1969). High levels of occupational self-direction would thus lead to an emphasis on the development of internal resources in children necessary for the exercise of self-reliance and autonomy in their own future work.

Research by Kohn and others (Bronfenbrenner, 1958; Gecas and Nye, 1974; Rosen, 1964; Sears et al., 1957) has also provided evidence for the second link in the causal chain. Class differences in values are reflected in parental behavior. Several studies have shown that social class is related to parental disciplinary practices, with greater use of reasoning and more concern with the intent of acts (instead of their consequences) at the higher levels.

> Working class parents are more likely to punish or refrain from punishing on the basis of the direct and immediate consequences of children's actions, middle class parents on the basis of their interpretation of children's intent in acting as they do. (Kohn, 1969:104)

Parental concern with self-direction thus fosters interest in the child's intentions; when parental emphasis is placed on conformity, the consequences of children's actions become more salient. In further support of the linkage between parental values and behaviors, Kohn reports "a direct connection between a particular parental value and a propensity to punish children for behavior that transgresses that value" (Kohn, 1969:105, note 7).

With respect to the last linkage in the model, between the parent's and child's values and behaviors, there is a mere paucity of direct evidence. According to the logic of Kohn's analysis (1977, 1980), self-directed styles of parenting would foster self-direction in children as well, facilitating adaptation to those educational and occupational tasks requiring independent thought and behavior. This self-direction would foster socio-economic achievement in the next generation (see also Bowles and Gintis, 1976). While Campbell (1978) showed that parental values relating to self-direction and conformity influence the child's adaptation to the sick role, this sphere of behavior is not directly relevant to achievement. Moreover, Morgan et al. (1979) found no significant relationship between parental self-directed values and high school seniors' locus of control. It should be noted, however, that these tests of Kohn's model incorporate no measures of parental behaviors or of the character of the parent–child relationship that would likely influence the transference of values.

Reinterpretation of some of the literature on social class and socialization, however, provides considerable indirect support for Kohn's entire causal model. First, it has been conclusively established that parents of higher-socio-economic level have the more communicative and supportive relationships with their children (Elder, 1962; Furstenburg, 1971; Gecas, 1979; Kerckhoff, 1972; Kohn and Carroll, 1960; Komarovsky, 1976: Chs. 6 and 7; McKinley, 1964; Rosen, 1964; Rosenberg, 1965; Scheck and Emerick, 1976). Parental support might reasonably be considered a direct outcome of self-directed parental values. The parent's concern with fostering self-direction in children would likely increase their involvement in the socialization process and heighten their supportiveness. In fact, Kohn (1969:117) found that middle class fathers were more involved in child rearing than their working class counterparts, and that "the higher fathers' valuation of self-direction, the more supportive of their sons and daughters they claim to be" (1969:115). Gecas (1979:398) has likewise linked parental supportiveness and affective involvement to concern with enhancing self-direction.

Furthermore, there is evidence establishing a clear linkage between these parental behaviors and socialization outcomes. Parental support has been found to be related to a host of child attitudes and behaviors that would facilitate socio-economic attainment: self-esteem (Bachman,

1970; Coopersmith, 1967; Rosenberg, 1965)[1], internal control (Scheck et al., 1973); and the potency dimension of the self-concept (Gecas, 1971; Thomas et al., 1974: Ch. 2). In a now classic study, Rosen and D'Andrade (1959) found that the parents of boys with high need for achievement were warmer and more encouraging, and the fathers less directive than parents of those with less need for achievement. Kerckhoff (1974) has reported that parents' concern with school work and their respect for their child's judgement (likely reflections of interest and support) were associated with less fatalism on the part of the sons. Gordon (1972) showed that parental encouragement was related both to children's educational aspirations and to their self-esteem. Finally, Komarovsky (1976:215), on the basis of an interview study of male college seniors, concluded that occupational "floundering" and commitment are highly associated with the quality of the father–son relationship.

We thus find that there is substantial evidence for causal linkages from parental socio-economic status to parental behavior, and from parental behavior to socialization outcomes. Social class, a crucial dimension of social structural location, influences parental supportiveness and encouragement, which, in turn, foster achievement-related attitudes and behaviors in children. But while the crucial explanatory variable in Kohn's analysis, that of occupational self-direction, is for the most part missing in this body of research, there is reason to believe that socio-economic status and self-direction in work are highly interrelated phenomena. Spaeth (1976b) has demonstrated a rather high correlation ($r = .80$) between occupational prestige and a scale representing the complexity of work with data, with people, and with things, a major component of Kohn's self-direction construct. Spaeth even goes so far as to conclude that "to all intents and purposes, occupational prestige and substantive complexity of the work are the same thing" (1976b:171; see also Morgan et al., 1979: 163).

If occupational prestige and substantive complexity may be considered approximate indicators of one another, and if occupational self-direction is related to parental values fostering a concern with building self-direction in children, one would expect to find that higher status parents are the more supportive. The consistent associations between parental social class, parental support, and child attitudes conducive to achievement therefore provide considerable evidence, albeit indirect, for Kohn's theoretical framework.

Like many other studies, in this research we have no information from parents, so we cannot assess the impacts of their values directly.

---

[1] For a summary of research on the effects of paternal nurturance on boys' self-esteem, see Biller (1976:104–105).

We do have data, however, concerning both the socio-economic level of the family and the supportiveness of the father–child relationship as it is perceived by the son. We therefore can examine the process by which socio-economic origin influences sons' achievement-related attitudes and values via the character of the father–son relationship. If a process of interpersonal communication and support underlies the association between socio-economic background and achievement orientations, we would expect that a close and understanding father–son relationship mediates the transmission of work-related psychological orientations from fathers to sons. Though mothers may influence vocational development as well as fathers, the father is the more likely occupational role model. Previous studies have demonstrated the importance of the father's occupation in influencing the vocational socialization of sons (see Biller, 1974:59–62 for a summary; Werts, 1966) and earlier analyses of this data set (Mortimer, 1974, 1975, 1976) provide further evidence for this conclusion.

Although we view the transmission of achievement-related orientations as of central importance in mediating the influence of the family on occupational attainments, our data allow examination of the direct effects of socio-economic status and father–son relations on behaviors following graduation from college. Thus we can ascertain whether the family affects post-graduate educational attainment (perhaps through the provision of necessary economic assistance), the pattern of stability or instability in the son's early work career, and the process of job search, net of those psychological variables that may be influenced by family background in an earlier phase of life.

Orientations to Work and the Process of Attainment. It is implicit in our discussion thus far that work-related psychological orientations influence socio-economic attainment, but we have not examined this assumption directly. The effects of psychological orientations on the process of attainment have long been of interest to social scientists. Attention has been directed to the achievement motive, aspirations and plans in relation to educational and occupational attainment, and the work ethic. Some early studies (Crockett, 1962; Littig and Yeracaris, 1965) attempted to demonstrate the importance of psychological variables by comparing the strength of the need for achievement among persons who had exhibited different patterns of intergenerational occupational mobility. Similarly, Duncan and Featherman (1972) examined Protestant ethic work values in a cross-sectional study of occupational attainment.

But there are those who allege that achievement orientations have no causal role in the attainment process, that they are merely products of attainments rather than as factors having independent influence on the direction of the work career (see Becker, 1979; Roberts, 1968). According to this line of argument, people adjust their attitudes according to their experiences; their orientations to work and achievement are for the most part responses to their educational and occupational attainments.

Certainly, in the absence of longitudinal data it cannot be determined whether differences in psychological orientations, found among persons of varying socio-economic level, are the causes or the effects of adult attainments. Strong achievement orientations, in adolescence and early adulthood, could have contributed to occupational success. Alternatively, they could be the consequence of occupational attainment, reflecting the effects of work experiences on attitudes and values.

There is evidence, however, based on long-term longitudinal studies, demonstrating the predictive utility of adolescent work-related attitudes. Psychologists (Jordaan and Super, 1974; Super and Bohn, 1970: 124-5) have noted the importance of early vocational maturity for subsequent socio-economic attainment and work adjustment. Vocational maturity has been operationalized in numerous ways, including measures of achievement motivation, the crystallization of occupational choice, the development of vocational interests, information about job requirements, and commitment to implementing a vocational preference. Moreover, data from the Fels study (Kagan and Moss, 1962) suggest that achievement imagery in early adolescence predicts achievement behavior in the twenties. Consistent with this latter finding, McClelland's follow-up of Wesleyan students showed that the need for achievement, measured in the senior year of college, predicted the entrepreneurial character of the work role 14 years later (1965).

It should be noted that psychological orientations have been found to have significant effects on subsequent attainment, even when numerous relevant control variables are included in causal models. Sewell and Hauser (1976:19) reported direct effects of achievement orientations on attainments 7 years beyond high school graduation. College plans predicted educational attainment, and occupational aspirations influenced occupational prestige, even when controlling socio-economic background, student ability and academic performance, and significant others' influence. Featherman (1971), on the basis of his multivariate analysis of longitudinal data from the Princeton study, also concluded that work orientations have independent impacts on socio-economic achievement over a 7- to 10-year period in adulthood.

Researchers who have included psychological variables in models of the status attainment process have focused on the following question: To what extent do achievement orientations mediate the effects of background variables on adult attainments? Although the differential attainments of social class, racial, and ethnic groups are often explained in terms of variations in their orientations to achievement—e.g., the unwillingness to delay gratification as endemic in the "culture of poverty," or the low internalization of the Protestant work ethic on the part of some ethnic minorities—several empirical studies have shown that psychological variables only partially mediate the effects of social origins on destinations. But while they have been found to constitute only weak intermediaries between social background and achievement, it is generally agreed that they affect attainments directly, independent of their association with social class origins (Duncan et al., 1972; Featherman, 1971; Sewell and Hauser, 1976).

The present study further pursues this set of issues by examining the implications of three kinds of work-related psychological orientations, all measured in the senior year of college, for achievement-related behaviors and attainments 10 years thereafter. We investigate the importance of these psychological dimensions as intervening variables, mediating the impacts of socio-economic origins and family relations on adult attainments. They include a work-related dimension of the self-concept, the individual's sense of competence; work involvement or commitment; and occupational reward values. Because of the centrality of these variables to our investigation, we describe each of these psychological constructs more fully in the following pages.

The Competence Dimension of the Self Concept. There is a voluminous literature on the self-concept, particularly relating to self-esteem (Wells and Marwell, 1976; Wylie, 1979), and widespread recognition of its importance for adequate personality functioning. While authors have used the term "self-esteem" in referring to various dimensions of the self-image, Rosenberg (1976) has clearly distinguished self-esteem, or the individual's general evaluation of self, from other components (see also Gecas and Mortimer, forthcoming). The present analysis focuses on another dimension of the self-concept, self-competence or personal efficacy. Rosenberg refers to this dimension as "self-confidence," or "the anticipation of successfully mastering challenges, obstacles, or tasks . . . it is closely associated with an internal locus of control" (p. 12). Self-esteem, the person's overall self-evaluation, refers to a sense of goodness, with strong moral connotations. Self-esteem and the sense of personal competence may generally be positively related. However, following Rosenberg, we view them as conceptually distinct components of the self-concept. It is likely that the individual's assessment of the value of instrumental control would moderate the association between the sense of competence and self-esteem (Rosenberg, 1976:12; and 1979:18–19, 288; Turner, 1976).[2]

There is evidence, from studies of both self-esteem and internal control, that the self-concept influences occupational attainment. Self-esteem has been found to be positively related to socio-economic status (Gurin and Gurin, 1976; Jacques and Chason, 1977; Luck and Heiss, 1972) and self-direction in work (Kohn, 1969; Kohn and Schooler, 1973: 103, 115), and inversely related to occupational stress (Luck and Heiss, 1972). However, the relative importance of selection and socialization processes in producing these associations is not known.

In favor of the "selection hypothesis," of primary concern to us in this chapter, high adolescent self-esteem has been found to be associated with high occupational aspirations (Bedeian, 1977; Douvan and Adelson, 1966; Gordon, 1972), expectations of success in attaining one's goals, and persistent striving for achievement (Rosenberg, 1965). Moreover, it is widely assumed that a positive self-image promotes occupational achievement (Korman, 1970). Hall (1971), for example, hypothesizes that high self-esteem and confidence engender information search and risk-taking, activities that facilitate the mastery of occupational tasks. Morrison's (1977) cross-sectional data are consistent with this position; managers who had adapted successfully to changing role demands had higher self-esteem and risk-taking propensity than those who did not. Providing more direct evidence for the selection hypothesis, Bachman and his colleagues (Bachman and O'Malley, 1977:373; Bachman et al., 1978:113) have reported a small but positive relationship between self-esteem, measured during high school, and occupational status 5 years following graduation.

Andrisani and Nestel's (1976) panel study focussed on the locus of control, a psychological dimension more closely related to the sense of personal efficacy or self-competence, and therefore more directly relevant to us here. Individuals with an initially high sense of internal control, when studied 2 years later, had achieved higher status and income than those with a more external control locus. The authors attribute the advantages of the "internals" to their confidence, frequent exploratory behavior, and propensity to take risks (see also Andrisani, 1978; Gurin and Gurin, 1976). Furthermore, Schooler (1980) reports that a construct reflecting responsibility for one's own fate, which appears quite similar

---

[2] This usage diverges from that of other investigators who describe self-esteem instrumentally—stressing efficacy and competence (see Korman, 1970; Weidman et al., 1972; and Kohn and Schooler, 1973, who view "self-confidence" as a dimension of self-esteem). Like Rosenberg (1979), we conceptualize self-esteem as self-acceptance, self-liking, and a sense of personal worth, independent of mastery or achievement potential (see Wells and Marwell, 1976:62–64).

to internal control, predicted status attainment over a 10-year period, even after other relevant psychological variables and the characteristics of previous jobs were controlled.

Building on this earlier work, we hypothesize that self-competence, measured prior to labor force entry, will foster the attainment of autonomous, extrinsically rewarding, and interpersonally satisfying work experiences. Those who perceive themselves as highly competent would have stronger expectations of success in reaching their goals, and there is considerable experimental evidence that such expectations become self-fulfilling prophecies in facilitating subsequent attainments (Jones, 1977). We also expect, on the basis of studies reviewed in the previous section of this chapter, that the sense of competence will be stronger among students of higher socio-economic background, and that this pattern will be mediated by close and supportive father–son relationships.

Work Involvement.   Investigators have conceptualized work involvement in a variety of ways. According to Locke (1976:1301), "a person who is involved in his job is one who takes it seriously, for whom important values are at stake in the job, whose moods and feelings are significantly affected by his job experiences." Dubin (1956; Dubin et al., 1976) considers work to be a "cent...l life interest" to the extent that workers prefer to engage in activities in a work-related, as opposed to a nonwork context. Lawler and Hall (1970) define "job involvement" as "the degree to which the job situation is central to the person and his identity." Other investigators have used the terms work (or occupational) "commitment" (Becker, 1960; Beynon and Blackburn, 1972; Elder, 1974; Kohn, 1969:178–81), "identification" (Becker and Carper, 1956), and "centrality" (Mannheim, 1975) to connote similar attitudes. While the conceptual and operational definitions of these terms are somewhat different, all refer to the same basic phenomenon—the extent to which work is considered a central and important sphere of life activity.

There is evidence that work involvement is significantly related to job satisfaction, though it is conceptually and empirically distinct (Lawler and Hall, 1970). Thus, some research suggests that when individuals are highly involved in their work, they become more critical and dissatisfied with their jobs than they would otherwise be (Beynon and Blackburn, 1972; Gurin et al., 1960). The person who attaches little importance to work may not be as disturbed by low levels of reward. However, a positive relationship between job satisfaction and work involvement has also been reported (Mannheim, 1975). There is evidence that work involvement is positively related to ambition and an "upward anchorage" in orientation to career (Goldman, 1973; Lodahl and Kejner, 1965) and to commitment to the employing organization (Dubin and Porter, 1975). In one study (Dubin and Champoux, 1974), job-oriented blue-collar male workers were rated by their supervisors as high in initiative and application, cooperation, and quantity of work. But they were also low in adaptability, perhaps because of their great emotional investment in their jobs.

As in the case of self-competence, we hypothesize that a high level of importance attached to work *prior to* labor force entry will facilitate occupational attainment. This orientation would likely heighten the motivation to obtain diverse occupational rewards—intrinsic, extrinsic, and people-oriented—and encourage effort and persistence in striving for these gratifications. The findings of the Berkeley studies, linking adolescent attitudes to adult attainment, are quite supportive of this hypothesis. High commitment to work and high occupational aspirations were found to predict vocational achievement and adjustment many years later (Block and Haan, 1971; Clausen, 1976; Elder, 1974: Ch. 7; Elder and Rockwell, 1979). We also expect, paralleling our previous discussion of the development of personal efficacy, that high socio-economic background, mediated by a favorable father–son relationship, will enhance occupational involvement in late adolescence.

Occupational Values. Occupational reward values are assessments of the importance of the various rewards offered by work. College students aspiring to different occupations have repeatedly been found to have varying levels of concern with the several types of rewards potentially available to them at work (see Davis, 1965; Rosenberg, 1957). In the many studies of adult workers, two major value dimensions have repeatedly been distinguished. Extrinsic values concern rewards that are derived from the job but are external to the work itself (e.g., income, prestige, and advancement). In contrast, intrinsic values involve rewards directly obtained from work experience (e.g., interest, challenge, responsibility, autonomy, and similar gratifying features). Studies of college students, however, generally report two intrinsic dimensions as well as the extrinsic one (Davis, 1965; Rosenberg, 1957). The first, which we will call intrinsic, involves the use of abilities, expression of interests, and creativity. The second is a people-oriented set of concerns—the chance to work with people and to be useful to society.

The widespread interest in occupational reward values on the part of vocational and industrial psychologists, as well as sociologists, is attributable to their influence on career decision-making. While initially they affect occupational choice, later in the work history they influence job and career changes. The consistent relationships between occupational values and work preferences (Holland, 1976) support the hypothesis that occupational choice is a rational process in which persons attempt to maximize the occupational rewards that they most highly value (Blau et al., 1956). Job satisfaction, and the propensity to change jobs, are also widely viewed as contingent on the interaction of work experiences and values. As a result, people will respond differently to the same occupational experiences according to their values and prior expectations (see Belcher and Atchison, 1976; Kahn, 1972; Lawler, 1973). While this "fit" or interaction hypothesis is rather controversial,[3] there is some evidence that incongruity of reward values and work experiences increases job dissatisfaction (Kalleberg, 1977; Locke 1976: 1304). According to prominent theories of career development, incongruence between values and rewards also fosters attempts to change jobs in order to realize a better fit (Andrisani and Miljus, 1976; Holland, 1976). Thus, Lofquist and Dawis (1969: Chs. 5 and 6) view the individual, during the course of the work career, as continually attempting to maximize the correspondence between personal needs and the "reinforcer system of the work environment" (see also Hall, 1971; Jordaan and Super, 1974; and Super, 1970).

Though some sociologists (Becker, 1979; Roberts, 1968) tend to discount values as causal factors in attainment, their importance probably increases with the socio-economic position of the job choosers and their standing in the labor market. Upon entering the labor force during the economically favorable period of the mid-sixties and early seventies, the college graduates in this study had high educational qualifications, enhancing their market position, and a wide range of occupational opportunities from which to choose. This situation would appear to maximize the potential for the implementation of values.

Even for such persons, however, it is usually not possible to maximize all occupational rewards at once. Temme (1975: Ch. 4), on the basis of extensive occupational level analyses, has shown that valued rewards of an intrinsic and extrinsic nature are not highly correlated with one another. Thus, some occupations may provide considerable opportunity for the fulfillment of intrinsic or people-oriented values and provide much poorer prospects for the attainment of extrinsic rewards. His analysis suggests that important compromises or "trade-offs" are necessary in career decisions, as the individual seeks to obtain positions whose rewards are valued most highly. As attempts are made to maximize these rewards, however, occupational experiences that are assigned less priority may have to be sacrificed. (See also Taubman, 1975:17–19).

These considerations, as well as the findings of previous studies of

---

[3] See Herzberg (1966), Kohn (1977:liii), Kohn and Schooler (1973:109), and Stone (1976). Mortimer (1979) provides a review of research bearing on the fit hypothesis.

occupational choice and job change, lead us to expect that occupational reward values will influence the character of attainment, including its socio-economic and nonvertical dimensions. Upon entry to the labor force, persons will choose occupations, and thus select their work experiences, on the basis of their values. The individual will attempt to select a work role which maximizes rewards that are deemed most important. If value preferences are not initially fulfilled, an attempt may be made to change employment so as to achieve a greater congruence between values and rewards. As a result, persons with high extrinsic reward values would gravitate toward occupations with great income-generating potential; those placing high priority on the people-oriented rewards would move to occupations providing opportunities for work with people; and individuals with strong intrinsic values would attempt to maximize interest and self-expression in their work.

We therefore hypothesize that occupational reward values play an important part in the process of occupational attainment. Like self-competence and work involvement, we also expect to find that these values are influenced by socio-economic origin and the character of the father–son relationship. Since the rewards encompassed by each dimension of value tend to be more prevalent in occupations of higher standing, it is reasonable to suppose that fathers in the more prestigious, economically rewarding, and interpersonally satisfying occupations would transmit such values to their sons.

Interrelations of Self-Competence, Work Involvement, and Occupational Reward Values.   While the three work-related psychological orientations of interest to us here are all expected to influence the attainment process, there is reason to believe that they are not independent of one another. In attempting to develop a justifiable causal ordering among the five constructs, all measured at the same time, we assumed that occupational values are the more proximal influences on occupational choices and attainments. Choice, by its very nature, implies the implementation of values (Blau et al., 1956; Williams, 1970:442–443), and several studies have verified a direct connection between occupational reward values and career decision-making (Davis, 1965; Mortimer, 1976; Rosenberg, 1957). We consider the competence dimension of the self-concept and work involvement to be causally prior to the three value dimensions (see Figure 2-1).

A sense of competence likely enhances the individual's perception of the chances of obtaining intrinsic, people-oriented, and extrinsic occupational rewards. We therefore anticipated that self-competence would have positive effects on all three dimensions of occupational reward values. This expectation is consistent with current conceptualizations of achievement-related motivations as dependent on self-perceptions (Spenner and Featherman, 1978:384–387) and expectations of success (Atkinson et al., 1976:38). Persons will be unlikely to set high goals, or to strive for the attainment of particular occupational rewards if they perceive themselves incapable of implementing their goals. According to Bandura,

> . . . expectations of personal efficacy determine whether coping behavior will be initiated, how much will be expended, and how long it will be sustained in the face of obstacles . . . (1977:191)

Highly related to a sense of competence and personal efficacy is the level of internal control (Rotter, 1966), though they are not identical psychological phenomena (Bandura, 1977). Perceiving oneself as competent, strong, and capable of mastering problems will promote a perception of one's life situation as dependent on one's own actions. Conversely, the belief in external control is likely to be associated with a sense of impotence and incapacity. Rotter and Mulry (1965) have posited that internal-external control orientations influence values, and present experimental evidence suggesting that internals value skill-determined more than chance-deterined reinforcement. There was some tendency for the reverse to be true for externals. Since occupational rewards are largely skill-determined, it would be consistent with Rotter and Mulry's research to find that evaluation of the rewards to be obtained in the work setting are responsive to a sense of personal efficacy.

In view of these considerations, we expect that individuals with a strong sense of competence will view occupational rewards as within their reach. The potential satisfactions to be found in the work sphere will, therefore, be quite salient to them. In contrast, the person with a sense of personal inadequacy will likely seek other kinds of satisfactions, requiring less instrumental effort and less demanding coping behaviors. Gordon's (1972: Ch. 5) finding that measures of self-competence are positively related to occupational aspiration is quite consistent with this reasoning.

We follow a parallel line of argument in specifying that work involvement also precedes occupational reward values in the causal model. We expect that work involvement, like self-competence, will engender a tendency to seek life satisfactions in the work sphere, reinforcing the importance of all three occupational rewards. It is therefore hypothesized that the level of commitment to work, as indicated by the individual's expectations, while still in college, of the degree of importance of work in the future, will have positive effects on each of the three value dimensions.

However, no hypothetical causal relationships are specified among the three dimensions of occupational reward values, nor between work involvement and self-competence. While it is plausible to assume that the occupational reward values are related to one another in a complex reciprocal manner, these interrelations cannot be adequately specified on the basis of prior studies. In addition, work involvement and competence may be reciprocally interrelated, as interest in work, and the achievement-related effort and performance fostered by this attitude, enhance one's perception of competence, and as the sense of personal efficacy encourages further involvement and commitment to the work sphere. Given the difficulty in specifying the preponderant direction of influence in these relationships, on either theoretical or empirical grounds, we have chosen to leave them indeterminate in the causal model.

As noted earlier, we hypothesized that self-competence and work involvement would influence all three dimensions of occupational attainment. It is not possible, however, to specify in advance the causal processes through which these psychological orientations affect the occupational outcomes. Their effects may occur indirectly, mediated by occupational reward values or by work-related achievement behaviors following the completion of college. Early work involvement could increase the likelihood of a stable career progression. A firm commitment to work, and the high level of effort which this involvement promotes, could make problems such as subemployment and unemployment less likely. Similarly, self-competence may facilitate post-graduate educational achievement, diminish the likelihood of career instability and lead to more active job search. Alternatively, competence and work involvement may influence the occupational attainments directly, independent of the variables placed later in the causal chain. Moreover, it is unclear whether the effects of values on attainments will be entirely direct, or whether some or all of their influence will be mediated by differences in post-graduate educational attainment, the pattern of the early work career, or by differences in job-seeking behaviors. We now turn to these achievement-related behaviors.

Post-graduate Achievement Behaviors as Determinants of Occupational Attainment

This brings us to the final set of issues under consideration in this chapter—the implications of achievement-related behaviors, following college graduation, for occupational attainments in the early work career. As noted above, we examine three kinds of behaviors, each of which has been addressed in the stratification literature: post-graduate education, the stability of the early work career, and the mechanisms of job search. Both their direct effects on attainments, and their functions as intervening variables, mediating the influence of earlier factors on later achievements, are of interest.

Higher education is well recognized as an important dimension of human capital investment, fostering higher income attainment (Douglass, 1977; Strumpel, 1971). Indeed, the effect of higher education, particularly at the post-graduate level, on income may become increasingly manifest as individuals move into the middle and later phases of professional and managerial careers, given the relatively high and late income peaks in these occupations (Kelly, 1973). The effect of education on work autonomy has also been subject to some scrutiny (Kohn, 1977; Kohn and Schooler, 1973; Spaeth, 1976a). Kohn and Schooler's (1978) longitudinal analysis suggests that the direct effects of education on the substantive complexity of work may diminish over time.

In their senior year of college, the distribution of the respondents' career choices showed them to be highly attracted to the professions of medicine, law, and college teaching, and to various managerial and administrative occupations (Mortimer, 1974). While post-graduate education is a necessity for the first three professions, it has also become increasingly important as a requirement for entry to career tracks leading to the most prestigious and rewarding managerial positions in business and government. These occupations involve service to clients or substantial involvement in other kinds of interpersonal relations. In this panel, post-graduate education may therefore be a significant influence on our third dimension of attainment, the social content of work, as well as on the other two (income and work autonomy).

The effects of education on occupational attainments may be mediated, at least partially, by two subsequent variables in the causal model: the stability of the early work career and the reliance on formal vs. informal job search procedures. First, it is reasonable to suppose that post-graduate education, because of its great cost in time and money, would engender career stability, given the losses associated with change in the career (Super and Bohn, 1970:114). Post-graduate degree holders are also apt to have had access to the most desirable entry positions—especially in terms of future prospects—which would lessen their inclination to change careers. Strumpel (1971:64) reports that advanced degree holders, in comparison to B.A. recipients, have more stable work histories, being more likely to have had only a few jobs in the same occupation during the course of their careers. In this study, we define career stability in terms of two related phenomena: a shift in occupational focus after college graduation, and difficulties in finding and maintaining appropriate employment. Career changes, as well as periods of unemployment, involuntary part-time employment, and sub-employment (working in a job that does not require one's training and skills), suggest difficulties in attaching oneself to a satisfying career ladder. These problems are expected to have deleterious consequences for early occupational attainments.

The four years of college are a time of vocational exploration and change for the majority of students (Davis, 1965; Sharp, 1970). This exploration is sometimes accompanied by uncertainty and inner turmoil, as an attempt is made to match values and abilities with the rewards and requirements of future careers. But by the time of graduation, most have settled on a career, and proceed to implement their vocational goals. On the basis of a national longitudinal study of 16,000 male 1958 B.A. recipients, Sharp (1970:6) concluded that the undergraduate major "represents a strong vocational commitment." Between 1960 and 1963, 74 percent of the men remained in the same occupation (72). She also reports that, in the 1958 class, 8 or 9 years younger than the cohort considered in the present study, those who did change were unlikely to enter a profession, but instead went into less prestigious and remunerative work, such as sales and clerical positions in business. According to Sharp (1970:12),

> A college graduate who chooses or is forced to make a radical field switch after graduation either has a fairly lengthy retreading operation ahead, or else he will end up in a professionally marginal position. The smoothest careers, in terms of graduate study and jobs, are enjoyed by those who do not deviate from the area which they selected for themselves during their undergraduate years.

Career stability is expected to be significantly influenced by the psychological orientations of the individual, placed earlier in the causal chain, as well as by educational attainment. Specifically, those with a greater sense of competence, high work involvement, and strong occupational reward values are expected to be more successful in smoothly implementing their initial occupational goals.

The final intervening variable in our causal model refers to the mode of job search—the means by which the most recent occupational position was located. Granovetter's (1974) work has drawn attention to the importance of informal contacts in occupational attainment. According to his analysis, placement in social networks that provide job information is a crucial factor in achievement. His study of recent job changers, men in professional, technical, and managerial occupations, indicated that those who had informal sources of job information found the higher paying and more satisfying jobs. Those who relied on formal mecha-

nisms, such as employment agencies, advertisements, and direct application, were clearly disadvantaged in these respects. Granovetter attributes
the large unexplained variances in predicting socio-economic success to
analysts' failure to take into account the factors which affect placement
in important information networks.

Granovetter's study focuses on weak dyadic ties, since linkages to the
more lucrative jobs were work relations of relatively low intensity and
involvement. He examined features of the career which facilitate or
impede the formation of such ties, e.g., work in a people-oriented vs.
technical job; previous career mobility leading to the development of
contacts; and the length of time spent in the career. While the data at
hand would allow us to investigate some of these issues, we are more
concerned in the present analysis with the implications of earlier variables in the model—socio-economic background, father–son relations,
work orientations, and post-graduate education—for the utilization of
different job search procedures, and the effects of these, in turn, on
occupational attainments.

One of the mechanisms by which fathers in higher socio-economic
positions might influence their sons' chances later in life is by providing
job information and contacts that facilitate movement into the more
desirable jobs. It is also plausible that persons who have more positive
orientations to work—those who feel more competent, who are more
committed to work, and who assign higher value to occupational rewards—would be more assertive in seeking out personal acquaintances
for job information, using more informal (in addition, perhaps, to formal) modes of job search. Finally, studies of professional education have
emphasized the strong peer subculture and friendships which develop
in the course of professional training and may continue throughout the
worklife (Becker et al., 1961; Moore, 1969:878–880). Work-related contacts may thus be made in graduate and professional school that prove
useful in later job search.

In addition to investigating whether job search procedures mediate
the effects of variables earlier in the model, we extend previous research
to consider their implications for *three* dimensions of attainment: income,
work autonomy, and the social content of work. Only the first of these
occupational attainments (along with prestige) has been considered in
prior studies of job search.

This concludes our description of the central variables in the causal
model. Like many previous investigators, we are interested in the processes through which social class origin influences the socio-economic
attainments of the following generation. But we have attempted to incorporate a broader range of processes into our causal model, considerably extending the study of the attainment process. First, by drawing

on the related work of family sociologists, concerned with the processes of socialization and development, we have a major focus on the father–son relationship, considered as a mediator of the effects of social class position on sons' achievement-related psychological orientations, and as a variable of importance in its own right. We have seen that specification of paternal support as intervening between family social class background and sons' attitudes and values is highly consistent with Kohn and Schooler's theoretical framework, directed toward explaining the associations among social class, parental values and behaviors, and children's attitudes and attainments.

Secondly, instead of studying the socioeconomic level of occupational plans and aspirations, of great interest in prior investigations, we are examining a range of social psychological determinants: the sense of competence, work involvement and occupational values. Our emphasis is partly attributable to the particular character of the panel under study; their aspiration levels and plans are quite restricted, given their socio-economic backgrounds, high educational attainment, and the character of their occupational choices. However, we believe that a wider range of psychological orientations is relevant to the attainment process, regardless of socio-economic origin, and may help us to predict the particular features of occupational destinations.

Third, the fact that we are studying a 10-year period following college graduation has allowed us to consider behavioral processes that are relevant to attainment: post-graduate educational achievement, the stability of the early work career, and the modes of job search. Finally, in comparison to prior research, we broaden the occupational outcomes to include three dimensions of attainment—work autonomy, income, and the social content of work. We hope that extending the investigation of occupational attainment in these directions will enhance our understanding of the processes through which the family of origin influences the occupational destinations of sons. Because our study is confined to a panel of highly educated men, it remains for future studies to examine the variations on these processes that may occur in other segments of the population.

We now turn to our operationalization of these variables.

MEASURES

Father's Socio-economic Status

Socio-economic level is represented by a single construct with three indicators: the father's occupational prestige (Siegel, 1971), the father's education, and family income, all obtained while the respondent was still in college. (The specific questions are given in Appendix B.)

It has been argued (Duncan et al., 1972: 42; Otto, 1975) that the various measures of social class standing often have impacts of different kind and magnitude on dependent variables, and therefore should be considered separately in causal models. We have followed this strategy in some previous analyses (Mortimer and Lorence, 1979a, b), with somewhat anomalous results. We found (1979a: 1377), for example, that family income had a positive effect on all three measures of sons' occupational attainment—income, work autonomy, and the social content of work—even when controlling the sons' senior occupational reward values, grade point average, and the mother's education. But when included in a multivariate causal model, the father's education and occupational prestige had no significant impact on these attainments. At the same time, the mother's education had a negative effect on the son's work autonomy and the social content of his work.

It is perhaps pertinent to an understanding of these anomalies to point out that each of the socio-economic background indicators contains errors of measurement (due to question wording, other test effects, etc.) which are not taken into account when entered as single variables in causal models. Since the reliabilities of these indicators for young, well-educated professional and managerial workers are not known, we assumed in these previous analyses that each was measured without error. Each indicator may also contain unique variation that is not associated with the other measures. However, by using the measures of socio-economic status as multiple indicators of a more general, latent construct, we can separate measurement error and indicator-specific variance (both considered as "error") from the "true score" variance of each indicator. By defining the construct in terms of the covariation of the indicators, its effects, taken as a whole, can be examined. Given the positive intercorrelation among the socioeconomic variables[4], and the widespread conceptualizations of socio-economic position as determined by educational achievement, occupational prestige, and income, this strategy seems most reasonable. It is also more parsimonious, greatly reducing the total number of parameters to be examined.

Since the focus of this analysis is on the transmission of socio-economic position from father to son, the mother's education is not included in the construct. While the mother's education did not show the same relationship as the other social class indicators to all subsequent variables in the model, it is likely that inclusion of the mother's education in a

---

[4] The zero-order correlation of father's prestige and education is .648; father's prestige and family income, .568; and between the education and income variables, .410.

Table 2-1. Distribution of Fathers' and Sons' Occupations

Occupations	Fathers[a]	Sons[b]
Doctor	3.7	17.6
Dentist	1.4	3.3
Lawyer	6.3	18.2
Physical & Biological Scientist	2.0	6.6
Social Scientist	.8	7.0
Teacher	3.7	4.7
Artist, Writer	1.0	4.3
Other person-oriented occupation	44.3	22.7
Other technical occupation	21.3	11.7
Blue collar occupation	9.2	1.8
Other	.6	1.0
Missing data	5.9	1.2
Total	100.2[c]	100.1
	N 512	N 512

[a]When the son was in college.
[b]In 1976.
[c]Columns do not sum to 100.0 because of rounding.

socio-economic background construct would yield very similar findings.[5] Though 40 percent of the mothers were employed during the respondents' senior year of college, only 28 percent worked full time. We have no information concerning the mother's contribution to family income. Since the wife's contribution is usually considerably smaller than that of the husband (U.S. Department of Labor, 1975b), our measure of family income mainly reflects the father's income.

Table 2-1 shows the occupational distributions of both fathers and sons. Given conventional definitions of mobility, based on occupational prestige, it is evident that this panel is a rather upwardly mobile group. Whereas less than 1 out of 5 fathers (17.9 percent) were in the professions of medicine, dentistry, law, teaching, college teaching, and science, the majority (57.4 percent) of the sons were found in these occupational categories in 1976. Almost two-thirds of the fathers are in managerial (the category "other person-oriented" in the table consists mainly of

---

[5] Kerckhoff (1974:64) added the mother's education as an exogenous variable to causal models (including the father's education and occupation, and the son's IQ). While the mother's education was significantly related to educational expectations in the 9th and 12th grade, it did not contribute substantially to the explained variance nor alter the other parameters "appreciably." Schooler (1980) reports a direct effect of the mother's education on sons' educational attainment, even after controlling the father's education and occupational prestige.

managers) and technical occupations, mostly middle-level positions in business, while this kind of occupational designation applies to only about a third of the sons. Finally, just under 10 percent of the fathers are in blue collar work, while this is a very rare career destination among the sons (1.8 percent).

While it must be admitted that this panel of college graduates comes from relatively advantaged occupational backgrounds, there is still considerable variation in their socio-economic origins. This is evident not only from the occupational distribution of fathers, but in the fathers' educations and the family incomes (see Appendix B). More than 1 out of 5 fathers had no more education than high school, an almost equal proportion had only some college. Seventeen percent had incomes under $10,000 in 1966–67. The analysis which follows enables an assessment of the extent to which such differences in socioeconomic background influence the process of occupational attainment, even given the fact that all sons are college graduates.

Paternal Support

Paternal support was defined by two indicators: the father's level of empathy or understanding, as perceived by the son, and the son's feeling of closeness to his father. (See Appendix B.) For the most part, sons reported rather positive relations with their fathers, as might be expected given the positive relationship between social class and parental support, consistently found in previous studies, and the relatively high socio-economic background of the panel. But it is noteworthy that one out of four sons felt their fathers understood them "not too well" or "not at all," and close to half (43.7 percent) felt "not very close," or only "fairly close" to their fathers. Again, since we are interested primarily in the father-son relationship as a mediator of the effect of social background on sons' achievement orientations, the measures of relationship with mothers have been excluded from the analysis.[6]

It might be argued that since the indicators of the quality of the father–son relationship are derived from sons' perceptions and reports, they may be contaminated by the sons' psychological characteristics. That

---

[6] By excluding the mother from this analysis we do not mean to imply that she has only negligible influence on sons' career decisions and attainments. Previous analyses of occupational values (Mortimer, 1975) lead us to expect that the insertion of relations with mothers into the causal model would not alter the findings. Moreover, the high interrelation of variables indicating support from parents would make an estimation of the independent influence of each parent difficult, if not impossible. (The zero-order correlation of closeness to the father and mother was .70; for the measure of understanding, it was .78.)

is, sons' sense of self-competence, their work involvement, and their occupational values might color their perceptions of relations with their fathers. If this were the case, the causal relationships among the paternal support and personality variables could be reversed or bi-directional, not unidimensional as suggested in Figure 2-1. Though these alternative causal specifications are possible, we view the sequence specified in Figure 2-1 as the most plausible and consistent with the socialization literature.

A large body of research has demonstrated clear linkages between prior parent–child relationships and developmental outcomes. Longitudinal studies have especially highlighted the significance of close and supportive parent–child relationships for healthy personal outcomes in adulthood. Regardless of the specific conceptualization of the dependent variable—e.g., overall adjustment, absence of symptomatology, competence and adaptive capacity, strong interpersonal relationships, or level of functioning in adult roles—the quality of earlier relationships in the family is outstanding in its predictive power (King, 1968; Offer and Offer, 1975; Peskin and Livson, 1972; Siegelman et al., 1970; Vaillant, 1974, 1976). Cross-sectional research on self-esteem likewise points to the importance of parental interest, involvement (Rosenberg, 1965: Ch. 7), acceptance, and understanding (Carlson, 1963) for the child's development of a positive sense of self. Moreover, previous studies indicate that parent–child relationships are highly stable in childhood and adolescence, particularly for sons (Crandall, 1972; Hunt and Eichorn, 1972), and our own analyses of this data set (Mortimer and Lorence, 1981; see also Chapter 3 of the present volume) confirm this pattern.

We therefore believe that it is more plausible to assume that support from the father influences the development of positive orientations to work during adolescence, if not earlier in life, and that these particular psychological dimensions will have relatively little influence on the quality of the father–son relationship.

Self-Competence

A semantic differential measure of the self-concept provided the indicators of self-competence. The respondents described themselves on a seven-point scale with reference to 29 bi-polar characteristics. On the basis of a previous exploratory factor analysis, four items were chosen to represent the competence dimension of the self: strong–weak, active–quiet, successful–not too successful, and competent–not too competent.[7] High scores on these items suggest a well-developed sense of personal efficacy. This construct seems to capture elements of Osgood's (Osgood et al., 1957) "potency" as well as "activity" dimensions. Franks and Marolla (1976), using a semantic differential scale administered to college students, identified a very similar competence factor which they called "inner self-esteem." Given the character of the panel, it is not surprising to find that these measures are positively skewed; very few respondents placed themselves at the most negative points of these scales.

Work Involvement

The college seniors were asked to assess the importance which they expected nine "areas of life" would have for them in "your life after college." Career or occupation, the dimension of interest here, was evaluated along with marriage, parenthood, friendships, community involvement, and other activities. As in the case of self-competence, the seniors' response to this question was positively skewed; 38 percent felt that work would be "crucially important" in their lives in the future, and about half thought this sphere would be "very important." Though there is only one indicator of work involvement in the senior year of college, we have drawn on the same measures in the freshman year and in 1976, and have used the method proposed by Wiley and Wiley (1970) to estimate the error component.

Occupational Reward Values

In the senior year of college, the respondents assessed the importance of 14 work features in making their career decisions. On the basis of an exploratory factor analysis, three value dimensions, corresponding to those found in previous studies of college students, were identified: people-related, intrinsic, and extrinsic orientations. Items with high loadings on these three factors were used as indicators of the multiple-item constructs. For the people-oriented construct, the indicators tapped interest in working with people rather than things, and concern with being helpful to others and/or useful to society. Intrinsic orientation was defined by interest in opportunities to exercise one's abilities and skills, to

---

[7] In a previous analysis (Mortimer and Lorence, 1979b), the item "confident–anxious" was used as an indicator of competence. Since this measure was subsequently found to load on another self-concept dimension, elsewhere labelled "well-being" (Mortimer and Lorence, 1981), we substituted "successful–not too successful" for this item in subsequent analyses of competence. This change was made to simplify causal models including multiple aspects of the self-image, and to make the present work consistent with these studies. This modification of the construct has no effect on the substantive conclusions of the research.

express one's interests, and to be creative and original. Items concerning occupational prestige, opportunities for advancement, and high income were the indicators of extrinsic orientation. As shown in Appendix B, the students generally considered the extrinsic rewards as less important than the intrinsic and people-oriented ones. The most important single item, endorsed as "crucially important" by 38 percent of the students, involved self-expression: "this occupation is a unique expression of my interests, something I really like."

Educational Attainment

The 1976 respondents were asked to give their educational histories since graduating from college. Their written responses were coded in four categories (see Appendix B). As noted in Chapter 1, the graduates are characterized by a high level of educational achievement: 52 percent had received Ph.D's or professional degrees, and an additional 26 percent had masters level degrees. Only 5 percent had not gone beyond the B.A.

While this level of educational achievement seems quite extraordinary, the amount of graduate school attendance reported by these men may not be unusual for a sample of college *graduates*. Sharp (1970) studied a national sample of 1958 degree recipients, about 8 or 9 years younger than our cohort, and reported that 61 percent of the men had attended graduate or professional school by the summer of 1963. This amount of post-graduate study is quite high, considering that the men in her sample graduated from college when graduate schooling was less common than in the late sixties. Similarly, Davis (1964:85) reports a high level of aspiration for graduate study among 1961 male degree recipients—only 20 percent had no plans for graduate study. Astin and Panos (1969), in a more recent survey, discovered that 70 percent of 1965 college graduates, just 1 to 2 years behind our panel, planned to go on for post-graduate study. Turning from these national samples to one more like the Michigan panel, Korn (1968:217) has reported that, of men who entered Stanford in 1961 and subsequently graduated, 65 percent were in graduate school by 1966. The present panel, entering college in 1962 and 1963, may therefore be unusual not so much in their post-graduate educational participation, but in their high level of eventual success in obtaining advanced degrees.

Career Stability

There were two indicators of career stability. The first assessed the difficulties the graduates had experienced in finding satisfactory work:

problems of unemployment, underemployment (working below one's level of education and training), or involuntary part-time employment. Given the well-educated and otherwise advantaged character of this panel, it is not surprising to find that these problems were relatively infrequent; only one-fourth the panel had experienced any of them. The second measure assessed whether change had occurred in career direction since graduating from college. Just over half the panel (55 percent) said they were in the same occupation in 1976 that they had planned to enter upon leaving college. Twenty-six percent had changed, and 17 percent reported no specific plans when they graduated (the latter were assigned a code value intermediate between those indicating change and stability).

It may be considered somewhat problematic that our measure of change is a self-report, since the sociologist's assessment of what constitutes an occupational or career change may not necessarily coincide with that of the respondent. To assess the discrepancy between the two, we compared this subjective measure with an objective indicator of change, based on the senior year career choices and the 1976 occupations of the graduates, both coded in the 11-category classification shown in Table 2-1. Of those found in the same occupation in the senior year and in 1976 (that is, those for whom the senior career choice is the same as the 1976 occupation), 73 percent reported no change and 14 percent said they had no specific plans when they graduated (see Table 2-2). Among those who were in the same occupational category at both times, and thus by our "objective" judgment, considered to be stable, only 13 percent

Table 2-2. Association of Objective and Subjective Measures of Occupational Change

OBJECTIVE CHANGE	SUBJECTIVE CHANGE[a]				
	Yes	No specific plans at graduation	NO	%	N
Senior choice same as 1976 occupation	73.4	13.5	13.1	60.0	282
Senior choice different from 1976 occupation	30.9	22.3	46.8	40.0	188
%	56.4	17.0	26.6	100.0	
N	265	80	125		470[b]

[a]Question: Is your present occupation the one that you planned to enter when you left Michigan?
[b]The total N does not equal 512 because of missing data.

reported an occupational change. On the other hand, of those who changed by the objective criterion, 47 percent reported a career change, 22 percent indicated no specific plans in their senior year, and 31 percent said they were in the same occupation that they had planned to enter earlier.

Overall, there is a moderate association between these measures (eta = .43), with more disagreement occurring between the two when the objective measure indicates that change has occurred. Given the nature of the occupational classification, we believe there may be more risk of misrepresenting the respondent's career pattern in using the objective than the subjective measure. For example, if a respondent had moved from a technical to a managerial position, which is a typical career progression in many fields, he would have likely reported no change, while this movement would be reflected in the objective classification by a shift in categories. Moreover, there is much room for career change within these classes, especially in the "people-oriented" and technical categories, which would not be reflected in the objective indicator. Given these possibilities, we chose to use the respondent's report as an indicator of change rather than our "objective" measure. The general agreement between the two measures is heartening, however, because it suggests that the respondents, in considering whether they had changed occupations, were often using a conceptual framework that corresponded quite well to our objective classification.

Job Search

The respondents were asked how they obtained their present jobs (as well as their first jobs), and were given a checklist containing 15 possible methods. Following Granovetter (1974), an attempt was made to discover the variety of ways the respondents sought and found their jobs, not merely the most proximal or effective influence. When asked about their first jobs, they were probed, "Check all that helped you in any way, e.g., by telling you about the job, by giving you the name of someone who later offered you a job or gave you other useful leads, etc." (This probe was not repeated prior to the question regarding the current job, since it followed quite closely in the questionnaire.)

The distribution of the modes of search for the present job is given in Table 2-3. It is evident that the responses are quite widely dispersed among the methods, with very little concentration in any single category. Direct application is the most frequent mode, indicated by 25 percent, a method found in previous studies of young people to be highly popular as well as effective (Reubens, 1977: Ch. 7; U.S. Department of Labor, 1975a; Young, 1974). Granovetter's study of recent professional, tech-

Table 2-3. Modes of Seeking Current Jobs

Methods	Percent*
Formal Methods	
The University of Michigan's placement office	5.5
An employment agency or personnel consultants	3.7
An advertisement in a newspaper, magazine, trade, or technical journal	8.2
I applied directly to the organization	25.0
Informal Methods	
A relative	5.7
I entered the family firm	2.0
A University of Michigan faculty member	4.1
A faculty member in a post-graduate educational program	5.7
A fellow undergraduate at the University of Michigan	1.4
A fellow student in a post-graduate educational program	5.3
Another friend or acquaintance	18.0
I worked for the organization while I was still in school	3.9
I was transferred or promoted from within my organization	6.1
Someone I didn't know from *another* organization contacted me about the job	5.3
I became self-employed	13.7

*This column does not sum to 100 because respondents indicated *all methods* they used.

nical, and managerial job-changers reports a similar usage of direct application (19 percent). The second and third most frequent mentions are "a friend or acquaintance" (18 percent) and "self-employment" (14 percent). No other category contains even 10 percent of the panel.

Given our interest in the implications of socio-economic background for the mechanisms used to obtain jobs, it would have been useful to consider the family separately as a source of job information. This was not feasible, however, within the context of the multivariate model, since the respondents rarely reported that their relatives helped them. Only 6 percent found their jobs through a relative; and only 2 percent entered the family firm. Therefore, whatever general association exists between social class background and the mode of job search would have to reflect other, more indirect, family influences.

It is reasonable to assume that in seeking jobs, persons of higher socio-economic background would have a variety of advantages channeling them toward the better positions. For example, they might have access to a wider range of professional and managerial contacts because of the occupational networks in which their fathers were already embedded. Alternatively, a high social class background may be conducive to the development of interpersonal skills which provide facility in initiating and maintaining relevant social relationships. Advantaged socio-economic origins could have also promoted access to early employment positions that led to better current jobs.

Given these possibilities, and the distribution of the variables, our classification of job search methods diverges somewhat from that of previous investigators (Granovetter, 1974; Ornstein, 1976). We attempted to develop an index that would distinguish those modes of job seeking and finding that are universalistic, open to all who wish to use them, from those that may be thought of as particularistic, dependent on special relationships or previous positions. Those activities found in the first, more universalistic category, which we call "formal methods," include the use of university placement services, registering in employment agencies, answering advertisements, and direct application to employers. Methods in the second cateory, designated "informal," include seeking information from friends, faculty members, fellow students or relatives, or entering the family firm. Methods were also placed in this second category if they depended on one's prior location in an organization—being on an "inside track," or having special access or visibility to organizational personnel, e.g., working for an organization while still in school, being transferred or promoted from within an organization, or being contacted by someone about a job. Becoming self-employed was likewise placed here, since self-employment tends to be available only to persons in certain restricted fields and often necessitates substantial resources, financial as well as interpersonal.

It was hypothesized that those from lower socio-economic backgrounds would have to rely more heavily on the more open, universalistic methods, while those from the more advantaged origins would have greater access to the second set of methods. It was also expected that positive work orientations, including a sense of competence, commitment to work, and high evaluations of occupational rewards, would promote use of informal methods involving greater use of contacts and personal initiative. Finally, independent of social origins, it was expected that the more particularistic and informal methods would entail special advantages for the job-seeker, channelling individuals toward the more rewarding jobs.

The distribution of the job search index is given in Appendix B, distinguishing those using formal methods only, those exclusively employing informal methods, and those respondents using methods in both categories (given an intermediate code value). (Remember, the respondents could check as many as applied.) The informal methods were the more popular, utilized exclusively by almost half the respondents. About 30 percent restricted their search activities to formal methods, while 11 percent used methods in both categories. It is interesting that the degree of overlap between the types is so small.

Occupational Attainments

Work Autonomy. The three observed indicators of work autonomy were the amount of innovative thinking required by the job, the degree of challenge encountered at work, and the respondent's decision-making latitude. These indicators, adapted from Kohn and Schooler (1974), assess the opportunity for self-directed and autonomous thought. As shown in Appendix B, the respondents generally perceived their jobs quite positively on these dimensions. About one out of four claimed "complete autonomy" and "a tremendous amount" of innovative thought, while more than half described their jobs as "very challenging." This pattern is quite expected given the professional and managerial occupations in which most of these men are located.

Income. The respondents were asked to give the gross annual income in wages or salary earned from their main job. This measure was chosen, rather than total personal or family income, because it was considered an appropriate indicator of *individual* occupational attainment and success. As shown in Appendix B, the median income is quite high—$20,000 to $24,999 in 1976. Only about one out of five respondents had an income under $15,000.

The Social Content of Work. In developing a measure of the social content of work, it was assumed that work involving welfare, teaching, and service functions is the most interpersonally involving and, for those who value such experiences, the most rewarding. Other work with people, as in selling, administration, and committee work, was thought to invoke a lesser amount of interpersonal involvement and satisfaction. The first indicator was based on the people-oriented work activities reported by the respondent; the second drew on the current occupational title. Work activities and occupations included in each of the categories, along with the response distributions, are given in Appendix B. It is noteworthy that, while 20 percent of the respondents were in technical, data-oriented, or blue-collar occupations, almost none report "no work with people." These variables, like the other measures of occupational attainment, are generally quite positively skewed: 61 percent of the men report teaching, advising, or service to clients; 51 percent are found in professions whose main functions entail these activities.

THE DATA ANALYSIS

Model Estimation Procedures

Maximum likelihood analysis of structural equations (Joreskog, 1973; Joreskog and Sorbom, 1977; Werts et al., 1973) was used to estimate the causal model. As described briefly in our discussion of the socio-economic construct, when using this statistical method, unobserved or "latent" constructs are defined in terms of the covariation of their measured indicators. The variance of each indicator is represented as two components: a part that is dependent on the latent construct, and the remaining or residual variance, which may be considered the result of errors of measurement or of any other unique source of variation that is unrelated to the construct. The factor loadings, expressing the relationships of the indicators to the constructs, the residuals of the indicators, and the correlations among the residuals are designated the "measurement parameters." These are to be distinguished from the "causal parameters," expressing the relations among the latent constructs.

In longitudinal research this procedure has two important advantages over conventional regression (ordinary least squares) techniques. First, since both random and systematic measurement errors can be specified in the causal model, more precise parameter estimates are obtained. Secondly, this procedure incorporates a goodness-of-fit test (chi-square divided by the degrees of freedom) which allows one to determine whether the parameter estimates of the hypothesized model are reasonable. As chi-square values approach the degrees of freedom, an increasingly good fit to the data is obtained.

The parameters of the measurement models were estimated by the computer program, LISREL, utilizing a maximum likelihood algorithm (Joreskog and van Thillo, 1972) adapted for our use by Ronald Schoenberg. LISREL IV (International Educational Services, 1972) was used to estimate the final causal model. The input to the program for all analyses was a variance-covariance matrix of the observed measures. Because of the large number of variables in the causal model, listwise deletion of missing data would have excessively limited the number of cases for the analysis. Therefore, the input matrix was based on pairwise deletion. To be conservative in making judgements of statistical significance, the smallest N (432) was used for calculating the standard errors.

Several of the constructs in the model had been utilized in previous, more restricted analyses of this data set (Lorence and Mortimer, 1981; Mortimer and Lorence, 1979a, b). In estimating the causal models, the measurement parameters for all multiple-indicator constructs were fixed at the values found earlier. For other constructs, not previously examined, the measurement parameters were estimated and then fixed. The general procedure used to estimate the measurement models is described elsewhere (Mortimer and Lorence, 1979a). To obtain optimal estimates of the measurement parameters for the psychological constructs, the models included the same constructs over time, including the senior year and 1976 indicators. The other measurement parameters were obtained by estimating reduced models, including more than one construct to increase model identification. With the exception of work involvement (whose reliability was estimated by drawing on a third freshman indicator using the procedure suggested by Wiley and Wiley, 1970), the single item constructs—educational attainment, job search, and income—were assumed to be perfectly measured. Corresponding to this assumption, the error variances of these items were fixed at zero. The lambdas, expressing the relations of constructs to indicators, and the correlated error terms of the indicators are given in Appendix B. In recognition of the likelihood that the unique variance (that is, variance that is unrelated to the construct) and error variance of *the same* indicators would likely be related over time, the correlated residual variances of the same indicators were included in the initially-estimated measurement models. These were retained in the final measurement models if found to be statistically significant.

Due to the large number of indicators and parameters to be examined, it was not feasible to estimate a fully recursive causal model, or to investigate all possible reciprocal effects.[8] Instead, the designation of causal paths was guided by the theoretical considerations developed earlier in this chapter, the empirical findings of previous studies, and the findings derived from the partial causal models that were estimated earlier.

After estimating an initial causal model, the first-order partial derivatives were examined (Sorbom, 1975) to be certain that no important causal paths had been overlooked. The first-order partials give an approximate indication as to whether allowing previously fixed parameters to be freely estimated would significantly improve the fit of the model. The partial derivatives for this model were generally quite small, and did not suggest the addition of new causal paths among the constructs. It should be noted, however, that the partial derivatives provide guidance for changing the model only when the causal ordering of the variables has been correctly specified.

---

[8] To incorporate the variables necessary for consideration in the third chapter, the actual model that was estimated included, as final endogenous constructs, the five psychological dimensions measured in 1976. All parameters were estimated in one analysis, instead of in two distinct phases, to improve model specification and to save computer time. The fit of this entire model, as measured by the chi-square value divided by the degrees of freedom, was 1.71.

In the final stage, the model was re-estimated, again fixing the measurement parameters, and fixing all paths found in the first stage to be statistically insignificant at zero.[9] This final model is shown in Figure 2-2. To simplify the figure, the measurement parameters are not shown. (All measurement parameters are given in Appendix B.)

We will now describe the findings, grouped according to the major questions of interest.

FINDINGS

Socio-economic Origin, Father–son Relations, and Work-related Orientations

As anticipated, social class background had important implications for the process of attainment; some of these effects were direct, others were mediated by subsequent variables in the model. Socio-economic origin was found to have significant direct effects, all positive in direction, on paternal support, sons' work involvement in the senior year of college, and sons' 1976 educational attainment. The path from the social class construct to paternal support (.192) shows that sons of higher socio-economic origin have more favorable relationships with their fathers, as they report feelings of greater closeness and empathy. This path replicates the findings of many previous studies of social class and family relationships, reviewed earlier in this chapter. Thus, in spite of the restriction of the panel to men of rather high socio-economic origin, the central conclusion of prior research, conducted with more representative samples, has been confirmed: fathers having higher occupational prestige, education, and family income are perceived by their sons as closer and more understanding.

Sons of higher social class background also manifested greater work involvement (.145). Fathers of relatively high socio-economic position, acting as role models for their sons, might be expected to have greater involvement in their work, which could influence sons' anticipations of what their futures might be like. Sons' high work involvement could also reflect a desire to retain a high socio-economic standing. The significant direct path from socio-economic background to post-graduate educational attainment (.169), net of the psychological variables, may indicate

---

[9] Parameters that were twice their standard errors were considered to be statistically significant. Due to the nonrandom character of the sample, the use of significance tests is not strictly appropriate. However, even in circumstances such as these, Winch and Campbell (1969) contend that such tests can indicate whether findings are systematic or random. The significance tests did not appear to be overly stringent since parameters found to be statistically insignificant were generally very small in magnitude.

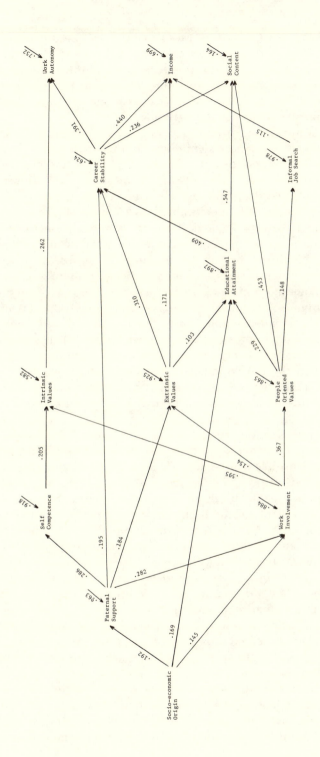

Figure 2-2. Causal Model of Occupational Attainment

75

differences in parental ability to support sons financially through lengthy post-graduate schooling. (The correlations between the three indicators of family socio-economic status and sons' educational attainment were, however, of approximately equal magnitude.)

What is most interesting from our perspective, however, is the wide range of significant influences stemming from paternal support. Sons who reported a more positive relationship with their fathers had a stronger sense of self-competence (.286), feeling stronger, more active, competent, and successful; they exhibited greater work involvement (.282), and they assigned higher evaluations to extrinsic occupational rewards (.184). If these psychological attributes indeed foster occupational attainment, sons with highly supportive fathers would certainly have an advantage. From the parameters shown in Figure 2-2, it would appear that the influence of socio-economic background on sons' work-related psychological orientations occurs largely indirectly, through the character of father–son relations. In fact, when paternal support is taken into account, the socio-economic construct has only one independent effect on work attitudes; it fosters work involvement (.145). This pattern of findings confirms our expectations regarding the significance of paternal support in the development of work-related orientations, and highlights the quality of the father–son relationship as an important factor relevant to socio-economic differences in occupational socialization.

The interrelations among the psychological dimensions is consistent with our hypothetical ordering of the constructs. The significant paths suggest that work involvement and, to a lesser extent, competence, foster positive evaluations of occupational rewards. The importance of work involvement for occupational value development is particularly striking. The seniors' assessments of the importance that work would have for them in the future had a marked influence on their intrinsic values (.595), a more moderate though substantial effect on their people-oriented values (.367), and a smaller but still significant impact on their concerns with the extrinsic rewards of income, advancement, and prestige (.154). The relative magnitude of these effects is especially interesting. They suggest that high work involvement is most conducive to increasing the salience of rewards to be gained from work itself—its intrinsic and people-oriented satisfactions. Work involvement strengthens the evaluations of extrinsic rewards to a much lesser extent. Those who felt a greater sense of self-competence in their senior year of college also assigned greater importance to intrinsic rewards, to the expression of their interests, abilities, and creativity in their work (.205). They may have felt more capable of meeting the challenges which such work offers.

The true causal ordering of these psychological constructs cannot be conclusively determined, since they were all measured at the same time. A more definitive resolution of these psychological dynamics awaits further longitudinal study. The pattern of relationships among the variables, however, is quite compatible with our reasoning that those who attach more importance to work and those who feel more competent, prior to entering the labor force, will assign higher evaluations to the rewards and satisfactions that are potentially available to them in the work sphere.

The pattern of relations among the psychological constructs indicates that paternal support may affect occupational values indirectly (as well as directly), by stimulating competence and work involvement. By enhancing work involvement, the father–son relationship heightened all three dimensions of occupational reward values. By fostering competence, paternal support indirectly encouraged an intrinsic value orientation as well. According to the logic of path analysis, the total effect of paternal support on intrinsic values, combining the two indirect linkages $(.286 \times .205 + .282 \times .595)$ would be .226. Its total effect on extrinsic values is .227 $(.184 + .282 \times .154)$, while its impact on people-oriented values is a weaker .103 $(.282 \times .367)$. Although the effect of paternal support is only indirect for two of the three reward value dimensions, computation of these total effects indicates the relevance of support from the father for the development of all three occupational values.

We thus find that paternal support has positive direct effects on three of the five work-related psychological orientations under consideration, and indirect effects on the three occupational reward value dimensions by enhancing work involvement and a competent self-image. Clearly, these findings are consistent with our hypothesis that a positive father–son relationship affects sons' occupational attainments by instilling positive work orientations, at least in the upper middle class.[10] Furthermore, it is particularly interesting to find an additional direct path from paternal support to career stability (.195), even after the substantial influences of educational attainment and extrinsic values on the career pattern are controlled. Sons who have had more positive relationships with their

---

[10] The significance of the father–son relationship as an intervening mechanism by which the father's work-related values are transmitted to sons is underscored by sub-group analyses comparing the process of attainment for professional and business families (as defined by the father's occupation). Using ordinary least squares regression, in professional families a close father–son relationship stimulated the development of intrinsic values (b = .269, beta = .208 $p < .05$), while this path was not significant in the business families (b = .110, beta = .081, n.s.). Due to the preponderance of business fathers (N = 303), the final model shown in Figure 2-2 more adequately represents the process of attainment in business families. The different patterns of relationships between family relations and values in business and professional families is further explored in Mortimer (1975) and in Mortimer and Kumka (1982).

fathers during college have less problematic work histories during the following decade, being less likely to change their careers since graduation and to experience problems relating to employment. Altogether, the findings provide substantial support for the conclusion that the father–son relationship is important for vocational development and attainment.

The fact that both parental support and the psychological constructs are measured before full-time entry to the labor force is extremely important, since work experience—another potential influence on these attitudes and values—has probably, for most of these students, been rather minimal. The findings suggest that the influence of the family on vocational socialization occurs in the pre-adult years, though we cannot ascertain, with the data available from this study, the exact timing of familial influence. There is reason to believe that the effect of the family on vocational socialization occurs prior to college, in early or middle adolescence. Though most students changed their career choices during college, it is pertinent that the pattern of intergenerational mobility, as indicated by the distributions of sons' occupational choices by their fathers' occupations, remained quite similar from the freshman to the senior years (Mortimer, 1974:1283). Moreover, previous analyses of the data showed significant relationships between paternal support measured in the freshman year of college and occupational values 4 years later (Mortimer, 1976). Since these work-related psychological orientations may be rather stable over time (Mortimer and Lorence, 1981), the effects of even earlier influences in the family will likely extend to later periods.

While prior studies have been restricted to examining the relationships between social class origin and achievement orientations (Gordon, 1972; Kerckhoff, 1974; Sewell and Hauser, 1976:17), this research extends the domain of psychological variables to self-perceptions, attitudes toward work, and values relating to prominent occupational rewards, and suggests the merit of further specifying and elaborating the intervening mechanisms, within the family itself, which underlie the transmission of work-related attitudes and values. The relationship between father and son has generally not been included in previous studies of status attainment, but appears from our analysis to be rather crucial in enhancing those psychological orientations that may heighten subsequent achievement. While the significant paths from paternal support to the four succeeding constructs (three psychological dimensions and career stability) are not exceedingly large, the consistent pattern of influence is impressive. Taken together, the results suggest that the father–son relationship has considerable importance for the development of a self-image and work attitudes that are conducive to achievement. Moreover, they indicate that the development of positive work-related psychological orientations, through paternal support, is a significant intervening process by which socio-economic origin may influence adult attainment.

Clearly, the results are consistent with Kohn's model of the effects of parental socio-economic position on the process of socialization, though two critical components of his theory (parental occupational self-direction and parental values) have not been directly measured.[11] As stated earlier in this chapter, it is plausible to assume that fathers of higher socio-economic status experience more autonomy in their work. This work experience, in turn, is likely to engender greater concern with the psychological development of children, and therefore more close and empathic parent–child relations. In this study parental social class (as measured by the socio-economic construct) has been found to influence parental behavior (as indicated by the son's report of the character of the father–son relationship). Paternal support, in turn, has significant effects on those attitudes of the late adolescent child—his competence, work involvement, and work values—that may have an impact upon his later occupational achievement.

Orientations to Work and the Process of Attainment

We must further examine the model to ascertain whether the psychological orientations found to be stimulated by paternal support are indeed relevant to the process of attainment. The path coefficients from the psychological constructs to the subsequent variables express the effects of attitudes and values, measured in the senior year of college, on experiences and attainments up to a decade later. These parameters confirm the importance of prior attitudes and values for subsequent attainments. In accord with our expectations, there are direct paths from the psychological orientations to all three dimensions of occupational attainment. First, intrinsic values directly influence work autonomy (.262). Those who assigned high importance to self-expression and creativity in work while they were still in college are found to have the more innovative, challenging, and autonomous occupational experience 10 years later. It is noteworthy that this effect is entirely direct. Intrinsic values had no significant influence on any of the intervening behavioral

---

[11] Kohn (personal communication, May 8, 1980) has expressed some reservation about the connection between parental valuing of self-direction and a supportive parent–child relationship. While the data support our interpretation of his model, a better, more accurate test of Kohn's thesis requires data expressing the father's occupational self-direction and his parental values.

variables—educational attainment, career stability, or the mode of job search.[12]

The pattern of relationships linking extrinsic values with income is considerably more complex. The direct path (.171) from extrinsic reward values to income shows that those seniors who placed a high value upon income, advancement, and prestige have higher incomes a decade later. But while this direct path is rather weak, there are also substantial indirect paths connecting the two constructs. Extrinsic values enhanced career stability (.310), which, in turn, has a sizable effect on income (.440). Thus, extrinsic values heightened the likelihood that the individual would have a smooth career progression in the decade following college graduation, without shifts in occupational direction and without experiencing the various problems of employment, and this kind of career pattern enhanced income attainment. Furthermore, there is a small positive path from extrinsic value orientation to post-graduate education (.103) which also contributes to the stability of the early career. It is reasonable to suppose that persons who value occupational prestige, advancement, and income would consider this further investment in education worthwhile.

According to the logic of path analysis, we should combine these direct and indirect influences to derive the total effect of extrinsic values on income. This total effect is .326 (.171 + .310 × .440 + .103 × .409 × .440). This rather substantial influence is almost identical to that reported as a direct effect (.328) in our previous, more restricted model, in which there were no constructs intervening between the occupational reward values and attainments (Mortimer and Lorence, 1979a:1377). Whereas, before, we were able to demonstrate that extrinsic values influence income, the present more refined analysis further contributes to our understanding of the process of income attainment by making explicit the intervening processes, via the career pattern and educational attainment, through which this influence occurs. This model also shows that the previously reported influence of the extrinsic value dimension

---

[12] Intrinsic values had no significant effect on income in the final causal model. In a preliminary analysis using ordinary least squares regression, intrinsic values had a negative effect on income when work autonomy was entered as an additional independent variable, predicting income, into the equation. Because there are positive effects of intrinsic values on autonomy, and autonomy on income, the negative effect of intrinsic values on income is masked when the effects of work autonomy on income are not taken into account. This negative effect gives further credance to Temme's (1975) concept of "tradeoff": to obtain high levels of work autonomy, those with high intrinsic values may have had to sacrifice high income to some extent. While it is plausible to assume that work autonomy is a determinant of income, the difficulty in specifying a justifiable causal order among all three occupational attainments, and the further complexity which such an ordering would introduce, deterred us from doing so in the final model.

on work autonomy (see Mortimer and Lorence, 1979a:1373) is wholly mediated by its effects on career stability and educational attainment.

The third value dimension, people-orientation, has a marked effect on the subsequent attainment of work with high social content (.453). Those who were more interested in working with people and helping others during their senior year were more likely to have occupational experiences involving social service and high interpersonal content a decade later. There are, in addition, indirect pathways linking people-oriented values and social content, through education and career stability. The total effect of this value orientation on the social content of work is therefore .600 (.453 + .229 × .547 + .229 × .409 × .236). The present analysis therefore reproduces the previously reported finding that people-oriented values have a strong impact on the social content of work (.608, Mortimer and Lorence, 1979a:1377). As before, the present more complete analysis has illuminated the processes through which this effect occurs. People-oriented occupational reward values increase the likelihood of advanced post-graduate education, which, in turn, enhances career stability and enables entry to occupations, such as the client-centered professions, involving high social content.

A further, rather striking feature of the model is the absence of direct effects from competence and work involvement to the three dimensions of attainment. These two constructs also had no direct effects on the achievement-related behavioral variables—educational attainment, career stability, and job search. The effects of competence and work involvement on occupational achievement, as specified by this causal model, are entirely indirect, through the occupational values which they stimulate.[13]

Though not all hypothesized relationships are borne out by the analysis (for example, competence and work involvement had no direct effects on occupational attainments when occupational value orientations are included as intervening variables), the general pattern of findings leaves little doubt that psychological orientations to work, measured prior to full-time labor force entry, have important implications for subsequent attainments.[14] According to this analysis, the most crucial psychological

---

[13] Whereas on the basis of a previously estimated partial model of the development of the self-concept (Mortimer and Lorence, 1979b), we reported a small direct effect of competence on income, that effect was reduced to insignificance in our first preliminary analysis (beta = .077, t = .99) when the effects of the other variables in the model were taken into account.

[14] Previous articles (Lorence and Mortimer, 1981; Mortimer and Lorence, 1979a,b) have reported the effects of senior psychological orientations on occupational attainments when estimated in the context of much reduced causal models. Minor discrepancies in the parameters estimated in those studies and those reported here are attributable to differences in the models (e.g., new constructs have been added), the use of listwise instead of pairwise deletion of cases, or to slight differences in the composition of the constructs. The substantial similarity of the results, regardless of these differences, attests to the robust character of the findings.

dimensions for occupational achievements are occupational reward values—the degree of importance attached to the particular rewards that are potentially obtainable in the work setting. Finally, the model shows that the effects of the family of origin, particularly the father–son relationship, on attainments are largely mediated by the work-related psychological orientations which this relationship stimulates.

Post-graduate Achievement Behaviors as Determinants of Occupational Attainments

Already we have noted that the relationships between occupational values and attainments are partially mediated by the intervening behavioral variables in the model—educational achievement and career stability. We now examine these most proximal linkages more directly.

Consistent with the human capital model, post-graduate education has significant implications for early attainments, but it directly affects only one outcome, the social content of work. When the large direct effect of .547 is added to the indirect path of .096 through career stability, a most sizable total effect is observed—.643. The strong magnitude of this effect is certainly due to the fact that those professions with the most extensive service or interpersonal components (medicine, dentistry, law, and the ministry), and the most stable career patterns, also have advanced educational degrees as prerequisites for entry.

Post-graduate education influences the other two attainment dimensions—work autonomy and income—entirely indirectly, through career stability (.409). Because of the high costs of advanced education, both in terms of educational expenses and income foregone, it was anticipated that those with more education would be less likely to have changed their careers since graduation. They were also expected to have had fewer employment problems such as subemployment, unemployment, and involuntary part-time employment. These expectations are borne out by the data. Though, in a more representative sample of workers, one might expect to find a direct linkage between educational attainment and income, we see that this effect is mediated here entirely by the career pattern. This probably occurs in our panel largely because post-graduate degrees permitted entry to the more stable, and also more lucrative, professions and managerial positions. (Though it is possible that, for some respondents, career change and employment problems preceded the completion of post-graduate education, the work history data suggests that the temporal order implied by this model is correct for the vast majority of respondents. Most seniors who were to obtain post-graduate education proceeded directly after college to graduate or professional schools.)

The dominant position of the construct representing the career pattern in the model is especially interesting. Career stability has rather substantial effects on two of the three occupational attainments, income (.440) and work autonomy (.391), and a smaller, but still significant effect on the social content of work activities (.236). These pervasive implications of the stability of the early career suggest the importance of crystallizing the career decision prior to college graduation, and indicate the depressive effects on early occupational attainment associated with career change and problems of employment. Given the prominence of career stability in this final causal model, the fact that it is significantly fostered by paternal support (.195) lends further credence to the significance of father–son relations in the process of intergenerational attainment.

It is also noteworthy that but one psychological variable directly influenced career stability. The path (.310) from extrinsic values to the career pattern shows that those who expressed greater interest in income, advancement and prestige in their future life's work have made the more steady early career progress. While the total effect is partially achieved by attaining more advanced education (.103 × .409), the main influence of extrinsic values on the career pattern is direct. Overall, the results suggest that problems of career instability stem, in this group, from two factors. The first is the lack of advanced education providing the credentials for the most secure occupational positions. Of almost equal importance, however, is the level of emphasis on extrinsic rewards. Income, advancement opportunity, and prestige would certainly be jeopardized by employment instability and career change during the early work history.[15]

The final intervening construct in our model is the mode of job search. Confirming one of our hypotheses, the use of informal search mechanisms was found to enhance income (.115). However, contrary to prior expectation, this variable had no significant effects on the two other attainment outcomes. Moreover, the socio-economic status of the family and paternal support exhibited no significant relationship to job search.

---

[15] Those who experienced employment problems also spent *more time* in the military. But while there is an association between military service and career instability, it is not possible with the data at hand to establish a causal connection between the two. There is some evidence that the military "selected" individuals who had not yet crystallized their career decisions. Those who entered the military were more likely than other respondents in 1976 to report that they had had no specific plans for a career when they graduated from college. It is also probable that the transition from military to civilian employment was difficult for some respondents. Still, as reported in chapter 1, military service did not strongly predict the socio-economic outcomes.Moreover, with military service measured as a binary variable (served in the military vs. not), it was not significantly related to these employment problems.

From this analysis, informal contacts or other help in finding jobs do not appear to constitute a general intervening mechanism by which fathers of high socio-economic level enhance the occupational attainments of their sons.[16] The sole path to this construct, from people-oriented work values, suggests that those seniors who were more committed to work with people may have had stronger interpersonal skills, and therefore greater capacity to develop instrumentally useful contact networks.

CONCLUSION

The central contribution of this analysis is its explication of the processes through which socio-economic origin, psychological orientations to work, and achievement-related behaviors influence three dimensions of occupational attainment. There has been considerable study of the determinants of occupational status or prestige, and some research on income attainment. But in the vast literature on intergenerational mobility, with rare exceptions (Schooler, 1980; Spaeth, 1976b; Spenner, 1981), little attention has been directed to the nonvertical features of work autonomy and the social content of work as dimensions of occupational attainment. The present research is also rather unique in including a measure of the quality of the father–son relationship as a central mechanism mediating the effects of social origins on occupational socialization and attainment. Moreover, most previous studies of the attainment process have focused on aspirations or expectations for achievement as the sole mediating psychological variable, consistent with their unidimensional focus on socio-economic attainment. In this study, five psychological constructs that are relevant to future work experiences and attainments have been examined. Finally, the model includes a construct representing the stability of the early career, which is generally absent from prior studies.

The final causal model suggests the merit of extending the scope of study of occupational attainment in several new directions. First, it reveals a quite pervasive impact of the father–son relationship on work-

---

[16] In a further analysis using ordinary least squares regression, subgroups based on the fathers' and the respondents' occupations were examined. When both fathers and sons were in the business sector, close father–son relations did predict the use of informal methods of job search ($b = .196$, beta $= .396$, $p < .001$). There was no such association for businessmen's sons who went into the professions ($b = -.070$, beta $= -.136$, n.s.), among professionals' sons, nor in the sample as a whole. These findings suggest that under certain specific circumstances, that is, when the son has "inherited" the father's position in the business sector, fathers can and do enhance their sons' income attainment by assisting them in locating jobs. In this particular subgroup, moreover, there was a stronger path from the mode of job search to income than in the total sample.

related psychological orientations. This pattern has considerable relevance for the more general issue with which we began: whether the socio-economic position of the family of origin influences the attainment of children by stimulating achievement-related attitudes, or by providing assistance and support in early adulthood. The results provide evidence for both kinds of processes. Socio-economic origin had a direct effect on sons' work involvement and a pervasive indirect influence on the psychological orientations through the father–son relationship. Paternal support, including its direct and indirect effects, influenced the development of all five psychological orientations included in the model. These orientations were found to feed into subsequent attainments. But the family constructs also directly influenced achievement-related behavior occurring after college. Socio-economic origin had a direct effect on post-graduate educational attainment, net of the psychological variables, and paternal support contributed directly to stability in the early work career. Thus, our two measures relating to family influence—socio-economic status and paternal support—have effects on psychological attributes, measured prior to college graduation, as well as on behavioral constructs, measured 10 years following. It must therefore be concluded that the influence of the family of origin on adult attainments occurs through earlier socialization experiences, as well as by affecting early adult achievement behaviors.

Second, the analysis shows that attitudes and values held before labor force entry have substantial implications for the attainment of socially valued occupational rewards. Whereas most previous research on the effects of values and other psychological dispositions on occupational selection has dealt with persons not yet in the labor force, the present study documents the persistence of "self-selection." The individual's sense of competence, conceptualized as a major dimension of the self-image, indirectly influenced work autonomy a decade later through its effects on intrinsic values. Work involvement also affected the dimensions of attainment indirectly, by stimulating high evaluations of all three kinds of occupational rewards. The considerable importance of occupational values in the final model, including their direct and indirect effects, suggests that these work attitudes be given further attention in future studies of attainment. The findings are clearly compatible with the notion of tradeoffs in the early work history—occupational reward values come to have important consequences for the dimensions of occupational attainment that will be maximized. Surely, psychological orientations affecting the occupational attainment process are not limited to plans and aspirations.

Third, this panel study demonstrates the importance of certain behavioral variables, following college graduation, for attainments in the early work career. The effects of post-graduate education are very much in accord with expectations based on the human capital approach. But more important, due to the lack of attention to this variable in prior attainment models, are our findings concerning the career pattern. The significance of career stability in the process of attainment is shown by its positive influence on all three attainment outcomes. These findings accentuate the importance, for those who attend college, of finalizing the career decision prior to graduation, and the detrimental effects that employment problems can have on early occupational attainments. The significant path from our indicator of the mode of job search to income partially replicates Granovetter's findings, but the job search mechanism, whether formal or informal, did not constitute a mediating variable in the process of intergenerational attainment for the panel as a whole.

Finally, the findings are consistent with the pattern of linkages specified in Melvin Kohn's conceptualization of the effects of social class on socialization. The present study can be considered only an approximate and partial test of his model due to the absence of data (on occupational experiences and parental values) from the fathers. The work of Kohn and Schooler and other researchers that have been stimulated by his paradigm has concentrated on the effects of social class on parental values. We reasoned that socio-economic position could be considered an approximate measure of the father's occupational self-direction. We also thought that paternal support would be a natural behavioral outcome of self-directed parental values. As a result, a positive association between these two family-related constructs was expected, and this expectation was confirmed by our analysis.

This study, however, bears most clearly on the last two linkages in Kohn's causal chain, those that have heretofore been quite neglected. This analysis is most relevant to those hypotheses linking parental values and behaviors to those of the child, and children's characteristics to subsequent socio-economic attainments. Kohn hypothesized that self-directed parental values and behaviors would stimulate psychological orientations in children which encourage their own socio-economic attainment. We find that paternal support, a likely expression of self-directed parental values, fostered the development of five work-related psychological phenomena—self-competence, work involvement, and three occupational value dimensions. These psychological attributes, in turn, had substantial effects on achievement-related behaviors and occupational attainments in the next generation. Kohn's "occupational linkage model," at least with respect to these final linkages, has been confirmed.

In summary, this chapter provides evidence for a multi-faceted process by which the family influences the occupational attainments of sons.

This process merits further investigation, including the several determinants that we have identified, in more representative samples of the population, including women and more diverse socio-economic, racial, and ethnic groups.

CHAPTER 3

Work Experience and Psychological Development

In this chapter we continue our exploration of the interrelations of work experience and psychological development. Chapter 2 examined the process of occupational attainment, including key psychological dimensions—self competence, work involvement, and occupational values—as partial determinants of that process. We now turn to the implications of work experience for change in these psychological constructs over the 10-year period following graduation from college. In doing so, we reconceptualize our earlier occupational outcome variables; while in the previous chapter they were considered dimensions of occupational *attainment,* they are now conceived as central work *experiences* with significant implications for personal change. Moreover, the psychological attributes that were previously among the *determinants* of attainment are now seen as the *effects* of that very process in a subsequent phase of life. The longitudinal design of this study enables an analysis that would be impossible with only cross-sectional data. It allows examination of the effects of early psychological attributes on occupational attainments, as well as the implications of these attainments and the work experiences which they imply, on later psychological change.

We now focus on the following question: After entering the world of work, do people change in response to the experiences encountered there, or are the psychological differences among people with distinct work experiences attributable to the fact that they chose their work (or were selected for it) in accord with its compatibility with their already-formed psychological traits? Put another way, do work experiences have independent effects on the adult personality, when early psychological differences, prior to labor force entry, are controlled? As before, in addressing this issue, we examine self-competence, a major dimension of the self-image; work involvement, the centrality of work as an important sphere of life activity; and evaluations of the importance of intrinsic, people-oriented, and extrinsic occupational rewards.

The potential of work experience as a determinant of adult personality is not a new idea, but a hypothesis that has been the subject of lively speculation throughout the modern era. In commentaries on the process of modernization and social change in the West, scholars have continually debated whether work is a potentially liberating or dehumanizing force, given the ever-increasing occupational differentiation.

According to one major current of thought, the complex patterning of the division of labor, emerging as an outcome of industrialization, enables the person to express diverse capabilities and talents that remain only latent possibilities in simple, mainly agricultural economies. As long ago as 1776, Adam Smith wrote,

> The difference of natural talents in different men is, in reality, much less than we are aware of; and the very different genius which appears to distinguish men of different professions, when grown up to maturity, is not upon many occasions so much the cause, as the effect of the division of labor. . . . But without the disposition to truck, barter, and exchange, every man must have procured to himself every necessary and conveniency of life. All had the same duties to perform, the same work to do, and there could have been no such difference of employment as could alone give occasion to any great difference of talent. (1913:12)

The division of labor thus provides the opportunity for persons to practice and master their trades and professions, allowing the development of human potential in diverse ways, and the channeling of energy to attain higher levels of efficiency and productivity.

Pursuing the same argument, Emile Durkheim speculated that, as work becomes more highly differentiated, the personality likewise becomes more individuated and autonomous. In *The Division of Labor in Society*, first published in 1893, he declared,

> . . . far from being trammelled by the progress of specialization individual personality develops with the division of labor . . . individual natures, while specializing, become more complex. (1964:403–404)

This view, that a complex division of labor is a liberating force encouraging self-expression and individual personality development, has its counterpoint in the argument that this very occupational differentiation is stultifying and constrictive, limiting human expression. Karl Marx, the foremost proponent of this position, argued that personality is reduced when individual activities are confined to specific occupational tasks. He argued,

For as soon as the division of labour begins, each man has a particular, exclusive sphere of activity, which is forced upon him and from which he cannot escape. He is a hunter, a fisherman, a shepherd or a critical critic, and must remain so if he does not want to lose his means of livelihood; whereas in communist society, where nobody has one exclusive sphere of activity but each can become accomplished in any branch he wishes, production as a whole is regulated by society, thus making it possible for me to do one thing today and another tomorrow, to hunt in the morning, fish in the afternoon, rear cattle in the evening, criticize after dinner, in accordance with my inclination, without ever becoming hunter, fisherman, shepherd or critic. This crystallization of social activity, this consolidation of what we ourselves produce into an objective power over us, growing out of our control, thwarting our expectations, bringing to naught our calculations, is one of the chief factors in historical development up to the present. (1964:97)

Marx pointed out that extremely simple and fragmented work proliferates in the early stages of industrialization, as craft-like occupations are replaced by machine production. The simplification of work tasks involved in this process limits the worker's control over the process of production, and is personally destructive and dehumanizing. To Marx, the essence of labor in its ideal state, its "exclusively human form," is its self-directed and autonomous quality:

The labourer . . . not only effects a change of form in the material on which he works, but he also realizes a purpose of his own that gives the law to his modus operandi, and to which he must subordinate his will. (1964:88)

But when workers no longer have control over the activities, productive means, and uses of their labor, they become alienated, detached from their own true natures as well as from the society at large. Marx believed that alienation from work is endemic in modern industrial societies. His concept of alienation underlies the loss of autonomy and self-expression in work:

In what does this alienation of labour consist? First, that the work is external to the worker, that it is not a part of his nature, that consequently he does not fulfil himself in his work but denies himself, has a feeling of misery, not of well-being, does not develop freely a physical and mental energy, but is physically exhausted and morally debased. (1964:169; excerpts reprinted by permission; © 1964, McGraw Hill)

In this passage, and elsewhere in his early work, Marx proclaims the primacy of work experience in personality development. It not only influences behavior and attitudes at the workplace, but has pervasive impacts on the individual—on his general sense of well-being and fulfillment, his energy, and his morality.

This "generalization thesis," that work has widespread effects on personal development, is thus clearly evident in the classic writings of Adam Smith, Emile Durkheim, and Karl Marx, and, in more recent times, has been developed by Kohn (1969) and others (Inkeles and Smith, 1974; Kanter, 1977a; Kohn and Schooler, 1973; Seeman, 1967; Schooler, 1972). In a contemporary test of Marx's hypothesis about the origins of alienation, Melvin Kohn (1971) found that lack of occupational self-direction in work is of crucial importance in producing a sense of alienation. Moreover, the deleterious consequences of highly routinized and fragmented work have been described in several studies of the assembly line (Blauner, 1964; Kornhauser, 1965; Walker and Guest, 1952). But it is not necessary to take a stand in the debate as to whether work in modern society is more often dehumanizing or liberating, to acknowledge that generalization processes may operate in both kinds of circumstances.

As a result of these processes, individuals in different lines of work often have distinctive and recognizable personality characteristics which have been a persistent subject of sociological inquiry. In 1925, Park and his colleagues called for the study of the diverse "vocational types" to be found in the city, to better understand the newly developing urban environment. Later, Sorokin (1947) proclaimed that "each occupation tends . . . to remake its members in its own image."

> When the same occupational operations are performed from day to day for many years, they effectively modify the mental, moral, social, physiological, and anatomical properties of their members in accordance with the nature and requirements of the occupational work. (p. 211)

While Hughes (1958) and his followers have pursued this insight in their many observational studies of particular occupational groups, our major concern, following Kohn (1969:235–36; Kohn and Schooler, 1973:98–99), is to identify the *dimensions* of work that have significant socializing impacts. It could be argued that each occupation represents a distinct configuration of work experiences with its own unique socializing effect. However, focusing analysis on occupational group differences has the marked disadvantage of obscuring the specific work dimensions that cross-cut occupational categories and influence the personality. Moreover, while the "occupational group approach" might produce intriguing results, it precludes the generalization of findings necessary for theoretical development (see Spenner, 1977; and Temme, 1975 for similar arguments).

Consistent with our emphasis on occupational attributes, a large number of surveys have systematically documented that there are psychological differences among persons with varying *dimensions* of work experience. This survey evidence is most extensive with respect to job satisfaction and other subjective reactions to the work itself (for a review of the job satisfaction literature, see Mortimer, 1979). It has been conclusively established that persons in occupations of higher prestige, those with the more economically rewarding positions, and those with more autonomous and intrinsically satisfying work express more positive attitudes toward their jobs (Centers, 1948; Centers and Bugental, 1966; Gurin et al., 1960: Ch. 6; Kilpatrick et al., 1964; Kohn, 1969; Locke, 1976; Quinn and Staines, 1979; Quinn et al., 1974; Robinson et al., 1969: Ch. 3; Seashore and Taber, 1975; Wilensky, 1964).

However, according to the "generalization model" of adult socialization, attitudes, values, and ways of thinking are generalized and abstracted from the modes of successful adaptation to daily life pressures and situations, particularly those encountered in the workplace. This generalization model presumes that, since occupation is such an important role in the life of an adult, it will have quite pervasive effects on the personality, coming to influence both work and nonwork spheres. There is a "direct translation of the lessons of the job to outside-the-job realities" (Kohn, 1977). It is therefore consistent with this approach to look beyond the job in studying the psychological impacts of work experience. For example, there is considerable evidence from Kohn's work (1969), as well as studies in other national contexts (see Kohn, 1977, for a review), that orientations developed in the work situation, concerning the importance of self-direction and conformity, influence parental values. And there is increasing recognition among social scientists, as well as in the society at large, that work experiences are critical determinants of the overall quality of life, physical and mental health, and the potential for personal development (O'Toole, 1973; Veninga and Spradley, 1981).

It should be emphasized that this conceptual model of socialization in adulthood emphasizes occupational tasks and experiences as major sources of personal change. While interpersonal relations at the workplace (e.g., with supervisors, coworkers, and clients) may also influence the developing adult personality (see Lorence and Mortimer, 1979, for a discussion of this possibility in the context of political socialization), the generalization model does not presume that significant others or groups must intervene for this influence to occur (see Inkeles and Smith, 1974; Kohn, 1976:100–101; Kohn and Schooler, 1973:105; Spaeth, 1976a). Following this generalization model, we examine work experiences as sources of psychological change in early adulthood. (For a comparison of the generalization model with other theoretical approaches to adult socialization, see Mortimer and Simmons, 1978).

We believe that studying the five psychological constructs over time, the self-concept, work involvement, and occupational values, enables an appropriate test of the generalization thesis—that experiences at work extend beyond the particular job situation to influence attitudes about self and work more generally. Though each of them are pertinent to work, none directly pertain to the respondent's current job. The measure of self-competence contains no reference to the present work role, but indicates the respondent's overall assessment of himself—whether competent, strong, active, and successful. The question regarding work involvement does not ask about the respondent's involvement in his present job; instead, the reference is to "career or occupation" more broadly, as an "area of life." Similarly, the 1976 measure of occupational reward values specifically directs the respondent to look beyond his current position in considering his value priorities, "If you were offered another occupational position, how important would you consider each of the following work characteristics in deciding whether to accept it?"

There is evidence that each of these five psychological constructs is linked to work experiences in ways that are consistent with the generalization hypothesis, but this evidence is, for the most part, cross-sectional in nature. Self-esteem has been found to be associated with the socioeconomic level of the job (Gurin and Gurin, 1976; Jacques and Chason, 1977; Luck and Heiss, 1972; Rosenberg, 1979: Ch. 5), self-direction in work (Kohn, 1969; Kohn and Schooler, 1973:103, 115), and occupational stress (Luck and Heiss, 1972). This central dimension of the self-image is probably positively related, for most people, to what we have labelled self-competence.

Work involvement has similarly been found to be significantly related to occupational experiences that imply self-direction, that is, work that permits autonomy, creativity, and the use of abilities; work that is challenging and moderately difficult; and work that allows participation in decision-making (Lawler and Hall, 1970; Kohn and Schooler, 1973:103; Patchen, 1970; Siegel and Ruh, 1973). Extrinsic rewards, such as income, and opportunities for promotion have also been found to be positively related to work involvement (Mannheim, 1975). Finally, numerous studies have documented the differences among adult workers in occupational values, evaluations of the importance of specific work experiences and rewards, and have linked these differences to work experiences (Andrisani and Miljus, 1976; Belcher and Atchison, 1976; Kohn, 1969; Quinn et al., 1974).

Whereas the many cross-sectional studies of psychological differences among the incumbents of different kinds of occupations attest to the probable impacts of work experience, it is necessary to have longitudinal data, measuring individual change over time, to empirically demonstrate that this socialization process occurs. As we have observed, it is often assumed that occupations "mold" the personality (see Hughes, 1958; Kanter, 1977b; Moore, 1969; White, 1952, for further elaborations of this thesis). While cross-sectional differences are generally interpreted as demonstrating this molding effect, the "occupational socialization hypothesis" has rarely been examined over time.

Longitudinal study is essential to test this hypothesis, because cross-sectional differences, either among members of particular occupational groups, or associated with continuous occupational dimensions, could instead be attributable to earlier occupational *selection* on the basis of the very same psychological traits. There is substantial evidence for this contrasting "occupational selection hypothesis," that persons choose their work on the basis of previous dispositions. It has been the focus of numerous studies of occupational choice by psychologists as well as sociologists (Davis, 1965; Holland, 1976; Rosenberg, 1957; Strong, 1955; Super et al., 1963). This hypothesis is also a central concern of the present study, though, consistent with our general perspective, it is examined in Chapter 2 in terms of *dimensions* of occupational attainment, not choice of distinct occupational groups. Our causal model clearly demonstrates that work attitudes, measured prior to labor force entry, influence subsequent occupational attainments. Our study differs from most previous research on occupational selection since it examines *actual* work experiences, considered as outcomes of earlier attitudes and values, not mere preference for occupational membership at some future time.

While panel data on the same persons over time is necessary to determine whether work experiences do, in fact, engender psychological change, longitudinal research extending across broad phases of the life course has generally not focused on the impacts of work experiences on the individual (for a brief review of such long-term panel studies, see Mortimer and Lorence, 1981). Several recent longitudinal studies covering shorter time spans, however, have shown that work experiences influence the personality. Most notable among these is Kohn and Schooler's (1978) 10-year study of work experience and psychological functioning. Providing evidence for the socializing impacts of occupational experience, the substantive complexity of work was found to have a significant contemporaneous effect on intellectual flexibility. This socialization effect occurred in spite of the high level of stability of this psychological attribute. This analysis gives concrete evidence for the generalization model—the substantive complexity of work was found to influence intellectual flexibility, a basic psychological attribute that would have highly general ramifications for functioning, both on and off the job. Kohn and Schooler's longitudinal analysis also showed that "selection" processes operate: earlier intellectual flexibility predicted later job complexity, suggesting processes of work selection or "job molding" (modifying one's work) on the basis of prior psychological traits. The prominence of occupational experiences as sources of individual change has been further demonstrated with respect to several other psychological variables in their data, including parental valuation of self-direction, standards of morality, trustfulness, self-deprecation, and anxiety, using a similar analytic framework (Kohn and Schooler, 1982, 1983; Slomczynski et al., 1981). There is additional evidence from other panel studies, likewise interpretable within a generalization framework, that occupational successes and failures influence physical health (French, 1968; Kasl et al., 1975) and emotional stress (Pearlin and Lieberman, 1979). Our study of self competence, work involvement and occupational values builds on this research tradition.

As we noted in the introduction, by focusing on the effects of occupational experiences on adult psychological attributes, this study examines a central question in the study of personality—the degree of stability of personal characteristics as the individual moves through the life course. Psychoanalysts and some developmental psychologists believe that the main contours of personality are set by the end of childhood (Kagan and Moss, 1962; Lidz, 1968; Luborsky and Schimek, 1964), and this premise has been dominant among social scientists for a long period of time (see Gergen, 1977). Recently, however, sociologists interested in the life course have joined psychologists studying "life-span development" in arguing that the individual is responsive throughout life to new social experiences, particularly at the time of important role transitions or other significant life events (Brim and Kagan, 1980; Brim and Ryff, 1980).

This issue is complicated by the fact that the very stability of psychological traits may be strongly affected by the degree of persistence in environmental circumstances. Though psychological stability after the early years of life has been frequently demonstrated in longitudinal studies (Kagan and Moss, 1962; Kelly, 1955; Kuhlen, 1964), it is quite difficult to explain this phenomenon. Stability, in the very simplest case, may be attributable to the fact that once a psychological trait is developed, it persists over time, without being significantly influenced by the environment. Rosenberg calls this "static stability" (personal communication). Such persistence may mean constancy, such as a relatively unchanging characteristic like intelligence, or a persistence of advantage or disadvantage relative to others, like maintaining one's position at the top of the class. By early adulthood, the individual may have developed a sufficiently high level of work involvement to sustain continuously high effort throughout the career. Moreover, it is conceivable that a very strong sense of self-esteem, developed in the early years, could withstand occupational failures and disappointments in adulthood, particularly if the individual gauged himself against a different set of standards (see Rosenberg, 1979).

Alternatively, stability could be due to continuous external influence, as persistent social and environmental conditions support constancy, or the maintenance of one's position relative to others (see Bloom, 1964:223; Wheaton et al., 1977:89–91). Rosenberg (personal communication) calls this situation one of "dynamic stability"—individual attributes remain stable over time as a result of sustaining life experiences. In this case, the personality attribute or behavioral pattern changes when environmental support is withdrawn. For example, stability in achievement, in both education and the work sphere, could engender a continually high sense of competence. But under conditions of "dynamic stability," if this external validation of self were withdrawn in the face of setbacks and mounting competition, one would expect the sense of personal efficacy to diminish.

But even given a high level of responsiveness to environmental conditions, which the concept of "dynamic stability" implies, the individual should not be viewed as merely a passive recipient of external influence. We believe it is more likely that the person is an active selector and molder of the situational context. In Chapter 2 we showed that early psychological orientations influence subsequent occupational attainments. The respondents might thus be viewed as actively creating the occupational experiences which later affect the course of their personal development, selecting and molding those external circumstances that can engender psychological persistence or change over time.

The panel design of this study enables us to examine these processes of static stability, dynamic stability, and personal determination of subsequent life events. We assess the degree of stability of each of the five work-related psychological orientations, and the extent to which the stabilities are attributable to persistent achievement and success. We do this by comparing the level of stability over time, as measured by zero-order "true score" correlations of the senior and 1976 psychological constructs, shorn of measurement error, with our final estimates of stability, net of occupational and other influences, derived from our final causal model of psychological development. If the "zero-order" stability were found to be substantially larger than the "net" stability, we would conclude that the external variables in the model largely account for the true score correlations that were observed. By this method, we can investigate the extent to which the stability in these psychological dimensions is "static" or "dynamic," in Rosenberg's terminology, over the 10-year period.

In this chapter, we question the notion that significant socialization experiences occur only in childhood, and examine the process of psychological development in adulthood, following entry to the labor force. Specifically, we hypothesize that occupational experiences are major sources of psychological change. At the same time, we believe that they may be important in establishing an environmental context that is conducive to the preservation of initial psychological attributes. Given the significance of the occupational role in modern societies for social status and economic well-being, as well as the substantial amount of time that is spent at work, we expect to find that occupational experiences will have important implications for psychological change, as well as stability, during the period of transition to adulthood.

We will now develop our rationale for anticipating that the particular psychological constructs under investigation will be significantly influenced by occupational experiences during the early work career.

WORK EXPERIENCE AND SELF-COMPETENCE

Although the sources of change in the self-concept over time have been given relatively little attention (Rosenberg, 1976), the generalization model would lead one to expect that a central psychological orientation, like the self-concept, would be influenced by previous occupational successes. In support of this expectation, Bachman and his colleagues (Bachman and O'Malley, 1977; Bachman et al., 1978:114) report that occupational prestige is associated with increases in self-esteem during the early post-high school period, and Cohn (1978) has demonstrated changes in self-esteem in response to unemployment and re-employment. (See also Elder, 1974:246–47; Goodwin, 1977; and Gurin and Gurin, 1976 for further evidence). Andrisani (1978) has similarly provided evidence that high earnings may enhance a sense of internal control (see also Andrisani and Abeles, 1976; Andrisani and Nestel, 1976), and Elder (1969) shows that upward mobility fosters a sense of competence.

While these previous studies have, for the most part, focussed on extrinsic dimensions of occupational attainment (such as prestige, income, upward mobility, and employment security) as determinants of the self-image, some investigators have emphasized the importance of work autonomy in fostering a sense of competence and high self-esteem. According to Rosenberg (1979:146), ". . . someone who sees the visible outcome of his efforts, the products of his own decisions, would feel greater respect for himself than someone who . . . cannot attribute the results to himself." Similarly, Korman (1970), in discussing the sources of a sense of competence, posits a "task-related" component, responsive to experiences of autonomy in the work environment. Franks and Marolla (1976) distinguish "inner self-esteem," dependent on "one's own competent actions, and the rewards stemming from such actions," from "outer self-esteem," dependent upon the approval of significant others. The work of Kohn and his colleagues has demonstrated the relevance of work experience for change in the self-concept over time. Occupational self-direction was found to have a significant negative effect on self-deprecation (indicated by feelings of uselessness, being "no good", a lack of self-respect, and similar measures) even when the same lagged psychological state (10 years previously) was controlled (see Slomczynski et al., 1981). Their findings regarding the occupational sources of fatalism (Kohn and Schooler, 1982) and powerlessness (Kohn, 1976) provide further evidence that self-direction at work influences the individual's sense of personal efficacy and control over life events.

In Chapter 2, we showed that self-competence, measured prior to labor force entry, fostered the attainment of autonomous work experiences through its effect on intrinsic occupational values. In the present chapter, we build on the work of several other investigators, including Kohn and Schooler, Rosenberg, Bachman, and Andrisani, in examining the extent to which work experiences "feed back" on the self-image in a later phase of life. Specifically, we hypothesize that occupational experiences of autonomy, giving opportunities for the expression of competence, will enhance a sense of personal efficacy, validating the perception of self as strong, active, competent, and successful. Previous studies suggest that income attainment, because of the clear demonstration of achievement which it provides, similarly enhances this dimension of the self-image. However, our earlier analysis (Mortimer and Lorence, 1979b) showed that income had no significant impact on self-competence in this panel.

Furthermore, we go beyond previous research to investigate not only the impacts of work experiences on self-competence, but also the effects of the early career pattern. We assess whether early career stability has an effect on competence over the 10-year period of study that is independent of occupational experiences and rewards. We hypothesize that early career stability, a smooth career progression without major changes and employment problems, will enhance the sense of competence. In contrast, experiences of career uncertainty and problems of employment are expected to diminish self-competence over time. This pattern would be quite consistent with the findings of earlier studies of the psychological impacts of unemployment (Bakke, 1940:251–255; Cohn, 1978; Powell and Driscoll, 1973).

WORK EXPERIENCE AND WORK INVOLVEMENT

Whereas there has been some attention to change in the self-image in response to work experience, the level of involvement in work has been subject to very little systematic longitudinal study. Some investigators have attempted to identify the features of work experience which promote high work involvement by performing cross-sectional analyses of the attitudes of workers with different job characteristics. As noted earlier, their studies suggest that self-directed and intrinsically satisfying occupational experiences (Kohn and Schooler, 1973:103; Lawler and Hall, 1970; Patchen, 1970; Siegel and Ruh, 1973), as well as extrinsic rewards (Mannheim, 1975), heighten work involvement. Because this research is cross-sectional, however, the relationships could be attributable to the combined effects of selection processes, and the persistence of early work involvement over time. But it is plausible to assume that rewarding experiences on the job would heighten the centrality of work over time. When occupational rewards are low, one might expect that the person would channel interests and involvements toward nonwork areas of life, in an attempt to compensate for the absence of satisfactions in the work sphere. After analyzing the mechanisms people use to cope with persistent work strain, Pearlin and Schooler (1978:10–11) conclude that "people seek to control stress in occupation, through without much success, by keeping work itself in a place secondary in importance." (Faunce and Dubin, 1975, and Vaillant, 1976, present similar arguments.)

We therefore hypothesize that work autonomy will enhance work involvement over time. (Our earlier analyses showed that income and career stability had no such effects, see Lorence and Mortimer, 1981).

WORK EXPERIENCE AND OCCUPATIONAL VALUES

It is often assumed that occupational reward values are formed relatively early in life, before the completion of formal education, and that they persist very much in their original form throughout the work history. This premise pervades the literature on occupational choice, job satisfaction, and career development. It also appears to parallel the more general notion that personality, including central values and motives, is formed mainly in childhood and adolescence, while changes in adulthood only encompass more specific and superficial orientations. As a result, although there are many studies of occupational values as factors influencing job selection, satisfaction and change, the possibility that work experiences may lead to shifts in these values over time has rarely been examined empirically.

Still, it is sometimes argued that when the individual has inadequate economic resources, income and other extrinsic benefits of work come to assume the highest priority. When material needs are satisfied, the salience of extrinsic rewards decreases as the worker's attention turns to other, more intrinsic satisfactions (Flanagan et al., 1974; Maslow, 1954). In support of this reasoning, it has been shown cross-sectionally that concern with intrinsic occupational rewards steadily increases with occupational prestige; extrinsic rewards are more highly evaluated at lower occupational levels (Kilpatrick et al., 1964; Kohn, 1969: 75–78; see also Gurin et al., 1960:157–162). These trends would seem to imply a sequential process by which extrinsic values are replaced by intrinsic concerns as the individual progresses from lower to higher levels of socio-economic attainment. But such a process has not been confirmed longitudinally.

It would seem, however, that the generalization model would lead to somewhat different predictions regarding occupational value development. If the individual were generalizing from his actual experience, the distinctive rewards and measures of success to which he is exposed would likely acquire increasing salience over time. These would be the kinds of rewards that are emphasized in his line of work. Rewards that are obtained in one's job would thus come to have high priority. Moreover, the level of reward would probably set limits upon future aspirations. This formulation is consistent with Durkheim's (1951:249–54) conceptualization of anomie. In considering the effects of attainments on goals, Durkheim pointed out that in normal times, i.e., in the absence of major economic change or societal disruption, "each person is . . . in harmony with his condition, and desires only what he may legitimately hope for as the normal reward of his activity" (Durkheim, 1951:250). But, according to his argument, the rapid attainment of wealth fosters a desire for increasing rewards, as aspirations rise and potential success seems unlimited. Such a process would engender a positive relationship between individual income and extrinsic values. Conversely, the absence of personal experience with particular occupational rewards would lessen the individual's hopes of attaining them in the future. The perceived importance of such rewards would be reduced further in the presence of alternative sources of gratification.

Durkheim's discussion may exaggerate the processes of generalization, abstraction and goal setting that occur in "normal" times, in response to more conventional occupational experiences and attainments. If these processes do occur, high levels of extrinsic reward would be expected to increase the salience of income, prestige, and similar benefits, not to diminish these concerns. Previous emphasis on extrinsic values would not be replaced by "higher order" considerations. Similarly, opportunities for work with people would be expected to heighten the people-oriented value cluster; autonomous, challenging work would reinforce initial intrinsic concerns. As a result, value differences among the incumbents of occupations at any given time would be the outcome of socialization processes (as well, perhaps, of occupational selection), which heighten evaluations of those satisfying experiences that are encountered in the work environment. (For similar formulations, see Hall, 1971; Kolb and Plovnick, 1977; and Maccoby, 1976).[1]

But in spite of the consistent socio-economic differences in occupational values, with the important exception of Kohn's work (1969: Ch. 10), there has been little systematic investigation of the sources of values in the occupational experiences of workers. We investigate the effects of work autonomy, income, and the social content of work, three central work experiences, on changes in values over time. As suggested above, we hypothesize that income will heighten extrinsic orientations, work with high social content will enhance people-oriented values, and autonomous work will strengthen the evaluation of intrinsic occupational rewards.

Furthermore, the data permit examination of the impacts of the career pattern on values, independent of those occupational experiences that are associated with career stability (see Chapter 2). On the one hand, it might be argued that career instability, and the negative experiences in the labor force which this implies, would lessen the evaluation of occupational rewards, as the individual turns to other, more gratifying spheres of life for emotional gratification. A stable career pattern, according to this argument, would be expected to foster occupational reward values, just as we found that work involvement enhanced them in the period prior to college graduation.

On the other hand, it is also plausible that instability in the early career would heighten the importance of occupational rewards, producing inverse relationships between career stability and values. The lesson of the

---

[1] This conceptualization parallels Feldman and Weiler's (1976:375–376) discussion of "accentuation" at the individual level. Feldman and Newcomb (1969, especially pp. 193–94) described an accentuation process whereby students select college majors on the basis of their interests, attitudes, and values. These predispositions are then reinforced during college by faculty and peers. Moreover, students who are dissimilar to others in their major field are more likely to change their majors to achieve a better fit (see also Davis, 1965; Werts, 1967).

unstable career might be that such rewards cannot be taken for granted. Consistent with this line of reasoning, Elder (1974:189–193) found that prior experiences of unemployment and economic deprivation, both in their families of origin and in their own work lives, heightened men's concerns with employment security and other extrinsic rewards.

FATHER–SON RELATIONS AND PSYCHOLOGICAL DEVELOPMENT IN EARLY ADULTHOOD

The analysis presented in Chapter 2 showed the pervasive influence of paternal support on the development of work-related psychological orientations in late adolescence, before entry to the labor force. Paternal support had rather substantial direct impacts on sons' self-competence and work involvement. Excepting the direct effect of paternal support on extrinsic orientations, the father's influence on sons' values occurred indirectly, through the two more general psychological orientations. The same indicators of relationship with the father were included in the 1976 questionnaire. These measures enable us to examine the extent to which paternal support is stable and continues to influence the development of psychological orientations that are relevant to occupational attainment in early adulthood.

One might reasonably expect to find that paternal influence would diminish, following the "launching" of sons, as the primacy of relations with parents is supplanted by the acquisition of marital, parental, occupational, and other life involvements. It is also possible, however, that a positive father–son relationship would be a significant source of support and encouragement to the son in early adulthood, as he enters his own occupational role. Given the tendency of sons to prefer occupations like those of their fathers (see Mortimer, 1974), occupational demands on the son might be expected to be quite similar to those experienced by the father in the beginnings of his career. Given these considerations, paternal support might continue to be a significant source of competence, work involvement, and occupational values for the son in the early phases of adulthood. To our knowledge, this possibility has not heretofore been addressed empirically.

THE MODEL OF PSYCHOLOGICAL CHANGE

The Causal Ordering of the Constructs

The causal model to be considered in this chapter (see Figure 3-1) extends our earlier model of occupational attainment to include the five psychological dimensions, measured in 1976, as final outcomes. As before, the ordering of these variables reflects the assumption that self-competence and work involvement are causally prior to occupational values, as it was expected that a sense of competence and high work involvement would enhance the evaluation of occupational rewards (our rationale is given in Chapter 2). As noted earlier, this causal ordering cannot be considered definitive given the simultaneous measurement of these constructs.

Our main concern, however, is to examine the effects of occupational attributes and the career pattern on the psychological constructs. In order to assess the influence of these work experiences, it is necessary to control the stability of the psychological attributes over time. This control rules out the possibility that significant paths from adult work experiences to the psychological dimensions are attributable to processes of selection and subsequent stability. Therefore, a direct path has been estimated from each of the five psychological constructs, measured in the senior year, to the corresponding 1976 construct. These paths indicate the degree of psychological stability, independent of work and other adult experiences, over the 10-year period.

In the analysis of occupational attainment presented in Chapter 2, there was no question of the causal ordering of the work and psychological variables, since self-competence, work involvement, and occupational values were all measured 10 years prior to the occupational attainments. But in the present analysis both the work experiences and psychological attributes were measured at the same time, though we assign the work experiences causal priority in our model. The fact that the respondents have pursued their careers for an average of 5.5 years since completing their post-graduate schooling provides some justification for this causal ordering. (Though a decade elapsed between the two periods of data collection, most respondents spent considerable time in post-graduate schooling. Some also served in the military.) It is reasonable to suppose that occupational experiences within the context of the same career would involve similar levels of autonomy, income, and social content, in spite of change in specific employment positions. In the absence of career change, the work constructs would likely represent persistent occupational experiences.

Nevertheless, it is quite plausible to assume that the psychological variables are also quite stable over time. As a result, the psychological constructs may represent constant states during a previous, unspecified period of time. If, in fact, both the 1976 work experiences and the psychological constructs represent long-term phenomena, one might expect to find a pattern of reciprocal influence between them. Reciprocal causal paths would reflect an ongoing process of mutual influence, as persons choose and mold their jobs to conform to their personalities, and as work experiences continuously shape them. Such a pattern would parallel Kohn and Schooler's (1978) findings with respect to the inter-relations of occupational complexity and intellectual flexibility.

Because of the problem of model identification we could not initially explore all reciprocal relations of interest within the context of this full causal model. To investigate the possibility of two-way causation, we therefore examine the reciprocal interrelations of work experiences and psychological attributes only when significant causal paths are found between them, given our initial (one-way) specification of the causal ordering of the variables. Because of the high cost of reestimating the full causal model, we estimate these reciprocal relations within the con-text of much smaller, reduced models.

We expected, on the basis of the extensive theoretical and empirical work that has been reviewed, that work autonomy would be of central importance for adult psychological development. This expectation was confirmed by our earlier partial analyses, considering the development of self-competence, work involvement, and occupational values sepa-rately (see Lorence and Mortimer, 1981; Mortimer and Lorence, 1979a,b). These analyses, showing that work autonomy is a significant predictor of 1976 competence, work involvement, intrinsic orientation, and people-oriented values, guided the development of the full causal model, including all five psychological constructs. We therefore initially specified direct paths from work autonomy to these four constructs—to all the psychological variables except the extrinsic values. These paths indicate the "socialization effect," or the impacts of work autonomy on the psychological attributes after earlier psychological differences have been controlled.

As noted earlier, other studies have suggested that income attainment would also have a positive effect on competence and work involvement. We predicted on the basis of the generalization model that income would likewise enhance extrinsic values over time. Since, however, income was found in our own previous work to have no significant effects on com-petence and work involvement, only a path from income to extrinsic orientation was included in the initial causal model. Finally, correspond-ing to our hypothesis that satisfying experiences encountered in the work sphere will enhance the evaluation of the very same rewards, a direct path from the social content of work to people-oriented values was included.

In Figure 3-1, career stability is antecedent to the psychological di-mensions, as well as to current occupational experiences. The career pattern's causally prior position is justified because the measures of ca-reer stability (including career change and an indicator reflecting the problems of unemployment, subemployment, and involuntary part-time employment) cover the entire time span since college graduation. Post-graduate educational attainment likewise represents a temporally prior achievement.

Finally, repeating our model specification for the earlier time period, the construct representing 1976 paternal support is a cause, not an effect, of the 1976 psychological constructs. Because the relations between parents and children generally form in an early stage of life and remain quite stable over time (see Mortimer and Lorence, 1981), it seemed more plausible to assume that relations with the father would influence the son's adult work orientations than to posit the reverse causal ordering.

A description of the model estimation procedures follows.

Model Estimation Procedures

In this third chapter we are primarily concerned with the influence of work experiences and the career pattern on change in psychological orientations over time. Yet it is desirable to estimate these effects in the context of a full model including all prior variables, that is, all factors that have been found to influence the process of occupational attainment. Including all relevant constructs in a single model enables assessment of the entire causal process under consideration at once, and to assess the fit of the whole causal model to the input data. It also permits more accurate estimation of the parameters than if only selected variables relevant to this process were considered at one time. Furthermore, in conceptualizing the interrelations of work, family, and personality through late adolescence and the early life course, we have emphasized the effects of family origins and early psychological orientations on later occupational attainments, and the impacts of adult occupational experiences on subsequent psychological development. It is therefore intellectually appealing to analytically represent this complex process as a single, all-inclusive model.

When using the LISREL program, the amount of time necessary for model estimation increases markedly as additional indicators, constructs and parameters are included. Given the scope of the model under investigation, there were a large number of causal parameters of hypothetical interest. For example, in developing the analysis presented in Chapter 2, we wished to explore the possibility that certain variables early in the causal chain, such as the family's socio-economic status, would influence subsequent variables, like the son's 1976 income. One could estimate a fully recursive model using the maximum likelihood technique, though this would be quite expensive due to the large amount of time needed to estimate the many parameters which such a model would yield. Nor is such an exploratory analysis compatible with the essentially confirmatory logic of causal model specification and of testing the fit of the hypothetical model to data. We therefore attempted to specify the relations among the constructs as definitively as possible, thereby simplifying the model before estimation.

Causal paths were consequently deleted if they had been found to be statistically insignificant when estimated in the context of very similar, though partial, causal models. Paths from 1976 income to 1976 self-competence and work involvement were eliminated on this basis, since income was found to have no significant effects on these psychological variables (see Lorence and Mortimer, 1981; Mortimer and Lorence, 1979b). A path from career stability to work involvement was likewise fixed at zero in view of its failure to significantly predict this psychological attribute in our previous analysis.

In the initially estimated full model, we also removed theoretically interesting paths in view of the findings of other extensive exploratory analyses. To assess the relations among all the variables in a multivariate context, we first estimated a fully recursive total model, using ordinary least squares regression with factor-based scales substituted for the latent constructs. While this procedure does not take errors of measurement into account, and therefore generates less accurate estimates of causal parameters than would be obtained by the use of multiple-indicator models, such preliminary analysis would seem appropriate for exploratory purposes. Paths from the 1976 measure of paternal support to the 1976 psychological variables were dropped on this basis, given its extremely weak effects on the five dependent variables.

Thus the preliminary model that was estimated by the LISREL procedure represented the end product of three previous, partial analyses, considering each of the psychological constructs separately, and a thorough examination of the relationships among the variables. This sequential procedure in the development of the model was very useful, enabling considerable simplification and reduction of the number of parameters to be estimated.

First-order partial derivatives are provided by the program which can be used as a check to ascertain whether these preliminary analyses, given their approximate character (that is, their incompleteness and, with respect to the regression analysis, their inability to take measurement error into account), were generating erroneous conclusions and, consequently, a misspecification of the causal process. The first-order partials give an indication of whether parameters that were previously fixed at zero would be statistically significant if allowed to be freely estimated, thereby improving the fit of the model to data. It is, of course, hazardous to place too much emphasis on the partial derivatives, particularly if they suggest relationships for which there is no prior justification. The specification of causal paths should instead be guided by theoretical considerations. However, if the first order partials are very small, assurance is provided that no potentially important paths have been inadvertently left out of the model. On the other hand, large partials suggest that some relationships may deserve further scrutiny. Thus, estimating a simpler model including all pertinent constructs enables some assessment as to whether very early variables in the causal process have direct effects on later ones in the chain, without the need to estimate a more complex, fully recursive model.

As noted briefly in Chapter 2, our analytic procedure consisted of the following stages. We first estimated an intitial causal model, based on the theoretical and empirical considerations outlined above, including all relevant variables. All measurement parameters (i.e., the paths from the constructs to the indicators, the error terms of the indicators, and the correlations among these errors) were fixed at the values obtained from the previously estimated measurement models (see Appendix B).

In the second stage, insignificant causal paths were dropped and the partial derivatives for all fixed parameters (that is, those that were fixed at zero) were examined. These partial derivatives suggested no changes in the initial part of the model, among variables leading up to the occupational attainments. But two modifications were indicated in the subsequent specification. The partial derivatives suggested a correlation between the residual terms of two 1976 occupational value constructs, those representing the intrinsic and people-oriented reward values. This residual correlation was estimated, found to be significant, and therefore included in the third phase. The partial derivatives also suggested inclusion of a path from the 1976 measure of paternal support to work autonomy. This would indicate that the quality of the father–son relationship has a direct effect on the son's attainment of work autonomy during the period subsequent to college graduation. This path was also estimated in the second phase but proved to be insignificant. It was consequently deleted in the subsequent stage of analysis.

Before re-estimating the model in the third phase, all paths found earlier to be insignificant were fixed at zero. As in the previous stages, all measurement parameters were fixed. For this final model, all partial derivatives were found to be extremely small.

Finally, in the last stage of analysis, partial reciprocal effects models were estimated to clarify the causal ordering of the significant relations between the constructs representing the 1976 work experiences and the psychological attributes. Since no reciprocal paths from the psychological constructs to the work experiences were found to be statistically significant, they were not incorporated in the final model, which is shown in Figure 3-1.

Before turning to a discussion of the findings, it should be noted that the final model represents a very good fit to the data. A chi-square goodness-of-fit test was used to determine the extent to which the estimated parameters can reproduce the original input data matrix. Chi-square values which are large relative to the degrees of freedom indicate a poor fit, while those that approach the degrees of freedom suggest a good fit (Joreskog and Sorbom, 1977:290–291; Long, 1976:168–73). The observed chi-square value of 1364.88 with 799 degrees of freedom yields a ratio of 1.71 per degree of freedom, which would appear to be a quite adequate fit. Moreover, the absence of large first-order partial derivatives suggests that the fit of this model to the input data would not be significantly improved by respecification.

Further indication that the model is correctly specified derives from the general lack of significant residual correlations among the constructs. This absence suggests that the covariation of the constructs is adequately explained by the variables that have been identified as predictors. As noted earlier, there is only one significant residual correlation, between the constructs representing the people-oriented and intrinsic values, implying that the covariation of these work values is not sufficiently accounted for by the prior variables.

THE FINDINGS

To simplify the discussion of this complex model, we will first examine the development of each psychological construct separately, and then make some more general comments about the pattern of findings as a whole.

The Development of Self-competence Over Time

What is perhaps most striking about the analysis of self-competence is the high level of stability of this construct. The stability path (.731) should be considered quite precise, since both random errors of measurement in the indicators, and the correlations of the error variances over time, have been extracted in the estimation of this coefficient. It is noteworthy that the magnitude of the stability coefficient is quite similar to the stability path of .71 from 1964 to 1974 intellectual flexibility reported in Kohn and Schooler's prior study (1978:45). Bachman et al. (1978:291) report a slightly smaller path of .69 (corrected for unreliability) from

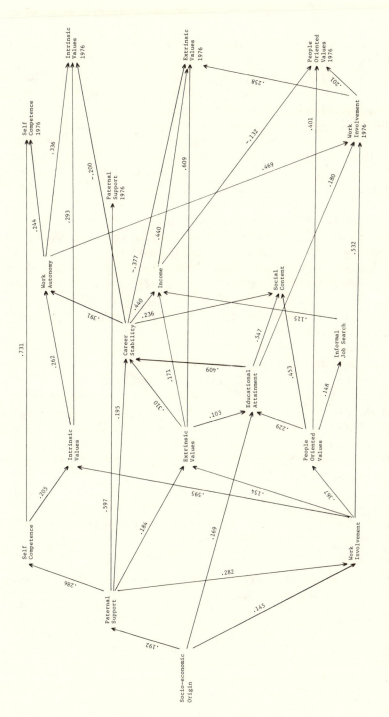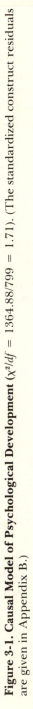

Figure 3-1. Causal Model of Psychological Development ($\chi^2/df = 1364.88/799 = 1.71$). (The standardized construct residuals are given in Appendix B.)

self-esteem during a shorter period from the senior year of high school to self-esteem 5 years after graduation.

It should be noted that in the earlier measurement model the stability estimate was .793. This estimate, in a model including no external variables, is almost identical to the stability path shown in Figure 3-1 (compare with Table 3-1). This suggests that, in spite of the significant impact of work autonomy on this dimension of self, which we will presently address, this experience hardly accounts for the high level of stability in the self-image dimension over time. Using Rosenberg's terminology, the weight of the evidence seems to favor the "static," rather than "dynamic," stability hypothesis.

The high stability of the competence dimension of the self-concept supports Erikson's (1959) thesis that the individual's sense of identity is largely formed by the end of adolescence. He posited that the establishment of identity is the critical developmental task of adolescence, after which the self-image remains quite stable. Several social psychologists have also postulated that the preservation of a consistent and stable sense of self is a major motivational goal (Epstein, 1973; Korman, 1970; Lecky, 1945; and Rosenberg, 1979). If this is the case, then the members of this panel have been quite successful in achieving this outcome. It has also been suggested that positive self-concepts are more resistant to change over time (Epstein, 1973:411). The generally positively skewed distribution of the senior self-competence indicators could then be an additional factor reducing the propensity to change.

Persistence of the self-image, as indicated by this high stability path, means that an individual's position, relative to others being studied, remains quite similar. Scores at one time thus predict subsequent score values. Using this essentially correlational criterion, and drawing heavily on the Fels data (Kagan and Moss, 1962), Bloom (1964:177) has estimated that approximately half the variance in a number of important adolescent characteristics (e.g., intellectual interest, dependency, and aggression) can be predicted by the age of 5.

But even this high degree of observed stability in self-competence

Table 3-1. Stabilities of the Psychological Constructs over a 10-year Period (derived from measurement models)

Psychological Constructs	Standardized Stabilities	Standardized Residuals of the 1976 Constructs
Self-Competence	.793	.371
Work Involvement	.705	.502
People-Oriented Values	.500	.750
Intrinsic Values	.364	.867
Extrinsic Values	.676	.544

does not imply that the measures have remained constant over the period of observation, though this could occur. Even with such strong stability, there could be quite uniform change among members of a group. For example, Rosenberg (1979, Ch. 9) has suggested that mean self-esteem scores fall as groups of children move into adolescence. At the same time, their positions vis-à-vis one another could persist. Examination of the mean self-competence indicator scores suggests that such a uniform, though small, change may have occurred. (These means are given in Appendix B.) The respondents perceived themselves as more competent in 1976 than they did when they graduated from college. (Two other indicators, strong–weak, and successful–not too successful, have shifted upwards only slightly in average value, while the last, active–quiet, has declined slightly.)

The generally positive shift in the perception of self as competent suggests that as adult roles are acquired—in work, the family and perhaps other institutional spheres—the individual's sense of personal efficacy is heightened. This may be especially likely if a successful adaptation has been made to the demands encountered in these new roles. Judging from their achievements, such success would seem to characterize the vast majority of the members of this panel.

Our primary concern in this chapter, however, is to assess the implications of work experiences in the early career for adult psychological change. The causal path from work autonomy to the self-concept indicates the extent to which differences in this occupational experience can account for variation in self-competence. It is evident that the competence dimension of the self-image is clearly responsive to experiences of autonomy in the work environment (.244). Because we have controlled the strong stability effect, the covariation between work autonomy and competence cannot be explained by earlier selection processes. Moreover, as demonstrated in our previous analysis (Mortimer and Lorence, 1979b), this relationship cannot be attributed to the covariation of work autonomy with income, educational attainment, or the socio-economic level of the family of origin.

A critic might still object that because work autonomy and self-competence have been measured simultaneously, the coefficient which we believe represents occupational "socialization" (.244) actually reflects another effect of "occupational selection," but one occurring subsequently to that manifested in the earlier period. This would be the case if, in 1976, persons were still actively choosing and molding their jobs to obtain greater congruence with their psychological dispositions. A person with a high sense of competence might repeatedly seek positions offering opportunities to do highly innovative and autonomous work, or continually take the initiative in performing work tasks that offer a sense of challenge.

It is not possible to resolve this issue with the data at hand, as a thorough resolution would require more frequent observations of both competence and work autonomy. But, as noted previously in this chapter, we can address the question by attempting to estimate reciprocal effects models of work experience and psychological change. To permit estimation of the reciprocal influences between a pair of constructs, it is necessary to have appropriate instrumental variables with which to identify each equation. Each of the instrumental variables must be directly related to only one construct in the pair. The configuration of predictors in the model permitted estimation of the reciprocal interrelations of work autonomy and self-competence, using senior self-competence, intrinsic values, and carer stability as instruments.

This "reciprocal effects" model, shown in Figure 3-2, lends further credence to our hypothesis that work autonomy has significant socializing impacts. In fact, the coefficient representing the effect of work on self-competence (.229) was hardly changed at all from what it was in our original model, allowing only one-way causation (.244). Furthermore, the path in the other direction, from 1976 self-competence to work autonomy, is a very small and insignificant .042.[2] It is therefore apparent from this analysis that the selection effects are lagged, occurring only in an earlier period of life. As we discussed in Chapter 2, senior self-competence enhances intrinsic values which, in turn, promote work autonomy.

These findings suggest that work autonomy may be of particular importance in the development of the adult self-image. While the path coefficient of .244 is not exceedingly large, its effect is almost one-third the stability coefficient, the direct effect of the same psychological construct measured in the senior year. In considering the magnitude of this path, it must be remembered that the men who participated in this research project generally have a high level of work autonomy. The restriction of variance in work autonomy would likely diminish the estimate of this socialization effect, even if in the broader population it is a crucial influence on the adult self-concept.

Furthermore, as Kohn and Schooler (1978) have emphasized, a small influence on a highly stable psychological attribute may be of greater

---

[2] In a previous analysis of self-competence (Mortimer and Lorence, 1979b:319), we attempted to estimate the reciprocal interrelations of 1976 competence and work autonomy using a different set of instruments. This analysis failed to produce a significant path in either direction between the two constructs, probably because of the weak instrumentation. In the present analysis, the addition of career stability as an instrument generates a more fully identified model and a different, and theoretically more plausible, pattern of findings.

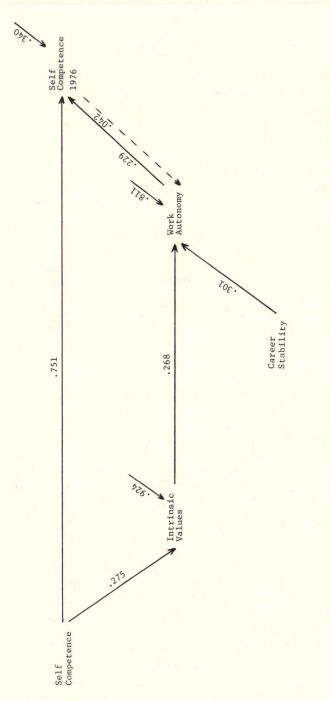

Figure 3-2. Reciprocal Analysis of Work Autonomy and Self-Competence (χ^2/df = 247.91/91 = 2.72)

113

significance for individual development than a large effect on an unstable trait. Bronfenbrenner, likewise, considers enduring change as the hallmark of human development: "To demonstrate that human development has occurred, it is necessary to establish that a change produced in the person's conceptions and/or activities carries over to other settings and other times" (1979:35). In discussing the effects of substantive complexity on intellectual flexibility, Kohn and Schooler assert:

> A path of .18 might not in ordinary circumstances be considered especially striking; but a continuing effect of this magnitude on so stable a phenomenon as intellectual flexibility is impressive, for the cumulative impact is much greater than the immediate effect at any one time. Continuing effects, even small-to-moderate continuing effects, on highly stable phenomena become magnified in importance (1978:42).

As we noted earlier, the stability of self-competence and intellectual flexibility is very similar, as shown by the two studies. Similarly, our "occupational socialization" path of .244 is quite close to that which emerged in Kohn and Schooler's longitudinal study, indicating that work autonomy has a comparable influence on these highly stable psychological attributes.

The hypothesis that the competence dimension of the self-concept would be enhanced by income attainment received no support from our analyses. As mentioned previously, this was shown by estimating a partial model of self-concept development (Mortimer and Lorence, 1979b). Though in the present analysis the zero-order (true score) correlation of the income and competence constructs was a statistically significant .195, this coefficient was reduced to insignificance (.071, $t = 1.38$) when senior self-competence was entered as a second predictor. This illustrates a situation in which the relationship between a dimension of work experience and a psychological attribute is fully attributable to processes through which the more competent individuals achieve higher income in later stages of life. (This selection process is not clarified by our model, however, since there is no significant path from senior competence to income in Figure 3-1, with the other variables controlled. Nor are there significant paths from senior competence to other constructs that influence income. Yet, the zero-order correlation between senior competence and 1976 income is a statistically significant .152.) The relationship between income and 1976 competence is reduced even further (to .006) when work autonomy is included in the analysis as a third predictor.

It is also noteworthy that there was no evidence for a direct effect of career stability on self-competence. Apparently, those individuals who avoided problems of employment, and who persisted in their original occupational intentions, did not enjoy a greater sense of competence than did those who had the more disrupted career histories since college graduation. The relationship between the career pattern and competence, as indicated by the model, is entirely indirect, resulting from the fact that career stability enhances the autonomy of work.

Turning to the 1976 measure of paternal support, it is perhaps somewhat surprising, given the pattern of our earlier findings, to find no relationship between the 1976 measure of paternal support and 1976 self-competence. Instead, the analysis suggests that the father has a direct influence on the son's self-image only prior to adulthood. But given the high stability of this dimension of the self-image, this early paternal influence should be considered of substantial importance. Moreover, it should be noted that early paternal support also affects 1976 self-competence through an indirect chain of influence. Paternal support was found to stimulate the development of both extrinsic and intrinsic reward values, as well as stability in the early career. As we have seen, the occupational values and career stability, by various direct and indirect linkages, facilitate the attainment of work autonomy. And we now observe that work autonomy has a significant influence on the development of competence over time.

Taken together, the results suggest that autonomous and challenging work experiences, requiring a high level of self-directed thought and independent judgement, have important impacts on the individual's conception of self. Furthermore, it must be concluded that of the dimensions of work experience considered in this analysis, only autonomy has any significant effect on the self-concept over time. Apparently, it is the self-direction and challenge of work experiences—the extent to which the individual is pushed to the limits of his potential (Kohn, 1969:156)—that support a sense of personal efficacy. In contrast to the autonomy of the job, its extrinsic rewards had no significant impact on competence among the members of this panel. Career stability also had no direct effect on competence, but only an indirect impact through work autonomy. Finally, paternal support, though perhaps crucial to the development of a sense of personal efficacy in an earlier stage of life, no longer exerts a significant direct effect on competence in early adulthood. This analysis suggests that as the individual makes the transition to adulthood, adult achievement takes the place of paternal support as a source of self-image development.

While previous studies have generally been restricted to the effects of socio-economic attainment on self-esteem, these results demonstrate the fruitfulness of extending the scope of investigation to the competence dimension of the self-concept and an important intrinsic dimension of occupational experience. They also confirm Kohn's (1969:183–186) suggestion that variation in the autonomy of work may partially account for the significant positive associations between occupational status and measures of self-conception that can be observed in more representative samples of workers.

The Development of Work Involvement over Time

As is the case for self-competence, the strongest predictive coefficient for work involvement is the stability path, representing the effect of the same measure in the senior year of college. As indicated by the true score correlation of the constructs over the 10-year period, the stability of work involvement is quite comparable to that of competence (see Table 3-1). The path of .705, obtained from our measurement model, including no external variables, indicates that about half the variance in the 1976 construct can be explained by the same measure in the senior year. The fact that the indicator mean has remained rather constant over the 10-year period, with only slight decline, suggests, further, that no major uniform shift has occurred over time (see Appendix B).[3] However, a rather substantial decline in stability is observed when this zero-order coefficient is compared with the net stability path of .532, that is, the stability that can be considered independent of the other variables in the model. This difference may be interpreted as showing that almost a fourth of the initially-observed, zero-order stability can be accounted for by the differences in educational attainment and work autonomy that have been experienced by the graduates after college.

Returning to Rosenberg's conceptualization, approximately 25 percent of the stability over time may therefore be considered the result of a "dynamic" process. The individual, on the basis of his earlier psychological attribute, either consciously selects or otherwise determines his experiences in later periods of life. These experiences, in turn, contribute to maintaining the continuity of his psychological trait. In the present case, those respondents with higher work involvement in the senior year of college tended to have the more autonomous work in 1976, as a result of the complex pattern by which senior work involvement was found to influence subsequent work autonomy (through the three occupational value dimensions, educational attainment, and career stability). Work

---

[3] This stability is also manifest in the cross-classification of the measures. In spite of the 10-year period intervening, 51 percent of the 478 respondents who answered the question concerning work involvement in the senior year and in 1976 had the identical response both times. There was a slight tendency for work involvement to decline, as 139 respondents considered "work or career" to be less important to them in 1976 than they did in their senior year, and 97 considered it more important. This small decline is reflected in the means of the items (see Appendix B).

autonomy, in turn, has a considerable influence on work involvement in 1976. Senior work involvement similarly enhanced post-graduate educational attainment, through its effect on people-oriented occupational values, and educational achievement likewise increases work involvement over time.

In sum, we find that the high stability of psychological involvement in work is substantially attributable to life experiences that are at least partially determined by senior work involvement. Persons thus maintain their work involvement over time by producing circumstances that serve to maintain their earlier levels of psychological involvement in work. As we have seen, this was not the case for the self-concept dimension, whose stability appeared to be rather impervious to later life experiences, or, in Rosenberg's terms, "static" in character. (The observed stability in competence could not be attributed to the variables reflective of subsequent life experiences, since there was virtually no difference in the two stability estimates—the zero-order path and the net stability derived from the causal model.)

But the most remarkable finding of our analysis of work involvement is the quite sizable path from work autonomy to this psychological dimension (.469). As indicated by the full causal model, the effect of autonomy is almost as great as the net stability of work involvement over time. As for the competence dimension of the self-image, we find that it is the challenge, independent judgement, and innovative thinking, inherent in work experience, which increase the level of work involvement, not its extrinsic rewards.

To ascertain whether there is any evidence for a two-way pattern of causation between the two constructs, it is again necessary to estimate a reciprocal effects model of work experience and work involvement. As before, the other variables in the model enable the identification of the reciprocal equations. Senior intrinsic values and career stability were utilized as instruments, identifying the equation for work involvement. Educational attainment and senior work involvement are the instrumental variables of the equation for work autonomy. This model, shown in Figure 3-3, demonstrates the identical pattern of results as we found when estimating the reciprocal effects of work autonomy and the self-concept. While the path from work autonomy to work involvement is somewhat reduced (from .469 to .370) by allowing the possibility of two-way causation, the reciprocal path, from work involvement to work autonomy, is not statistically significant (.118, $t = .752$). The latter suggests that present levels of work involvement do not influence work autonomy. There is, as a result, no evidence for the existence of processes of "contemporaneous selection" of autonomous work, or of "job molding" to

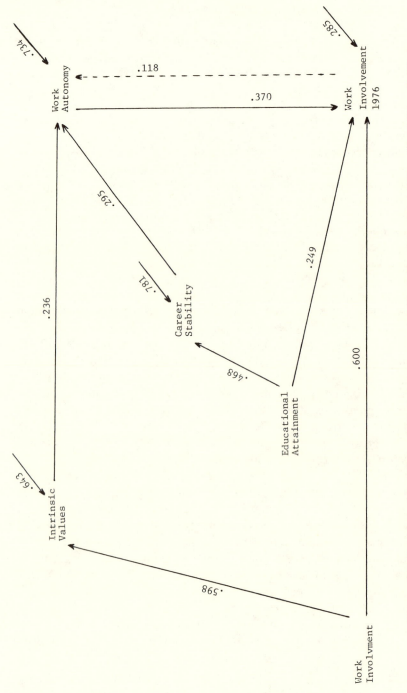

Figure 3-3. Reciprocal Analysis of Work Autonomy and Work Involvement (χ^2/df = 89.66/36 = 2.49)

increase the potential for work autonomy on the basis of current involvement in work.

The findings therefore provide substantial support for the "occupational socialization hypothesis" that occupational experiences influence
work involvement, but only with respect to the autonomy of work.
Though income, a major dimension of extrinsic occupational reward,
is positively correlated with work involvement (the true score correlation
between the constructs is .267), it has no significant effect on the psychological variable when the other constructs in the model are controlled.
Apparently, the association between income and work involvement is
mainly attributable to the covariation of income with work autonomy.
Using the maximum likelihood estimation procedure, the path from
income to work involvement is reduced somewhat when prior work
involvement is entered as a second predictor (to .204). However, the
major reduction in this path occurs when work autonomy is included as
a third independent variable. The coefficient from income to work involvement decreased to .041 when work autonomy was added to the
equation.

Figure 3-1 also shows that post-graduate educational attainment has
a positive effect on work involvement, net of the effect of work autonomy
which such education promotes (educational attainment increases career
stability, .409, which in turn has a substantial effect on work autonomy,
.391). In interpreting the path from education, it should be remembered
that, for the members of this panel, the measure of educational attainment reflects the years spent in professional and graduate schooling.
Among the central functions of socialization in these contexts is the
internalization of a commitment to the chosen career field, along with
the development of an appropriate occupational identity (see Moore,
1969:878–880). In view of these emphases, it is not surprising to find
that the effect of post-graduate education is to increase work involvement.

Taken together, the three constructs, senior work involvement, work
autonomy, and educational attainment, have rather high predictive
power, explaining 71.3 percent of the variance in 1976 work involvement. A quite comparable 63 percent of the variance in 1976 competence
was explained by our model. It is quite interesting to observe the similarity in the pattern of causation for the two constructs that we have
conceptualized as the more general and basic work-related psychological
phenomena. Both are clearly responsive to work autonomy, but do not
appear to be affected by the extrinsic rewards of work or by the stability
of the early career. Apparently, for these two quite general psychological
orientations, the intrinsic features of work experience—the innovative
thinking, decision-making ability, and challenge—are what matter. Ex-

trinsic rewards and security, as indicated, respectively, by income and by the stability of the early career, appear to make little difference.[1] And, as before, there is no significant path from 1976 paternal support to 1976 work involvement. The father appears to exert a direct effect on the son's psychological involvement in work only in a previous stage of life, prior to full time entry to the labor force. Thereafter, the influence of the father is only indirect, mediated largely by the substantial stability of this psychological attribute over time.

Occupational Reward Values over Time

Extrinsic Orientation. Of the three value dimensions, extrinsic orientation is the most highly stable. In fact, according to our measurement model (see Table 3-1), 46 percent of the variance in the construct in 1976 is explained by the same construct in the senior year of college. Figure 3-1 shows that this stability estimate is not substantially modified by the inclusion of the other variables in the causal model. There is only a small difference (.676 vs. .609) between the two estimates of stability, amounting to less than 10 percent of the zero-order stability. It might therefore be concluded that the stability of the extrinsic value dimension, like that of self-competence, is rather independent of the subsequent life experiences that are included in the model.

In addition to this relatively high stability, it is pertinent to examine the mean trend over time. There is evidence that the respondents have become more concerned about extrinsic values during the 10-year period, as each of the three individual item means have increased in average value (see Appendix B). This growing emphasis on the extrinsic rewards of work would appear to be consistent with the fact that most of the panel members have taken on the economic responsibilities of marriage and parenthood since graduating from college.

The causal paths show that income and the stability of the early career are the life experiences with significant effects on 1976 extrinsic values. Moreover, the predictive power of each of these variables is rather sizable. Consistent with the generalization model, having a high income reinforces the importance of extrinsic rewards (.440). At the same time, career stability has a negative effect on this value dimension (-.377). The wealthier respondents have thus become more concerned with extrinsic rewards over time, while, controlling this effect, those with the more stable careers have become less interested in the extrinsic rewards of

---

[1] Given this similar pattern of external causation, it was thought that the sense of competence and work involvement might become more highly correlated over time. However, the true score correlations of the constructs were almost identical in the two time periods (.267 in the senior year, and .276 in 1976).

work. As a result, it is those men with the more *unstable* early careers who have assigned higher priority to extrinsic rewards in 1976. Apparently, the career-related uncertainties associated with occupational change and problems of employment have heightened these respondents' concerns with income, advancement, and prestige.

It is interesting to note that the zero-order relationship of career stability and extrinsic orientation is positive. Career stability's positive correlation with extrinsic values (.223) is due to the substantial positive effects of career stability on income, and of income on 1976 extrinsic values. In this zero-order relationship, the real negative effect of the career pattern on extrinsic values is suppressed by income. It is therefore necessary to control income to observe the true inverse relationship of these constructs.

We do not examine the reciprocal influences of career stability and extrinsic orientation because the causal relationship between these constructs is established by their temporal ordering. Since the career construct incorporates information pertaining to the entire period since college graduation, it is clearly prior to 1976 extrinsic values.

Figure 3-4 presents a reciprocal analysis of the relations between 1976 income and extrinsic values. For the purpose of identification, we have respecified the model so that work autonomy is a predictor of income. As noted in Chapter 2, this was not done initially given the additional complexity which such an assumption would introduce into an already very complicated model. Moreover, while work autonomy is one determinant of income at the aggregate occupational level, this causal ordering of the variables is not so readily justified at the individual level of analysis. This respecification, while not entirely warranted, would seem permissible to enhance model identification. (However, it is apparent that this respecification is not very helpful in this regard, since work autonomy has no significant effect on income.) A second instrumental variable, helping to identify the equation predicting extrinsic values, is the mode of job search. Work involvement in 1976 is the instrument for the equation predicting income.

In Figure 3-4 we observe the same pattern that was found in our two other reciprocal models, assessing the effects of work autonomy on self-competence and work involvement, and the effects of these psychological variables on work autonomy. Though the one-way causative path of .440 from income to extrinsic values, shown in Figure 3-1, has now been partitioned in two, the path from income to extrinsic values has diminished only slightly (to .387). The reciprocal path, from extrinsic values to income is a very small and statistically insignificant .032.

We therefore discover, once again, that there is no evidence that the selection effects—from psychological traits to work experiences—occur

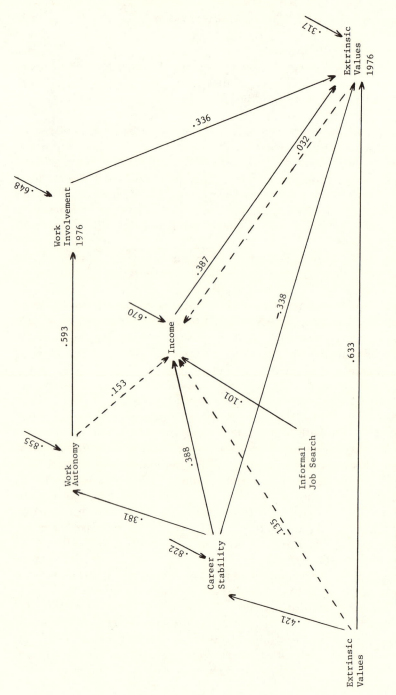

Figure 3-4. Reciprocal Analysis of Income and Extrinsic Values ($\chi^2/df = 147.97/63 = 2.35$)

contemporaneously. Current extrinsic values do not significantly enhance the extrinsic rewards of work. Instead, the evidence suggests that
the selection effect is lagged—extrinsic values, measured 10 years earlier,
have a positive effect on 1976 income (an insignificant .135 in the reciprocal effects model, with the insignificant path from work autonomy
controlled, and a statistically significant .171 in the final causal model
shown in Figure 3-1).

We find, further, that 1976 work involvement influences extrinsic
values (.258 in the final model), indicating that a high level of involvement in work enhances the importance of extrinsic rewards. This replicates the pattern found in the senior year of college, and the magnitude
of the effect is somewhat stronger than previously. We view this pattern
as only suggestive, however, given the fact that both psychological constructs were measured at the same time.

Finally, we again find that 1976 paternal support has no significant
effect on adult work-related orientations. Unlike the earlier period, there
is no evidence that 1976 paternal support enhances sons' extrinsic values,
either directly, or indirectly.

Intrinsic Orientation.   Turning to the intrinsic value construct in the
upper portion of Figure 3-1, it is evident that its net stability (.293) is
considerably smaller than that of the other psychological constructs.
Moreover, the zero-order stability of intrinsic values, .364 (see Table 3-
1), is reduced almost 20 percent when the other variables are included
in the analysis. It might therefore be concluded that the stability of the
intrinsic construct, though relatively small in absolute magnitude, is
somewhat attributable to the greater 1976 work autonomy of those who
initially placed a high emphasis on the intrinsic rewards of work. Thus,
the individual selects, or otherwise determines, his later occupational
circumstances, which, to some extent, increase the stability of his earlier
psychological trait. (The difference in the two estimates of intrinsic value
stability could also result partially from differences in later career stability. But because intrinsic values do not significantly predict the pattern
of the early career, the reduction of the zero-order stability that might
be attributable to this experience is less clearly "dynamic" in character.)

Examining the means of the individual indicators shows a trend quite
similar to the pattern observed for the extrinsic values (see Appendix
B). The respondents, for the most part, were more concerned with the
intrinsic features of work (that is, with expressing their interests, abilities,
and creativity) in 1976 than they were at the time of college graduation.
This trend is especially pronounced for concern with the expression of
one's abilities and skills.

Turning to the causal effects stemming from the life experience constructs, intrinsic value orientation, like self-competence and work involvement, is significantly enhanced by the autonomy of work (.336). Though the absolute magnitude of this path is not as great as the effect of work autonomy on work involvement, this causal path is still relatively large, especially when compared to the net stability of the construct (.293). The autonomy of work exerts a greater effect on intrinsic values than the same construct measured a decade earlier. Though we would have liked to estimate the reciprocal effect of intrinsic values on work autonomy, the pattern of relations among the constructs in the final model did not permit this mode of analysis. Because appropriate instrumental variables were not available, the equations would not be identified.

There is a second significant causal path to 1976 intrinsic values, from the construct representing career stability. As in the case of extrinsic values, its negative sign (-.200) suggests that respondents who experienced problems of employment have become more concerned with intrinsic values than their counterparts who had more stable early careers. The effect of career instability is therefore to increase the salience of intrinsic rewards.

Again paralleling the earlier finding regarding the relationship between career stability and extrinsic values, there is no significant zero-order association between career stability and the intrinsic value dimension ($r = -.062$, $t = .91$). In this case, the positive relationship between career stability and work autonomy, and the positive effect of work autonomy on intrinsic orientation, suppress the inverse relationship between the career pattern and intrinsic values. Including work autonomy in the analysis thus again becomes necessary to bring out the significant negative relationship between the variables.[5] Finally, we find no evidence that paternal support influences intrinsic evaluations of work in this phase of life.

People Orientation. Our third, and final, occupational reward value construct is people orientation, reflecting concerns with being helpful to others, useful to society, and being able to work with people rather than with data or things. Its level of stability, compared with the other two value constructs, is intermediate in magnitude. Its stability is .500 in the measurement model, suggesting that one fourth the variance in the 1976 construct is explained by the same construct ten years earlier. Judging from the stability estimate of .401 in Figure 3-1, about 20 percent

---

[5] Whereas before we reported a small negative path from income to intrinsic values (see Mortimer and Lorence, 1979a), this path becomes insignificant, -.042, when the career pattern is taken into account.

of this stability might be attributed to the other variables in the model. However, since senior people-oriented values were not found to influence income, the one experiential construct which affects 1976 people-orientation, this reduction in stability cannot be interpreted in terms of the dynamic process evident, for example, in the case of intrinsic values. Unlike the two other value orientations, the indicators of people-oriented values have decreased slightly in mean value in the decade under study, suggesting a lessening of concern with people-oriented rewards over time (see Appendix B).

This third value dimension is directly influenced by only one work experience construct, 1976 income. Income has a negative effect (-.132), indicating that those with the higher incomes have become less concerned with people-oriented rewards over the 10-year period. Though we attempted to estimate the reciprocal interrelations of income and 1976 people-orientation, the results of this analysis were inconclusive (see Figure 3-5). Using five constructs already in the model as instruments (senior extrinsic values, senior people-oriented values, career stability, job search, and 1976 work involvement), both reciprocal paths proved to be statistically insignificant. This analysis therefore provided no indication as to which path is of predominant causal importance.

While we had hypothesized that the social content of work would have a positive effect on people-oriented values, this path did not reach statistical significance in our preliminary causal model (beta = .085, t = .866).

As in the case of extrinsic orientation, there is a positive effect of 1976 work involvement on 1976 people-oriented values (.201). This path reproduces the earlier result in the senior year, again suggesting that higher work involvement stimulates interest in people-oriented occupational rewards. Whereas we previously reported (Mortimer and Lorence, 1979a:1377) that work autonomy has a positive direct effect on people-orientation, we now see that when 1976 work involvement is included in the analysis, this effect becomes indirect, transmitted entirely through the level of psychological involvement in work. Finally, paternal support again shows no significant impact on people-oriented values during this phase of the life course.

Work Experiences and Value Development: Implications of the Findings

Considering the three occupational value orientations together, these findings are important in providing further evidence for the socializing effects of work experience. Moreover, they identify the particular facets of work experience that have major importance for occupational value change. This analysis especially highlights the significance of work au-

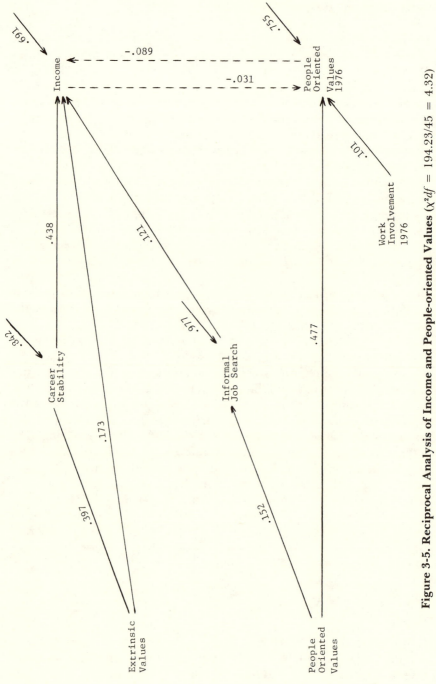

Figure 3-5. Reciprocal Analysis of Income and People-oriented Values ($\chi^2 df = 194.23/45 = 4.32$)

tonomy and income as significant occupational sources of value development. Work autonomy was found to have a significant direct impact on intrinsic reward values, and also influenced the people-oriented value construct indirectly, by stimulating work involvement. This pattern is highly consistent with Kohn's emphasis on the importance of occupational self-direction, a concept quite similar to our work autonomy, in understanding the effects of social class structure on the personality (Kohn, 1977). Income, a prominent extrinsic reward and indicator of occupational success, was found to enhance the extrinsic value construct, while lessening evaluations of people-oriented rewards.

The major implication of this pattern of findings is that occupational reward values develop by means of a simple process of generalization or reinforcement. As a result, the particular experiences that are encountered at work influence evaluations of corresponding occupational rewards. The positive coefficients from income to extrinsic values, and from work autonomy to the intrinsic value construct, represent this socialization effect. They provide clear support for the proposition that values change in response to reinforcing occupational experiences, as the rewards that are obtained in work increase in salience and value over time. Furthermore, the negative effect of income on people-oriented rewards suggests a process whereby the increasing emphasis on extrinsic occupational rewards supplants the importance of other values. Because the same value dimensions, measured in the senior year, have been controlled, the paths from 1976 work experiences to values cannot be considered spurious, dependent on earlier processes of selection. Moreover, we have shown that the effect of income on extrinsic values cannot be attributed to a contemporaneous process of selection. The reciprocal effects model showed no significant influence of 1976 extrinsic values on income.

These findings are perhaps pertinent to an understanding of social class differences in occupational values. As noted earlier in this chapter, intrinsic values have been found to be positively related to socio-economic position. Yet the results of this study do not support the prevalent assumption that high levels of extrinsic occupational reward engender a decrease in extrinsic concerns as attention turns toward "higher" and more intrinsic satisfactions (Maslow, 1954). In fact, the findings showed that income increased the evaluation of extrinsic rewards and reduced the salience of people-oriented values over time.[6] The positive effect of income on extrinsic values, though contradictory to Maslow's thesis, is

---

[6] For a similar pattern of findings, also contradictory to Maslow's formulation, see Hall and Nougaim (1968). Moreover, Andrisani and Miljus (1976) found no consistent relationship between income and intrinsic preferences in their cross-sectional study.

quite consistent with the fact that extrinsic values are very prominent in the business world, where income and advancement may be considered special symbols of occupational achievement and success (see Goodwin, 1969; Kilpatrick et al., 1964). This finding is also in agreement with prior studies showing positive effects of income (Agnew, 1980:60) and social class (Della Fave, 1974; Della Fave and Klobus, 1976) on success orientations.

Instead, an alternative explanation of the socio-economic differences in values is suggested. Since intrinsic rewards (as well as the extrinsic) increase directly with occupational status, the high evaluation of intrinsic satisfactions on the part of the higher social class groups may develop through processes of reinforcement. At lower occupational levels, it is more likely that the worker will find only extrinsic rewards on the job, though these will generally be of lesser magnitude. Furthermore, work autonomy, the occupational condition which was found to heighten intrinsic values, is largely absent in lower status occupational positions.

A second general finding concerns the effects of career stability on values. Its negative influence on both the intrinsic and extrinsic value orientations, net of the effects of occupational experiences, suggests that the lesson of the unstable career is to heighten the salience of occupational rewards. The positive paths from the construct representing career stability to the occupational attainments demonstrate the pervasive importance of a stable career progression for income (.440), work autonomy (.391), and the social content of work (.236). We now find that the career pattern is significant psychologically as well. Given the importance of attaching oneself to a stable career to assure continuous access to satisfying work experiences and rewards, it is not surprising to find that, when they are threatened by career shifts and the vicissitudes of employment, the salience of these rewards is enhanced.

We have seen that the overall pattern of influence of work experiences on occupational values is very consistent and plausible in light of the generalization model. But it is also somewhat paradoxical. While low levels of occupational rewards appear to detract from intrinsic and extrinsic values (as indicated by the positive path coefficients from work autonomy and income to these variables), the disruption and turmoil occasioned by career instability serve to enhance the very same values over time. This suggests that dynamic fluctuations in work experiences have somewhat different implications from stable patterns over time. Career change and employment problems, and the psychological uncertainties accompanying these experiences, are what enhance the salience and value of occupational rewards. Perhaps the individual is forced, at such times of difficulty and crisis, to reconsider his work (and life) situation, to sort out what, for him, is most highly valued, and to make new choices on the basis of this assessment. Continuingly low levels of income and work autonomy, however, have different psychological effects, which may result from their more enduring and routine character. Low income and the lack of autonomy in work were found to diminish extrinsic and intrinsic occupational values over time.

The Influence of Paternal Support Over Time

One of the most impressive features of the final causal model is the declining importance of paternal support for the development of work-related psychological attributes over the decade of study. In the earlier period, when the panel members were still in college, the quality of the father–son relationship exerted substantial direct and indirect effects on each of the five work-related value orientations. In contrast, no significant influence stemming from paternal support can be observed a decade later. While the construct reflecting the character of the father–son relationship is quite stable over time (.597), the pattern of relations shown in the final model suggest no significant effect of the quality of the father–son relationship, as measured in 1976, on the psychological outcomes, either directly, or indirectly through the work experiences. The difference that is implied in the father's influence from one time period to the next is certainly very striking.[7]

The overall pattern suggests that the father exerts a profound effect on sons' work-related psychological orientations, but this occurs only prior to the son's entry to the labor force. The family, largely through the supportiveness of the parent–child relationship, facilitates the occupational achievement of the next generation by enhancing those psychological orientations that we have demonstrated to be of importance for subsequent attainments. (It should be remembered that, while this analysis highlights the implications of the son's relationship with his father, given the high level of correlation between the quality of the son's relationship with the mother and the father, it is quite likely that the identical pattern would be observed if the mother's influence too were investigated.) The psychological orientations, as we have seen, tend to remain quite stable over time, thereby enhancing the significance of the family's initial influence.

It appears from this analysis, however, that after this early period of life the family's influence on psychological development occurs indirectly, through the orientations and achievements that have been en-

---

[7] It should be noted, however, that the effects of paternal support in the senior year may be artificially heightened by the failure to control the lagged psychological variables at that time.

gendered previously. This pattern is quite consistent with the idea that the experiences of early adulthood largely supplant the family of origin as direct sources of influence on individual attitudes and values.

We therefore conclude that the internalization of work-related psychological orientations in the family is of crucial importance for sons' occupational attainments and work experiences. Using the freshman and senior year data, previous analyses of the effects of fathers' occupations on sons' occupational choices and values (Mortimer, 1974, 1975, 1976; Mortimer and Kumka, 1982) pointed to the same conclusion. However, by the early adult period of the life cycle, following entry to the labor force, the father no longer has a direct effect on the son's psychological development. The father's influence on sons' competence, work involvement, and occupational values, the psychological attributes that were found to be of such great importance in influencing occupational choices and attainments in the immediate post-college period, now occurs only indirectly, through the earlier processes of socialization, stability, and attainment.

While the hypothesis that fathers continue to exert a direct influence on sons' work orientations in early adulthood was not confirmed by this analysis, some further investigation was undertaken to ascertain whether the patterns of fathers' influence might be more complex. That is, we wished to discover whether there was any evidence for interactions between work experiences and occupational origins in influencing adult sons' psychological responses to work. The family of origin could have a more complex, interactive effect on sons' subsequent psychological development, not observable within the context of an additive causal model. Specifically, it was thought that the implications of current work experiences for psychological change might be modified by the degree of similarity of fathers' and sons' occupational experiences. To explore the possibility of differences in sons' reactions to work experience, contingent on the father's occupation, a series of further analyses were undertaken.

First, it is plausible to assume that, through observation and discussion with their fathers, occupational inheritors might learn to anticipate important problems and strains in their future occupations. They could note their fathers' effective (and ineffective) modes of adaptation to these problems, and also come to appreciate their fathers' distinctive occupational satisfactions and rewards. As a result of these socialization processes, one might expect that inheritors, when compared with individuals from other occupational origins, would have more positive work orientations: feeling more competent, more involved in work, and having a pattern of occupational reward values that is more congruent with their particular occupational requirements and tasks.

Therefore, within specific occupational categories, the psychological orientations of men who had inherited their fathers' work were compared with those who had not. Using factor-based scales for the 1976 psychological variables, and t tests to investigate differences in means, the 1976 psychological orientations of inheritors were compared to those of non-inheritors in the four largest occupational groups (physicians, lawyers, managerial and other person-oriented occupations, and technical occupations). Of 20 such comparisons (four occupational groups and five psychological orientations), only one was statistically significant: technicians whose fathers were in the same occupational category were less people-oriented in 1976 than those in the same occupations who had different occupational origins. This result is consistent with the hypothesis that the father's work may have a continuing influence on sons' occupational values, modifying the effects of incumbency in a given occupational position. However, given the substantial number of these comparisons, this could also be a chance variation. Moreover, within the four occupational categories, there were few significant differences in indicators of job satisfaction (considering both facet-specific and overall satisfaction) or in perceptions of career progress between the two origin groups.

A second set of analyses more directly explored the possibility that interactions occur between work experiences and occupational origins in producing psychological change. It could be argued that because of their more effective anticipatory socialization, inheritors' self-concepts, work involvement, and values are less dependent on work experiences. According to this line of reasoning, family and occupational socialization would be more congruent, engendering, perhaps, more psychological stability over time for those who carry on the family work tradition. For those persons, occupational experiences could be less novel, more clearly predictable, and less significant sources of psychological change. Alternatively, a plausible though less convincing argument might be made that inheritors would be more responsive to work experiences, if these were made the more salient by their early vocational socialization in the family.

To test these possibilities, partial causal models of psychological change were estimated for inheritors and noninheritors in the managerial and other person-oriented occupational category, using ordinary least squares regression, and factor-based scales of the constructs. (Similar analyses in other occupational groups were precluded by small numbers.) These analyses included only those predictors that were found to be significant determinants of the five psychological constructs for the sample as a whole (as in Figure 3-1). Again, the pattern of findings provided no evidence of systematic differences between inheritors and noninheritors in their psychological responsiveness to work. Examination of the unstandardized regression coefficients for each predictor indicated an apparently random, not clearly interpretable pattern of differences in effects.

Thus far, our analyses have been quite consistent, indicating no evidence of interaction. Pursuing a similar mode of reasoning, it was thought that the psychological implications of income attainment might differ depending on whether the father were employed in the business sector. Previous analyses (Mortimer, 1975, 1976; Mortimer and Kumka, 1982) indicated the special salience of extrinsic values in business families. Specifically, closeness to the father in the business origin group mediated a process of extrinsic value transmission, while this did not occur for professionals' sons. However, the results of this investigation were also negative. Considering only persons who were employed in the business sector in 1976, a series of regression analyses incorporating interaction terms revealed no significant interactions between sector inheritance and income in influencing the five psychological constructs.

These supplementary analyses, taken together, indicate that work experiences in 1976 have similar socializing effects on individuals, regardless of their occupational origins. As a result, any differences in prior vocational socialization in the family associated with occupational inheritance, or incumbency of an occupational role that is similar to that of the father, appear to be insignificant as sources of variation in later psychological reactions to work. There was no indication that occupational origin interacts systematically with work experiences in producing psychological change. These analyses therefore support our earlier conclusion: that the family is important for the development of vocationally related orientations in an earlier period of life. By influencing occupational choice and sons' adolescent psychological orientations, the father exerts an important effect on occupational experiences and attainments, but only indirectly influences psychological development later in the son's life through these earlier processes.[8]

In summary, after an individual makes the transition from family and education to work, work-related psychological orientations appear to be rather independent of occupational origins, but contingent upon adult work experiences. This pattern provides further support for the "generalization model" of occupational socialization in adulthood. This model posits that work experiences tend to influence individuals similarly re-

---

[8] For a similar pattern of findings with respect to adult well-being, likewise showing a declining direct influence of the family of origin over time, see Mortimer and Lorence (1981).

gardless of the congruence of prior expectations and these events, or the "fit" of the person and the job.

Some Limitations of the Analysis

Before reflecting on the findings as a whole, some comments on the limitations of the analysis are in order. These limitations are most serious with respect to the measurement procedures and to the character of the panel upon which the findings are based. Of foremost importance, because all indicators are derived from individual self-reports and because they contain errors of measurement that cannot always be adequately taken into account in our analyses, the findings must be interpreted with caution. We noted in the introduction to this book that the special characteristics of this panel are very useful in simplifying our analysis and eliminating some confounding influences. But because the panel is of high socio-economic origin, is exclusively male, and includes persons who are only in the initial stages of their careers, the findings cannot be generalized to the wider working population.

In interpreting the findings, it must first be kept in mind that the constructs representing the work experiences are essentially subjective measures. Given the overall pattern of findings, this might be considered most problematic with respect to work autonomy. It could be argued that our indicators of work autonomy do not assess actual autonomy but rather the respondent's subjective assessment of his work. It would be interesting to compare the effects of both subjective and objective autonomy measures (such as ratings by a job analyst or by the worker's immediate supervisor) on the psychological orientations under consideration. While there is no general consensus on this issue, previous research on job satisfaction suggests that the perception of one's job attributes is a more potent influence on the psychological response *to work* than the "objective" situation (Seashore and Taber, 1975:350–352). It is unclear, however, whether the same conclusion would be appropriate when the dependent variables do not pertain to subjective reactions to the job, but instead to more general psychological phenomena. That is, the causal pattern may be different when generalization processes are being studied. It is therefore unclear whether it is the subjective perception of one's work as autonomous and demanding of innovative thought, or the actual presence of these work characteristics, which produce the psychological changes in question.

Of central importance in answering this question is the level of congruence of subjectively perceived and objective work conditions. The amount of challenge experienced in work is, however, by the very nature of challenge, a subjective phenomenon. Including this indicator in the autonomy construct was based on the assumption that autonomous work would be challenging, as it would allow the individual to utilize his own judgment, discretion, and independent thought in fulfilling work-related requirements. The covariation of the item gauging challenge with the other indicators provides some justification for this assumption. Further longitudinal research is necessary to identify the relative effects of subjective as well as objective measures of occupational experience, and to determine the relationships between them.

Second, while income is a highly objective characteristic, and apt to be reported quite accurately by highly educated respondents, there may still be measurement error in this indicator. But we have assumed in estimating the model that income is measured without error. While the failure to incorporate random measurement error in independent variables usually reduces the magnitude of causal paths (Heise, 1970), the biases in our estimates that are introduced by this assumption are not known.

The third measure of occupational experience, the social content of work, is based on two indicators: one that is more objective in character, based on the respondent's current occupation, and one that is more subjective, based on the respondent's report of his occupational activities. While there is less justification in the literature for positing that this work dimension is a significant influence upon psychological change than is the case for work autonomy and income, the absence of significant paths from this construct to the psychological dimensions could likewise be attributable to deficiencies of measurement.

Finally, there are two indicators of the construct representing the career pattern. The first summarizes the respondent's report of his experiences of unemployment, involuntary part-time employment, and sub-employment since graduating from college. This information was expressed in a single indicator because of the highly skewed distribution of each experience. Again, each of these component measures is likely subject to errors of measurement. The feeling that one's abilities and skills are not adequately utilized on the job (sub-employment) is, in essence, a subjective judgment. We have already discussed the discrepancy of our second indicator of the career pattern, self-reported career change, with our more "objective" assessment, and the fact that neither measure can be considered error-free.

Taken together, the subjective character of our measures of work experience cannot be denied. Only future research, including more objective indicators of these phenomena, can ascertain whether it is the objective work attribute, or the work as it is subjectively experienced, that is of more crucial importance for psychological development and change.

The restriction of the sample constitutes the second major limitation. This study elucidates the processes by which psychological orientations and work experiences are interrelated over time in a panel of highly advantaged young men. It must be emphasized that these "selection" and "socialization" processes were examined in a highly educated group of workers, most of whom entered their careers in the early seventies when the market for college graduates was quite favorable. This limitation attenuates the variance of the work experiences, as well as the psychological orientations. It may therefore introduce an element of conservatism into the findings and conclusions. If the implications of work autonomy and income on psychological development are so clearly significant in such a panel, they could possibly be magnified under conditions which enable study of the full range of independent and dependent variables. However, given the nature of the panel, considerable caution must be exercised in generalizing the findings to other segments of the working population. Because the members of the panel are for the most part found in the most intrinsically and extrinsically rewarding occupations, we cannot presume that the same processes would operate under other circumstances. They may be especially unlikely when there is little opportunity and under conditions of occupational reward deprivation, that is, when work provides little economic security, lacks gratifying social content, and gives few intrinsic satisfactions.

In addition to the restriction on socio-economic level, the respondents are all of approximately the same age. It has been argued that work experiences are most potent as socializing forces immediately after the individual enters a new occupational role (Hall, 1971; Schein, 1971; Van Maanen, 1976, 1977; Van Maanen and Schein, 1979). If this is the case, the fact that the men in the panel are all at the beginnings of their careers would heighten the potential of work experiences as sources of psychological change.[9]

There is also evidence that work involvement is stronger at this time of life than in subsequent periods. Several investigators of the mid-life "transition" or "crisis" have observed shifts in life interests and commitments later in life, as the individual turns attention to life spheres that may have been previously neglected (see Murphy and Burck, 1976; Riley et al., 1969; Sofer, 1970). Such a phenomenon would likely further reduce the psychological responsiveness of older individuals to their work experiences.

As a result, while the restriction on socio-economic status might weaken the findings, due to the attenuation of variance, the age limitation could strengthen the socializing effects of work experience. Be-

---

[9]This speculation is confirmed by a subsequent study (Lorence and Mortimer, in press).

cause the panel members have recently entered their careers and because they have not yet reached a period of mid-life re-evaluation and assessment, they may be more psychologically susceptible to the experiences which they encounter in their work environments. Further investigation is therefore necessary to assess whether the effects we have observed are unique to this particular phase of the career, or whether they persist throughout the worklife.

A further complication results from the fact that the study pertains to a unique period of time, encompassing rather favorable economic conditions at the beginning of the decade, and economic decline toward the end. It could be argued that the effects of work experiences on attitudes and values, along with other trends of stability and change, vary under different historical and economic conditions. Addressing this problem requires an examination of other cohorts making the transitions from family and education to work in different historical periods.

Finally, since this panel does not include women, it remains to be seen whether they respond in the same way to their work experiences. While the unique circumstances faced by employed married women, particularly their disproportionate responsibility for, and involvement in, family work, might lead one to expect that the socializing effects of work would be different for them, Miller and her colleagues have demonstrated by a series of cross-sectional analyses that married women and men manifest much the same reactions to work experience. This was found to be true for a wide range of psychological attributes, including subjective responses to work (Miller, 1980) as well as other psychological phenomena, such as intellectual flexibility and self-esteem (Miller et al., 1979). While this similarity between women and men would suggest that the findings obtained from a longitudinal study of comparable women would be essentially the same as those from the present study of men, this has not as yet been demonstrated empirically.

Psychological Development during the Transition to Adulthood: Implications of the Model as a Whole

The central conclusion of this chapter is that work experience, particularly work autonomy, is of major importance in influencing adult psychological development. Social structure thus influences the development of the individual personality well after the period of childhood and adolescence, the phases of life that have heretofore been the most intensively studied. One's position in the occupational structure, providing differential opportunities for work autonomy, income attainment, and career stability, may be particularly important in this regard. These are central components of position in the social structure of work which have a clear proximal influence on the developing adult personality (House, 1981).

In spite of the relatively high stability of the attitudes and values under consideration during the decade following college, work autonomy directly strengthened the individual's sense of competence, work involvement, and intrinsic reward values. It further enhanced the extrinsic and people-oriented values through its influence on the level of personal involvement in work. Income, our sole indicator of extrinsic reward and socio-economic achievement, had less pervasive psychological importance. It enhanced emphasis on extrinsic rewards, and diminished the people-oriented values. However, the positive correlations of income with competence and work involvement were shown to be spurious, either dependent on prior selection processes or on the covariation of income and work autonomy. The career pattern, a third measure of work experience, was important for psychological development mainly because of its effects on work autonomy and income. Because the degree of stability in the early career was a substantial determinant of these attainments, the career pattern indirectly affected the whole range of psychological orientations. Yet an unstable career, perhaps because of the uncertainties which occupational change and employment problems entail, was found to heighten evaluations of extrinsic as well as intrinsic occupational rewards, independently of the occupational attainments.

These findings demonstrate that psychological orientations that are relevant to work, though quite stable over time, should hardly be considered fixed from late adolescence through early adulthood. As discussed earlier in this chapter, this assumption has been the basis of many studies of the effects of attitudes on occupational choice, career change, and subjective reactions to work (such as job satisfaction). But this study shows that the relationships between work experiences and psychological attributes are instead highly reciprocal. Earlier attitudes and values influence subsequent work experiences, which, in turn, become significant determinants of psychological development at a later point in time.

A second set of findings concerns the level of psychological stability over time. The generally high degree of stability in these work-related attitudes and values accentuates the need for longitudinal investigations of development through the life course. High stability, coupled with the tendency of persons to select later life situations on the basis of their earlier predispositions, could, in many instances, fully account for psychological differences among persons with varying life experiences. This possibility makes the deficiency of cross-sectional research exceedingly apparent; with cross-sectional data, the effects of selection and subsequent adult socialization are entirely confounded. Moreover, longitudinal data are necessary to ascertain the significance of changes that are apparently induced by environmental circumstances. As pointed out earlier, it is plausible to assume that even a small change in a highly stable attribute will have important implications for the developing adult personality.

We began this chapter with a discussion of Rosenberg's distinction between static and dynamic stability. Static stability connotes a situation in which a psychological trait (e.g., intelligence) remains stable over time, seemingly unaffected by environmental contexts. Dynamic stability, in contrast, refers to stability that is dependent on sustaining environmental circumstances. For example, achievement values may be upheld over time by the continual presence of opportunity and actual experiences of success. In this study, we find illustrations of both processes. Self-competence was the most stable of the five psychological attributes, and its stability was seemingly the least affected by the subsequent life experiences, in the educational and work spheres, that were included in the model. It is noteworthy that competence is a dimension of self-perception, and therefore, according to Erikson (1959) and other developmental theorists, a psychological characteristic that should be quite established by late adolescence. Extrinsic values similarly manifested a pattern of "static" stability over time.

However, persistence in the other psychological constructs—work involvement, intrinsic values, and people-oriented values—seemed to be substantially dependent on adult experiences, particularly the degree of autonomy encountered in the work environment. The stability of intrinsic work values, for example, was clearly conditional on career stability and autonomy on the job. These patterns indicate that the respondents have maintained their work-related attitudes and values over time partially by creating the very circumstances and achievements that foster constancy of their original orientations. Senior work values thus influenced subsequent value development directly as well as by an indirect process—operating in a previous period to select or otherwise contribute to those subsequent experiences that have significant implications for psychological stability during the transition to adulthood.

These "dynamic" processes of stability have considerable importance for an understanding of human development over the life course. As noted earlier, there is mounting evidence, drawn from long-term longitudinal studies, that psychological attributes, including abilities, motives, and values, are markedly stable from early adolescence throughout adult life (Bachman et al., 1978; Block and Haan, 1971; Bloom, 1964; Kagan and Moss, 1962; Oden, 1968; Vaillant, 1974; for a review of this vast literature, see Moss and Susman, 1980). In fact, Costa and McCrae (1980a), on the basis of an extensive review of previous literature and examination of additional longitudinal data, have concluded that future investigators should turn their attention away from additional documentation of stability. Instead, they should focus on the processes by which individuals preserve their psychological attributes over time in the face of biological aging, changing social roles, and constantly shifting environmental circumstances. The results of this research would appear to provide some preliminary insight into these dynamics, at least in relation to one major sphere of life experience. The respondents, on the basis of their earlier attitudes and values, have been found to choose the kinds of work experiences that tend to reinforce their original constellation of work-related psychological traits. The individual may thus actively construct the circumstances which sustain psychological stability over time. These findings suggest that further investigation of these dynamic processes of stability, considering a wider selection of psychological attributes and life experiences, over a broader range of the life course, is a most promising direction for future research (see Mortimer et al., 1982, for additional evidence supporting such dynamic stability processes.) We will examine these processes further in the following chapter, in our consideration of work and the family of procreation.

Third, the results clearly demonstrate the changing pattern of developmental influences during the transition to adulthood. In the senior year of college, the degree of support from the father was important for the development of all five psychological attributes. By a decade following college graduation, the supportiveness of the father–son relationship was no longer a significant determinant, either directly or indirectly, of these work-related attitudes and values. The results of further analyses, undertaken to discover whether fathers' influence on sons' adult orientations was more complex and interactive, and therefore undetectable within the context of an additive causal model, were also negative. These findings underscored the pervasive influence of occupational experiences, particularly work autonomy. Regardless of differences in occupational origin, and related variations in anticipatory socialization, persons appear to respond quite similarly to the activities and demands which they encounter in the workplace. The overall pattern of findings implies that because of its influence on adolescent vocational socialization, the family of orientation is of great importance in determining subsequent occupational attainments. However, experiences in the workplace take precedence in determining the further course of adult development.

This research therefore upholds the idea, originating in the works of the classic sociological thinkers—Marx, Durkheim, Park, and Sorokin—and further developed in the contemporary work of Kohn and Schooler, Blauner, and others, that work has an important influence on individual psychological development. The "generalization hypothesis," that experiences encountered in the workplace have broad influence on attitudes and values, extending much beyond the work sphere, has been confirmed. But the results also suggest the complexity of these socialization processes: the features of work experience which engender psychological change appear to differ, depending on the specific psychological outcomes under scrutiny. This complexity suggests that the generalization model needs further specification and elaboration.

Whereas work autonomy had the most pervasive influence, affecting either directly or indirectly all psychological attributes under study, income attainment and the career pattern were also found to influence occupational values. Moreover, an earlier analysis (Lorence and Mortimer, 1979) of the development of political orientation showed that while work autonomy had no significant impact on political liberalism, this attitude was affected by income attainment and the sector of employment (i.e., whether business, legal, the military, etc.). And a final psychological construct that has been subject to longitudinal causal analysis, well-being (the perception of self as happy, relaxed, and confident), was found to be unresponsive to all experiences studied in the work environment. Well-being was, however, influenced by family-related variables, the family of orientation in adolescence and the family of procreation in early adult life (Mortimer and Lorence, 1981).

It would appear from these several analyses, taken together, that those attitudes and values that are most directly pertinent to work, such as the sense of personal competence, the level of involvement in work, and occupational reward values, are more responsive to occupational experiences than other psychological attributes, such as political liberalism or a general sense of well-being. It should be remembered, however, that only a limited number of work and psychological variables have been investigated in this study, and even these may have a highly restricted range, attenuating the relationships among them. Moreover, there is strong evidence from Kohn and Schooler's research (1978) that occupational complexity strengthens intellectual flexibility, a most highly general psychological trait. It is certainly premature to consider the pattern of findings arising from this study as definitive. What we have demonstrated is that work experience is of substantial importance in understanding the processes of adult psychological development, including change as well as stability. We must await the results of future longitudinal studies to designate the true parameters of this influence.

CHAPTER 4

Work–Family Linkage II: Work and the Family of Procreation*

We have shown in the preceding chapters that the family of origin is a prominent influence upon the development of psychological orientations that promote early adult occupational achievement. A supportive relationship between father and son was found to be particularly important in stimulating attitudes and values that are conducive to subsequent attainment. We have also demonstrated that these psychological orientations are not fixed in late adolescence, but they change in response to adult experiences encountered in the work environment. In the present chapter we turn to the interrelations of work, personality, and the individual's newly established family of procreation. Though young adults take on new family and occupational roles, generally in very close succession, these role transitions and their consequences are usually studied quite independently of one another. As a result, the linkages between them are not well understood.

Recent investigations have largely dispelled the "myth of separate worlds" surrounding work and the family (Kanter, 1977b), at least among social scientists. In spite of their institutional separation, they are linked together and dependent upon one another in numerous ways (Mortimer and London, 1984; and Mortimer and Sorensen, 1984 , review the relevant literature). In this chapter, we approach these con-

---

*This chapter draws on ideas presented in "The Varying Linkages of Work and Family" in *Work and Family: Changing Roles of Men and Women* (Mortimer and London, 1984). The analyses presented in the first section of the chapter were previously published in "Work and Family Linkages in the Transition to Adulthood: A Panel Study of Highly Educated Men," in the *Western Sociological Review* (Mortimer, Lorence, and Kumka, 1982). The analyses presented in the third section were published in "Occupation-Family Linkages as Perceived by Men in the Early Stages of Professional and Managerial Careers," in *Research in the Interweave of Social Roles* (Mortimer, 1980).

nections in three ways. First, paralleling the analyses presented in Chapter 2, we consider work and family linkages from the perspective of occupational attainment. Whereas before we examined the effects of the family of orientation on attainment, we now ask, what are the implications of the family of procreation for early occupational achievement? Do married men have any advantages over single men? It has often been suggested that family economic needs provide a major motivation for men to seek employment, and to be successful in their occupational careers (Piotrkowski, 1978; Rubin, 1976; Sennett and Cobb, 1972). But, in studying the effects of family roles on occupational attainment, researchers have largely confined their attention to the restrictions on women's accomplishments in the world of work posed by marriage and fertility (Card et al., 1980; Havens, 1973; Sewell et al., 1980). In contrast, there has been very little study of the effects of marriage on male occupational attainment. We test the hypothesis that mariage is an important "career contingency" for men as it has been found to be for women. But for men, the more likely effect of marriage is to foster, not limit, occupational achievement. In testing this hypothesis, we examine the implications of marriage for both objective indicators and subjective evaluations of occupational success.

In the second section of this chapter, we turn to a different but related question, again paralleling our earlier analyses. In Chapter 3 we demonstrated that work experiences, particularly work autonomy, have pervasive effects on psychological development. Here we ask whether marriage moderates the effects of occupational experiences on psychological change. That is, do married and single men differ, in any systematic way, in their responses to their work experiences? If they do, a moderating or "buffering" effect of marriage could possibly enhance occupational achievement and perceptions of success.

This second question encompasses a more general issue, crucial to an understanding of the relationship between social structure and personality. Do experiences associated with distinctive locations in the social structure have uniform effects on individuals? Or, alternatively, are there differences in these effects, depending on the unique attributes which the person brings to the situation? Such attributes could include the incumbency of other social roles, relationships with other persons, and particular personality features. According to the generalization model described in Chapter 3, work is such an all important life experience that it will have similar and pervasive effects on individuals, irrespective of the differences between them. The assumption is that, when confronted with the same occupational conditions, challenges, and requirements, persons will respond in very similar ways. Relatively few studies, however, have empirically tested this proposition by actually comparing the effects of work experiences in different segments of the employed population.

The traditional family is often described as a "haven," sheltering men from the ravages of competition and impersonality in the occupational sphere (see Fowlkes, 1980; Handy, 1978; Pahl and Pahl, 1971). Parsons (1955) considers the "stabilization" of adult personalities, promoting performance in the work role, as a major function of the family. But whether, in fact, the family moderates the effects of work experience on the personality remains to be demonstrated. In this research, we examine whether married and single men differ in their responses to their work experiences. Does marriage act as a "buffer," in a sense insulating men from the psychological consequences of their work environments?

Finally, in the third section of this chapter, we turn the question around. Instead of studying the influence of the family on occupational attainments and patterns of psychological change, we explore the effects of the husband's work experiences and orientations on the family and marital satisfaction. Clearly, occupation influences family life in numerous ways. For most families, work is the sole source of economic resources. It also sets strict time and spatial constraints on family activities. But equally important for our purposes, work may also affect the family indirectly through the psychological changes that are induced in the working member.

In past attempts to address these issues, most attention has again been given to the effects of women's work on the family. The rapid expansion of women's labor force participation, coupled with the concern that this new involvement would have deleterious effects on the family, has directed scholarly attention to the effects of the wife's occupational role on marital relationships and child socialization (Hoffman and Nye, 1974). By comparison, there has been relatively little research on crucial features of the husband's occupational role for his family roles.

Previous investigations of work and family linkages among men have focused almost exclusively on the socio-economic dimension of occupation. It is viewed as a critical source of family status, purchasing power, and style of life; that is, a factor which influences the family mainly through the provision of income. The consequences of the husband's adequacy as a provider for his power and authority in the family, for marital satisfaction, and for divorce have been central concerns (Aldous, et al., 1979; Hicks and Platt, 1970; Scanzoni, 1970). But in spite of growing interest and speculation surrounding the linkages of male work and family roles (Kanter, 1977b; Pleck, 1977), researchers have not fully delineated other features of the husband's occupational role—such as its career structure, the amount of time spent working, and the pressures experienced on the job—which may also influence the family (but see Clark et al., 1978; Fowlkes, 1980; and Pleck et al., 1980). The implications of male work orientations for the family, while the subject of some consideration in the dual career family context (Bailyn, 1970; Safilios-Rothschild, 1976), have been similarly neglected.

The Michigan panel represents a segment of the work force where one might expect to find particularly severe conflicts between work and family roles. Most of the men are in the early stages of demanding professional and managerial careers. At this time, family needs are also likely to be especially great. In addressing the effects of work on family life, we assess the extent to which both occupational experiences and the level of involvement in work generate strain in the family and come to influence marital satisfaction.

In summary, in assessing the interrelations of work and the family of procreation, this chapter addresses three different, but highly interrelated questions. First, how does marriage affect occupational attainment? Second, does marriage moderate the influence of work experience on the personality? And third, how do men's work experiences affect their family lives? These questions are clearly related to those considered earlier in this book. In the second chapter we examined the effects of the family of orientation—its socio-economic status and the character of relations with the father—on male occupational attainment. We now inquire as to whether the family of procreation is a more proximal source of occupational achievement in a later phase of life. In the third chapter we assessed whether work experiences induce change in attitudes and values, and we considered the moderating effects of family origins on these psychological outcomes. In the present chapter we examine whether marriage moderates the influence of work experience on personality in early adulthood. Finally, we trace the implications of work one step further, beyond the individual personality, to investigate whether occupational experiences and involvements influence the family life of the working member.

In this phase of our inquiry, the methodological strategy differs somewhat from the preceding work. This divergence is partly dictated by the less developed "state of the field" in the substantive areas to be considered. Specifically, our analyses have a more exploratory character than those reported earlier in this book. Instead of examining a tightly specified, complex causal model, incorporating all relevant influences pertaining to work and the family of procreation, we proceed in more tentative fashion. Rather than using confirmatory techniques, we construct factor-based scores for our major constructs of interest and examine zero-order correlations and simple path models using ordinary least squares regression. This alteration of procedure is also justified by the fact that many of our important independent variables (such as marriage and the wife's support) are based on single indicators.

THE EFFECTS OF MARRRIAGE ON OCCUPATIONAL ATTAINMENT

In contrast to the large body of literature on the effects of the family of origin on attainment (some of it is reviewed in Chapter 2), there has been little systematic empirical study of the family of procreation as a source of occupational achievement for men. Still, there is consistent evidence that married men have higher socio-economic attainment than unmarried men (as noted earlier, this is not the case for women). Duncan and his colleagues (1972:232–236), using the 1962 OCG data, show that the occupational prestige of married men is a full seven points higher, on the average, than the status of the divorced or separated. They found that the handicap of broken marriage is reduced about half, but not eliminated, when controls are introduced for social background, educational attainment, and the status of the first job. More recently, Abeles et al. (1980) have confirmed the higher status and income attainment of young married men, when compared to those who remain single, using data from the Project Talent panel, 11 years beyond high school graduation (approximately age 29). The never-married men had lower income and occupational prestige than the married even after adjustments were made for the effects of parental socio-economic status, academic aptitude, high school occupational aspirations, educational attainment, and years of work experience. While there is some disagreement in the literature as to whether the wife's own socio-economic characteristics (e.g., her education or her father's occupation) contribute to the husband's attainments, over and above his own characteristics,[1] there is a clear consistency in the pattern of advantage of married men. In fact, Abeles et al. (1980) document that early marriage, before completion of school, is associated with an even further increment in occupational prestige attainment.

How might we explain this consistent pattern? Though the processes by which marriage may influence attainment have been relatively neglected by status attainment researchers, there is reason to suspect that marriage is an important "career contingency," influencing the character of men's worklife transitions and early adult occupational achievement.

---

[1] Compare Blau and Duncan (1967: Ch. 10) and Duncan et al., (1972), who investigate occupational prestige, with Benham (1974, 1975) who examine the effects of the wife's characteristics on the husband's income.

Following Duncan and his colleagues (1972), we use the term "career contingency" to refer to an event "occurring subsequent to the determination of family background, that may have a bearing upon the level of ultimate occupational achievement" (p. 205).

First, there is an accumulating body of research, appearing in the literatures on work and organizations, sex roles, and stratification, documenting the sustantial contribution of wives to their husbands' work careers. A decade ago, Papanek (1973) coined the term "two-person career" to describe a prominent pattern in professional and managerial occupations: only the husband is officially employed, but there are clear expectations that the wife will engage in a range of activities whose manifest purpose is to enhance the husband's occupational career. In these occupations, there are heavy time commitments which draw the husband away from the family, placing the major burden of family responsibility on the wife (Bailyn, 1970; Pahl and Pahl, 1971; Young and Willmott, 1973: Ch. 5). Frequent social obligations, travel requirements, and geographic relocations also require the wife's active support (Greiff and Munter, 1980; Renshaw, 1976). The wife's participation in the "two-person career" has been most extensively studied in the managerial ranks of large organizations (Greiff and Munter, 1980; Handy, 1978; Helfrich, 1965; Kanter, 1977a; Whyte, 1956). But the pattern has been similarly described in other occupational contexts—politics (MacPherson, 1975) and diplomacy (Hochschild, 1969), the military (Finlayson, 1976; Goldman, 1973), academe (Fowlkes, 1980; Hochschild, 1975), medicine (Fowlkes, 1980), and the ministry (Douglas, 1965; Scanzoni, 1965; Taylor and Hartley, 1975).

Professional and managerial occupations are often structured as careers, sequences of positions involving increasing responsibility and rewards, through which individuals expect to move (Wilensky, 1960). The career pattern is important to the family because it establishes the upper limits of probable success and income attainment, given requisite effort, involvement, and family support. Thus, there may be considerable economic incentive for the wife to contribute to the husband's career (Greiff and Munter, 1980). Research on the "two-person career" has shown that wives often act as substitutes for employees, doing clerical work, keeping books in the office, making appointments, editing, attending meetings, or reading, all of which serve to enhance the husband's productivity. The wife may be responsible for extensive entertaining of business and professional associates. Wives serve as "image builders" for their husbands, since a good wife and family connote a stable, trustworthy worker. In the community, their volunteer work enhances the public images of their husbands' firms. It also permits them to make contacts which bolster husbands' businesses or professional practices. They may act as "sounding boards" or informal consultants, soothing their husbands after long days at work.

The question therefore arises, to what extent is the socio-economic achievement of men dependent on these activities of their wives? Such dependence would seem to be particularly likely in professional and managerial occupations, those in which the "two-person career" pattern is most strongly institutionalized. Is the man who aspires to success in this kind of work, but does not marry early in his career, disadvantaged with respect to early occupational attainment?

There is a second, more tangential, body of evidence, likewise suggesting the potential of the family of procreation as an influence on occupational attainment—studies of happiness, satisfaction, or, more generally, the "quality of life." While it is recognized that the economic needs of the family provide a crucial motivation to work and achieve, enhancing income attainment (Piotrkowski, 1978), married men may have some more general psychological advantages. Research in the "quality of life" tradition suggests that married men, when compared to those who are single, divorced, separated, or widowed, have psychological characteristics which could further contribute to their productivity and occupational advancement.

Married people, in comparison to the unmarried, have been found to express more positive global evaluations of, and satisfaction with, their lives (Andrews and Withey, 1976; Campbell et al., 1976). In summarizing research on the sources of happiness, Campbell and his colleagues (1976:25) note,

> Usually the strongest single correlate of these happiness reports involves the individual's marital status. Persons who are divorced or separated, or males who remain single after the customary period for marriage, are especially distinctive in their willingness to confess limitations on their happiness.

Young married adults (under 30), when compared with those who are single, also express the more positive feelings of well-being (Campbell, 1981). It is noteworthy that the psychological advantages of the married have consistently been found to be more pronounced for men than for women (Campbell, 1981:197).

Marriage may exert these salutary effects on the personality by providing companionship, intimacy, and emotional support, which contribute directly to a sense of well-being. And, in doing so, marriage may serve to protect the individual, mitigating the stresses derived from work and other external roles. (This supportive or "buffering" function of marriage, possibly modifying the impacts of life situations on the individual, is more fully discussed in the following section of this chapter). If marriage does significantly enhance the psychological adjustment and satisfaction of men, it is reasonable to suppose that this advantage would influence behavior in the work setting, enhancing productivity and occupational attainment.

There are, however, difficulties in interpreting the evidence—from both the "quality of life" and the "status attainment" literatures. To what extent are the socio-economic and psychological differences between married and unmarried men spurious, attributable to earlier processes of selection? That is, are men who marry, and who remain married over time, better adjusted psychologically, and perhaps more highly committed to work and achievement, even before marriage? Does early success in the work career predispose men to marry? Kerckhoff (1972) on the basis of cross-sectional data, argues that men with higher incomes are more likely to marry, and that this "income effect" is particularly strong among the highly educated. He asserts, "a higher level of education encourages the individual to set high standards of living for himself and his family" (p. 111). Hence, highly educated men with relatively low incomes would be unlikely to marry.

If such selection processes do operate, and if both psychological attributes (Mortimer and Lorence, 1981; Mortimer et al., 1982), and socio-economic characteristics remain relatively stable over time, the "effects" of marriage might, in fact, be spurious. These previous characteristics, leading to differences in the propensity to marry, might fully account for the advantages of the married. Campbell (1981) recognizes that differences by marital status in well-being could, at least to some extent, be due to selection processes. But he adds, "the kind of longitudinal study that would be necessary to test this hypothesis has not yet been done" (1981:185). With our panel of highly educated young men, we attempt to address this issue, considering both objective occupational attainments and some more subjective evaluations of life experience.

It is important to recognize that these alternative explanations of the advantages of married men are not mutually exclusive. Thus, selection to marriage on the basis of earlier psychological attributes and occupational achievements may partially account for the socio-economic differences between married and single men. It is probable that young men who have attitudes and values promoting success, or who are actually more successful occupationally, are also more successful in the marriage market. But, when these selection processes are taken into account, some of the advantage of married over single men could be due to the causal effects of marriage. Marriage could have a positive influence on achievement for a number of reasons. For example, men who are married may exert greater effort, they may be more committed to their occupations, and work longer hours than those who are not; married men may have the benefit of the wife's support in the "two-person career"; and married men may be perceived by others as more responsible, fostering more rapid promotion. While we certainly cannot fully examine all of the possibilities here, we will investigate, within the limits of the data, the relative merits of the "selection" and "causal" hypotheses.

By the time of the 1976 survey, 72.7 percent of the panel had married, 18.8 percent were still single, and 2.0 and 6.5 percent, respectively, were separated and divorced. (No respondent reported widowhood.) The proportion single in this panel is comparable to the figure reported by Abeles et al. (1980) for the Project Talent respondents, studied 11 years behind high school. In the Project Talent sample, about 4 years younger than the Michigan panel, 14 percent had not married (including men and women). Because of the relatively small number of separated and divorced men in our study, and because their characteristics and proc- esses of attainment may be different from those of men who never married, the divorced and separated have been deleted from the present analyses. Thus, we confine our comparisons to married and never mar- ried men. (There were 368 married men and 95 single men.)

Analytic Strategy

This investigation of the effects of marriage on attainment is presented in three phases. First, we examine whether there are differences in the attainments of married and single men ten years after college gradua- tion. We include the four objective measures of attainment that we have already studied in relation to earlier processes of family influence and psychological development: career stability, income, work autonomy, and the social content of work. We also assess six more subjective indi- cators, four of which parallel the objective achievements. Thus, we ex- amine career stability along with the individual's subjective evaluation of his career progress; income and extrinsic job satisfaction; work au- tonomy and intrinsic satisfaction; and the social content of work and the people-oriented dimension of job satisfaction. In investigating the dif- ferences between married and unmarried men, we also include the in- dividual's sense of competence, considered here as another subjective evaluation of success, and an overall measure of life satisfaction. This first analysis establishes whether there are differences in both objective and subjective attainments between married and single men.

Second, to investigate whether there is any evidence for the "selection hypothesis," we initially assess the extent to which attitudes and values, measured in the senior year of college, predict marital status a decade later. Do certain people, distinguishable by their earlier attitudes, select themselves into marriage? We then examine the possibility of self-selection on the basis of achievement: are men who are initially more successful in their careers the more likely to marry?

Third, we attempt to ascertain the independent effects of marriage on achievement by incorporating marriage in a modified model of attainment, similar to the one which was estimated in Chapter 2. We control the psychological attributes which were found to differentiate the married and single groups a decade earlier, prior to marriage, as well as other factors that were found in our previous analyses to influence attainments. Finally, to help interpret the findings, we present some additional data from the survey which indicate the kinds of occupationally-relevant, supportive activities that the wives of the panel members engage in, and their implications for their husbands' attainment.

The Findings

Let us now turn to the findings. Table 4-1 shows the zero-order correlations of marriage (coded 1 if married and 0 if single) and occupational attainments ten years after college. (Factor-based indices were constructed by summing the standardized responses to relevant items. The indicators of objective attainments are identical to those defining our earlier constructs. See Appendix B.) The first entry in the table shows that the married respondents had more stable career histories since college graduation ($r = .285$, $p < .001$); that is, they were less likely than the single men to change their occupations or to suffer problems of unemployment, sub-employment, or involuntary part-time employment. The analysis presented in Chapter 2 demonstrated the pervasive effects of career stability after college for subsequent occupational attainment. Changes in career direction and problems of employment were found to have deleterious effects on achievement. Here we find that marriage significantly enhances stability in the early work career.

Following our previous analysis, we also examine income, work autonomy and the social content of work activities, indicating the level of achievement of three different facets of occupational reward. Table 4-1 shows that the married are advantaged with respect to all of these outcomes. There is a rather substantial correlation between marriage and income ($r = .30$, $p < .001$). Marriage also has positive, though weaker associations with work autonomy ($.178$, $p < .001$) and the social content of work ($.096$, $p < .05$). The findings are thus far in substantial agreement with those of previous investigations of attainment (Duncan et al., 1972; Abeles et al., 1980). But we have extended those analyses to show that the married are advantaged with respect to career stability and the au-

Table 4-1.   Correlations of Marriage and Attainments A Decade after
College

	Objective Attainments			
	Career Stability	Income	Work Autonomy	Social Content of Work
Marriage[a]	.285***	.300***	.178***	.096*

	Subjective Evaluations of Success					
	Career Progress	Extrinsic Satisfaction	Intrinsic Satisfaction	People-oriented Satisfaction	Competence	Life Satisfaction
Marriage[a]	.251***	.246***	.139**	.103*	.183***	.212***

[a]Dummy variable. Coded 1 if married.
*$p < .05$.
**$p < .01$.
***$p < .001$.
    This table is reprinted with permission from "Work and Family Linkages in the Transition to Adulthood: A Panel Study of Highly Educated Men," by Jeylan T. Mortimer, Jon Lorence, and Donald Kumka. *Western Sociological Review, 13,* (1, 1982): p. 56.

tonomy and social content of their work, as well as their extrinsic occupational rewards.

The bottom panel of the table shows, not surprisingly, that the married also make the more positive evaluations of their success. To obtain a subjective assessment of the degree of progress in the career, an additive index was constructed from three positively interrelated indicators. First, the men compared their own career attainment with that of other people who started out at about the same time in their areas of work. Second, they assessed their prospects for future occupational advancement. Finally, they evaluated their level of work performance. (All subjective measures are also given in Appendix B.) In accord with their more stable work histories, the married men make more positive assessments of their progress than those who remained single over the decade ($r = .251$, $p<.001$). Not surprisingly, in view of their higher incomes, the married also express greater extrinsic satisfaction with their jobs ($r = .246$, $p<.001$). And in accord with their greater work autonomy and the higher level of social content in their work, the married also manifest greater intrinsic ($r = .139$, $p < .01$) and people-oriented ($r = .103$, $p < .05$) satisfactions.

Turning to our two more global subjective measures, the married men exhibited the more positive self-images, describing themselves as stronger, more competent, active and successful ($r = .183$, $p < .001$). Finally, when asked, "Consider how your life is going now, would you like it to continue in much the same way, or would you like it to change?" the married men showed greater satisfaction with their lives ($r = .212$, $p < .001$). This highly consistent pattern of findings is, again, very much in accord with previous research, paralleling quite closely studies of the "quality of life." As noted earlier, this literature reports clear differences between the married and other marital status groups in happiness and life satisfaction, and these differences have been found to be particularly pronounced among men.

But the question of selectivity remains. The socio-economic and psychological advantages of the married could derive wholly from processes of selection. It is plausible to assume that these objective and subjective advantages are attributable to important antecedents of marriage and are not its consequences. Are these differences caused by marriage, or are they spurious, resulting from the fact that certain men are more likely to marry? Are adolescents who will marry relatively early in their adult lives distinguishable from those who marry later, or who never marry? Do they have certain attitudes and values which facilitate subsequent occupational success? Or are men who are initially more successful in their work also the more likely to marry?

To investigate the possibility of initial psychological advantage for those who later were to marry, we correlated marital status in 1976 (again, coded 1 if married) and eight attitudinal measures, obtained in the senior year of college. Five of these were purposefully selected, on the basis of our analyses reported earlier, because of their relevance for future carer striving and attainment: work involvement (the student's anticipation of the importance of work in the future); the competence dimension of the self image; and extrinsic, intrinsic, and people-oriented occupational reward values. In a more exploratory vein, we also examined the relationship between marriage and three other psychological variables that could facilitate occupational success: risk-taking propensity, ambiguity tolerance, and stance toward change (see Hall, 1971; Morrison, 1977).

Of these eight psychological variables, only two were significantly associated with subsequent marital status: extrinsic value orientation ($r = .169$, $p < .001$) and the competence dimension of the self-concept ($r = .191$, $p < .001$). Those who would later marry, while still in college, attached greater importance to the extrinsic occupational rewards of income, advancement and prestige in choosing their future occupations. As seniors, they also manifested a stronger sense of competence—being more likely to rate themselves as strong, active, competent, and successful.[2] Because both extrinsic values and competence have been found to facilitate the attainment of income and work autonomy (either directly or indirectly), this pattern is consistent with the higher socio-economic achievements of the married men. There is thus some evidence that marriage "selects" people, or, more correctly, people select themselves to marriage, on the basis of attitudes that encourage occupational achievement. It should be remembered, however, that the other six psychological variables that were investigated bore no significant relation to subsequent marital status. We must conclude that there is rather scant evidence for this first version of the selection hypothesis. Earlier psychological variables are, for the most part, rather poor predictors of marriage.

There remained the possibility of selection to marriage on the basis of occupational attainment: are men who are initially more successful in their careers the more likely to marry? To examine the problem of causal ordering, we considered the timing of marriage in relation to career entry. We asked the married respondents how long they had been married. The number of years that the respondent had been working in his present career was recorded from a detailed job history. Part-time jobs during school were not counted. Nor were full-time positions, following the completion of formal education, if they were entirely unrelated to the present career, e.g., military service. By subtracting the number of years in the present career from the number of years married, we obtained a measure reflecting the ordering of these two life transitions.

The distribution of this variable provides additional refutation of the selection hypothesis. In fact, 55 percent of the married men married before embarking on their present careers. Thirteen percent both married and began their careers in the same year. Therefore, the socio-economic advantages of the married, shown in Table 4-1, cannot generally be attributed to a greater propensity to marriage on the part of the more successful. Only 32 percent, slightly less than a third of the panel, married after commencing their careers. Only for this minority

---

[2] The individual's sense of well-being in the senior year of college (feeling happy, relaxed, and confident) also predicted marriage ($r = .180$, $p < .001$). This well-being was further enhanced by marriage, even when the substantial stability of well-being was controlled. But because this earlier attitude bore no empirical relation to subsequent occupational achievement, and because these findings are discussed elsewhere (Mortimer and Lorence, 1981), it is not featured here.

of respondents could it be reasonably argued that occupational success occurred prior to, and fostered, marriage. (It is still possible, however, that marriage was fostered by the anticipation of occupational success, for example, by enrollment in a degree program leading to a lucrative career.)

These exploratory analyses are thus far consistent with previous studies. They have, for the most part, confirmed research in the status attainment and quality of life traditions, in showing that married persons are advantaged, both socio-economically and psychologically, in comparison to those who remain single. Second, we have presented some preliminary evidence that these advantages of the married are not due to selection processes. Only two attitudinal differences in the senior year of college, relevant to future occupational attainment, could be discerned between those who would marry, and those who would remain single during this early period of adulthood. Moreover, the vast majority of the respondents either married prior to embarking on their present careers, or undertook these two life transitions simultaneously.

Of course these analyses cannot definitively refute the selection hypothesis. That is, there may be other psychological attributes of the men, for which measures are not available in our senior questionnaire, or other earlier characteristics or experiences, which could foster both marriage and occupational attainment. And given the period of time elapsing between the senior year of college and marriage, there could have been substantial shifts in the psychological variables that we have been able to measure, to the advantage of the men who would marry. But, within the limits of the data at hand, selection processes do not appear to explain the clear advantages that have been observed in favor of the married members of the panel.

To investigate the interrelations of marriage and the attainment process more precisely, we performed a more comprehensive, multivariate analysis. We assessed both the antecedents and consequences of marriage within the context of a simplified causal model of attainment developed on the basis of the findings presented in Chapters 2 and 3. Thus, several important variables are included which were previously found to influence socio-economic achievement and psychological development (see Figure 4-1): family socio-economic status, paternal support, and the five psychological indices considered previously: competence, work involvement, and intrinsic, extrinsic and people-oriented values. These controls are necessary to insure that the covariation between marriage and both the objective and subjective attainments are not attributable to their mutual association with these prior variables. Incorporating marriage within a model containing these crucial variables also enables a better understanding of the causal processes underlying the interrelations of

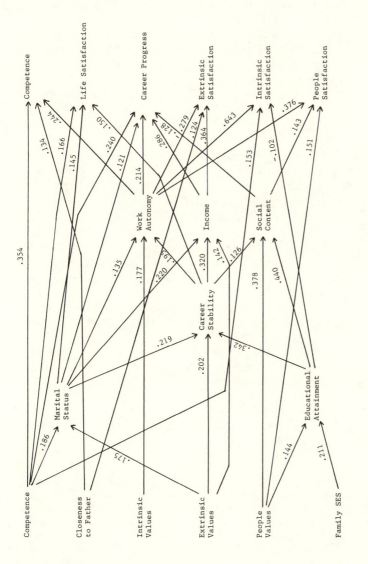

Figure 4-1. Causal Model of Marriage and Attainment

This figure is reprinted with permission from "Work and Family Linkages in the Transition to Adulthood: A Panel Study of Highly Educated Men." by Jeylan T. Mortimer, Jon Lorence, and Donald Kumka. *Western Sociological Review, 13*, (1, 1982): p. 60.

marriage and attainment. But, departing from our previous specification, because we are now focusing on the causes and effects of marriage, all variables prior to marriage are considered exogenous (see Figure 4-1). This reformulation considerably simplifies the model.

Educational attainment and marriage, measured a decade beyond college graduation, follow the family background and senior psychological constructs in Figure 4-1. While they are positively correlated ($r = .110$, $p<.01$), we cannot determine with certainty from the data at hand the precise timing of educational completion in relation to marriage. Most men married during, or shortly after, their post-graduate studies. Therefore, we do not specify a causal relationship between education and marriage.

As noted earlier, however, we can determine the temporal ordering of marriage and entry to the career. For this causal analysis, we have deleted all individuals (32 percent of the panel) who married after embarking on their present careers. The causal parameters from marriage to the attainment variables therefore reflect the effect of being married (before or at about the same time as career entry) as opposed to being single throughout the 10 years following college graduation. (To further clarify this investigation, only married persons in their first marriages are included in the analysis. This criterion led to the exclusion of nine additional respondents.)

Career stability, during the period since college graduation, follows marriage in the causal model,[3] and precedes 1976 income, work autonomy, and the social content of work. The six subjective evaluations—competence, life satisfaction, career progress and the three facets of job satisfaction (all shown in Table 4-1)—are the final endogenous variables. The model was initially estimated fully recursively (using ordinary least squares regression with pairwise deletion of missing data). In Figure 4-1, only the statistically significant parameters ($p<.05$) are shown. (Non-significant parameters were deleted in computing these estimates.[4]

First, it is evident from the analysis that the significant relationships

---

[3] Career stability refers to the entire duration of time since college graduation (see Appendix B). We could not determine from the questionnaire responses the particular timing of employment problems relative to marriage. In our judgment, however, the indicated causal order is the most justifiable, given the long duration of most of the respondents' marriages.

[4] The respondent's marital status is of central importance in this model—both as a predictor and as a dependent variable. Given that the use of a dichotomous dependent variable may result in biased and inefficient estimated coefficients (Hanushek and Jackson, 1977:179), the marital status variable was subjected to a logit transformation (Cohen and Cohen, 1975:258–259). This procedure is commonly used to correct for possible estimation problems with a dummy dependent variable. (The use of a dichotomous independent variable is not problematic in this regard.) The results presented in Figure 4-1 are substantively identical to the solution based on the transformed marital status variable.

between marital status and earlier attitudes, specifically, senior competence and extrinsic orientation, are not spurious, dependent on the covariation of both marriage and these attitudes with family socio-economic
status or paternal support.

Of much greater interest to us here, however, are the effects of marital
status on the occupational attainments and subjective evaluations of success. We find that the earlier (zero-order) relationship between marriage
and career stability (shown in Table 4-1) persists even when extrinsic
values and educational attainment, two other significant antecedents of
stability, are controlled. Thus, those who married prior to establishing
their present work careers experienced fewer problems of employment
since college graduation, and less frequently departed from their original
career intentions than did those who remained single (beta = .219,
$p<.001$).

Further, it is evident that marriage influences work autonomy and
income indirectly, through its effect on career stability. Due to the central
importance of stability in the early career for all three dimensions of
attainment—income, work autonomy, and the social content of work—the
salutary impact of marriage on career stability has widespread ramifications. But over and above these indirect influences, marriage has positive direct effects on both work autonomy (beta = .135, $p<.05$) and
income (beta = . .220, $p<.001$). The influence of marital status on the
social content of work, however, occurs solely through stability in the
early work career.

From these data, it may be concluded that the positive associations
between marriage and occupational attainments, initially observed in
Table 4-1, are not attributable to selection processes. Though unmarried
men who are already successful in their work careers may indeed be
more likely to marry, this propensity cannot explain the positive relationship between marriage and occupational achievement in the present
analysis. This is because the respondents who married after embarking
on their current careers were excluded.[5] Second, the positive impacts of
marriage on attainments are not due to the fact that those who marry
have particular psychological characteristics, prior to marriage, that are
conducive to both marriage and occupational achievement. Marriage
continues to have a direct positive effect on income even when prior
extrinsic values, which influence both marriage and income attainment,

---

[5] To ascertain whether any of the findings were specific to the particular selection of
cases included in this analysis (i.e., we deleted those men who married after initiating their
present careers and those in second marriages), we reestimated the model including all
married and single men. All significant parameters from marriage to the dependent
variables, shown in Figure 4-1, remained significant. All other parameters were substantially the same.

are controlled. Finally, we have shown, within the limits of the data, that the relationships between marriage and the attainments are not the result of other prior variables that may influence both marriage and occupational attainment processes, e.g., family socio-economic status, the quality of the father–son relationship, or post-graduate educational attainment.

We noted earlier that marriage had a positive zero-order association with six subjective evaluations of success (see Table 4-1), as well as the more objective attainments. In Figure 4-1, marriage continues to have significant direct effects on only two of the six—life satisfaction (beta = .145, $p<.05$) and career progress (beta = .121, $p<.05$). The three job satisfaction indices and the index of self-competence are affected by marriage indirectly, through the career stability and occupational attainments that are fostered by marriage. The indirect effects of marriage, through work autonomy, are particularly important for these subjective evaluations.

These results are again quite consistent with the findings from the quality of life literature. But they go beyond them, to show the processes through which marriage influences important subjective outcomes. Marriage has been found to have a direct effect on overall assessments of life satisfaction and career progress, independent of the effects of the occupational attainments (also facilitated by marriage) which contribute to these attitudes. Marriage influences the job satisfactions and the competence dimension of the self-image indirectly, through its impacts on work autonomy, income, and career stability.

To summarize thus far, we have shown that marriage has positive effects on objective occupational attainments, as well as subjective evaluations of self, work, and broader life experiences. The evidence suggests that these effects are not attributable to processes of selection to marriage. The status attainment and quality of life studies have demonstrated the generality of the relationships between marital status, on the one hand, and occupational achievement and well-being, on the other, in the population at large. But only with longitudinal data can we examine the temporal ordering of these major life transitions occurring between late adolescence and early adulthood, and begin to understand the causal processes underlying the observed associations. Thus, though the Michigan panel is certainly not representative of all working men, the data permit a clearer elucidation of underlying causal processes than is possible from earlier, mainly cross-sectional, research.

But what is it then, about marriage, that facilitates occupational attainments and contributes to feelings of career progress and life satisfaction? Aside from the social support, companionship, and intimacy which marriage can provide, which might encourage a sense of happiness and well-being, is there any more direct evidence in our data that marriage, in fact, enhances occupational achievement? Earlier we noted that marriage may strengthen the motivation to achieve in the workplace, with the added economic responsibilities—for spouse and children—which go along with family life. But there was no evidence in the data of a greater commitment to work on the part of the married. That is, there were no differences between the married and single men in their work involvement, in the effort which they exerted on the job, or in the number of hours worked.

Wives, however, may give quite tangible benefits to their husbands' careers. Unfortunately, no data were obtained directly from wives, and there are only a few items directly relevant to the dynamics of the "two-person career." The responses to one question, however, are quite suggestive. The men were asked to indicate the manner in which their wives became involved in their work, and were presented with a list of possible modes of involvement. Their answers show that their wives engaged in numerous activities which could directly enhance their career progress. Sixty-three percent of the married men said that she took part in "social activities with my co-workers and their spouses"; 50 percent reported "extensive discussions of my work and my experiences on the job." In substantial numbers of cases, the wives' support even extended to direct assistance with the "central role elements" (Weinstock, 1963) of the husbands' jobs. Nineteen percent reported that "she helps me directly in my work activities, e.g., by helping run the family business, by collaborating with me in writing, by editing, by assisting in office work, etc.," and for 8 percent, the wife made "contacts in the community which help to promote my business or professional practice." In fact, only 14 percent of the married panel members said that "my wife doesn't get involved in my work at all." When asked in a more general way, "Is your wife generally supportive of your occupation, and accepting of its demands?", 47 percent replied "extremely supportive," and 45 percent, "usually supportive." For only 1 percent (or four respondents) was the wife "not at all supportive" of their work. It is no wonder, then, that the married men have been shown to have an advantage, over those who never married, in the pursuit of their careers.

Furthermore, there was some more direct evidence that wives' support was instrumental to husbands' achievement. Among the married men, the general perception of the wife's support, though quite positively skewed, was positively related to work autonomy ($r=.128$, $p<.01$) and income ($.069$, $p<.10$). This item was also related to the men's subjective evaluations of their success—to competence ($.162$, $p<.001$), extrinsic job satisfaction ($.142$, $p<.01$), intrinsic satisfaction ($.130$, $p<.01$), people-oriented satisfaction ($.08$, $p<.10$), and overall life satisfaction ($.252$, $p<.001$). Moreover, both income and work autonomy were enhanced by the wife's contacts in the community ($.127$ and $.129$ respectively, for both, $p<.01$). These relationships indicate that the wife's support may be an important factor in the higher achievement of married, when compared with single, men.

Investigators of the "two person career" argue that wives often support their husbands' careers at the expense of their own (see Fowlkes, 1980; Hochschild, 1975). But thus far little systematic attention has been focused directly on the effects of their efforts on their husbands' occupational achievements. The findings presented in this chapter indicate that marriage is not only an important "career contingency" for women, but it also significantly influences male occupational attainments. Marriage was also found to influence six subjective evaluations of success, indirectly, through its occupational benefits, and, in two instances, directly as well. Though the socio-economic and psychological advantages of married men had been observed in earlier research, this study probes into the dynamics of these associations and suggests that these advantages are not easily explained by selection processes. In view of these findings, future investigators should examine more closely the specific processes through which the presence or absence of family life influences the occupational attainment and well-being of both men and women in early adulthood.

MARRIAGE AS A MODERATOR OF THE EFFECTS OF WORK EXPERIENCE

It is conceivable that marriage influences subjective evaluations of success and life satisfactions at least partially by modifying the consequences of occupational experience. If marriage is an important moderator or "buffer" of the effects of work, it could lessen the degree of psychological change resulting from experiences encountered in the work environment. Thus, persons would respond differently to the same objective job conditions, depending on their family situations. Men with supportive spouses may have more positive outlooks, even given setbacks and problems in their occupational careers. They might also be more resistant to the deleterious psychological consequences generally attendant on low income and the absence of work autonomy.

As noted in the introduction to this chapter, the possibility of significant interactions between marriage and occupational experiences, in determining the psychological response to work, relates to a more general question involving the interrelations of social structure and personality (House, 1981). Do experiences that people have because of their distinctive positions in the social structure have uniform psychological effects, or are there differences in these effects, depending on other individual attributes or the particular social roles occupied by the person? The generalization theorists (Inkeles and Smith, 1974; Kohn, 1977) would fall in the first camp on this issue.

Kohn, for example, emphasizes that occupational self-direction influences "such basic needs and values as to apply to most workers" (1976:124–125; see also Kohn, 1977:liii–liv). In one test of this proposition, Kohn (1976) investigated whether the conditions determining occupational self-direction have different effects on alienation (including the dimensions of powerlessness, self-estrangement, and normlessness) depending on the worker's occupational reward values (intrinsic vs. extrinsic), employing organization (bureaucratic vs. non-bureaucratic), status (white collar or blue collar) and situs of employment (a profit-making firm vs. government or a nonprofit organization). However, these important psychological and situational contexts in which employment occurs seemed to have little consequence for the manner in which self-direction influences alienation. No significant interaction effects were discovered.

But most research bearing on this issue concerns the effects of work experiences on job satisfaction and stress. In the job satisfaction literature, there is a major debate between those who argue that certain features of work, such as its complexity or the degree of "job enrichment," are of such overriding importance as determinants of satisfaction, that the special characteristics of the job incumbent will make little difference (see Herzberg, et al., 1959). This position is, of course, quite similar to that of Kohn. On the other side are the proponents of the "fit hypothesis," who claim that the worker's response to experiences on the job is highly dependent on the "fit" or correspondence between individual needs, values, or personality traits, and the particular features of the work (French and Caplan, 1972; Locke, 1976). While the second position is very popular among industrial psychologists and other social scientists, a comprehensive review of the job satisfaction literature has revealed greater support for the generalization model than for the "fit hypothesis" (see Mortimer, 1979).

But here we are concerned with a somewhat unique variant of this "fit hypothesis": What are the implications of marriage for the reactions of workers to their jobs? Does this important life circumstance impinge on workers in such a way that their responsiveness to occupational experience is significantly altered? If this were the case, married workers would respond differently than those who are single—to their work autonomy, their levels of income, and to other salient features of their occupations and careers. There are substantial reasons to believe that they might differ in this regard.

Most importantly, the married man has a stable intimate relationship with his spouse that can act as a significant source of support. Such support may be particularly important during times of difficulty or hardship in the work sphere, that is, under conditions of unemployment or subemployment, or when income or other occupational rewards are inadequate. This should not be construed to imply that single men have no such support, from friends (of either sex) or from their relatives. However, for the single man, the continuity and intensity of such relationships may be substantially less. Surveys of the "quality of life" consistently show that persons who live alone have lower scores on measures of well-being than those who live with others (Campbell, 1981). As noted earlier, Campbell (1981) emphasizes that the negative implications of singlehood are particularly severe for men.

A large body of research has addressed the possibility that social support can moderate stress, lessening the likelihood that persons will experience harmful consequences from the stressful situations which they confront in their lives (see Antonovsky, 1981; Kahn and Antonucci, 1980, 1981). According to House (1980), social support can act as a modifier in two ways. First, it may condition the relationship between objective events and perceived stress. Thus, persons with a great deal of support will interpret the same problems or objective conditions as less stressful than those with less support. Secondly, social support can condition the relationship between perceived stress and well-being. That is, at given levels of perceived stress, individuals with high support will suffer fewer negative consequences, such as mental strain or physical illness.

House (1980) has speculated on the processes underlying these modifier or conditioning effects. The first is a process of social definition. Positive definitions, applied to potentially stressful situations, could lessen the extent to which persons who are enmeshed in strong supportive groups perceive their life circumstances as stressful.

> . . . the perceptions and affects of persons in supportive relationships or networks may be simply less affected by objective environmental events, because the supportive network establishes its own definitions of reality. (1980:284)

Such a process of social definition (or redefinition) is consistent with Antonovsky's (1979) hypothesis that social support strengthens the individual's "sense of coherence," the feeling that events are comprehensible and that they will turn out as well as can be expected. According to Antonovsky, this "sense of coherence" reduces both stress and the negative consequences of prolonged stress.

A second possible process, considered by House, addresses the conditioning effect of social support on the relationship between perceived stress, when it does occur, and measures of well-being. This "buffering" or "strain responsive" function is due to the fact that social support is a "resource which can be drawn on in the face of stress to aid and bolster the person's adaptation to stress" (p. 283). That is, social support provides important resources of affect, affirmation, and aid (Kahn and Antonucci, 1981:392) which might prevent or mitigate the debilitating consequences of stress.

There is another mechanism, beyond these two that have been suggested by House, which might also underly the moderating effects of social support. It may be that close relationships with other people provide alternative sources of satisfaction which can be considered in some respects as substitutes for those derived from other spheres. As a result, deprivation in one arena, such as work, may not be perceived as so stressful to a person with strong support from others, nor would it be so debilitating to well-being. Thus, those who have meaningful attachments in several different life areas may be protected from a sense of overwhelming loss when there is disruption in any given role (Bengtson, et al., 1977; Maas and Kuypers, 1974).

House's research (1980) on the mental and physical health of factory workers has provided some evidence that support from the spouse acts as a buffer when the individual is confronted with stressful occupational experiences (see also Burke and Weir, 1977). Cobb and Kasl (1977) note a similar pattern when the worker experiences job loss. However, in House's study, work-related sources of support, especially from the supervisor, were more likely to be effective moderators of stress than support from the spouse (McMichael, 1978, comes to a similar conclusion).

There is, then, good reason to expect that marriage could act to moderate or "buffer" the effects of work experiences on the individual, generating differences between workers in their reactions to their jobs. But the alternative null hypothesis is also plausible, that marital status will make no difference for men's psychological responses to their occupational experiences. Because of the geographical separation of work and family life, and the relatively large number of hours that most people work, the family may have little ability to substantially moderate the psychological reactions of workers to their jobs. If men were found to respond similarly to their work experiences, regardless of their marital status or the degree of support obtained from their wives, a different conclusion would be indicated. Thus, a failure to confirm that fit hypothesis would support the generalization model. Universality in the effects of work experience, irrespective of marriage, would be consistent with Kohn's position that work is such an important arena of life experience that it influences people quite similarly, whatever the particular constellation of attributes which they may bring to the work situation, or the roles which they may hold outside of the work setting.

The research of Miller and her colleagues, based on the data obtained from the wives of men in Kohn and Schooler's 10-year panel, strongly supports the generalization model (or, in the context of this discussion, the null hypothesis of no difference). This work suggests that variations in family orientations and experiences make relatively little difference for workers' responsiveness to their occupational conditions. Miller's analysis of cross-sectional data suggests that married women and men manifest very similar reactions to their work experiences, in spite of the major differences between men and women in family responsibilities and involvements. This pattern held for a wide range of psychological attributes including job satisfaction (Miller, 1980), intellectual flexibility and the self-image (Miller et al., 1979).

In the analysis which follows, the five psychological dimensions considered in Chapters 2 and 3 are reexamined. We now investigate whether marriage moderates the psychological consequences of occupational conditions. We assess whether, for married and single men, the sense of competence, work involvement and the three occupational value dimensions exhibit similar patterns of change in response to work experience. These variables were chosen for this analysis, rather than job satisfaction or evaluations of career progress, because they were considered to be more general and enduring psychological attributes. We wished to assess the moderating effects of marriage with respect to relatively stable orientations and values, rather than more transient reactions to specific work situations.

Analytic Strategy

We investigated the "buffering hypothesis" by examining the moderating effects of two marriage-related dummy variables. The first is marital status (again coded 1, if married, and 0, if single). As before, the divorced and separated men were excluded from the analysis. The second variable reflects the level of support received from the wife. The married men were asked, "Is your wife generally supportive of your occupation and accepting of its demands?" Those responding "extremely supportive" (47 percent of the married group) were coded 1. Those making other responses, indicating less support from their wives (most indicated she was "somewhat supportive") were coded 0. This dichotomization of the wife's support (rather than using three or four categories) is merited, given the distribution of the variable and our desire to simplify the analysis. In analyses of the effects of marital status, all married and single men were included; analyses of the effects of the wife's support included only the married men.

We tested the conditioning effects of these family-related variables on the relationships between work experiences and the five psychological outcomes considered earlier, following the basic procedure described by House (1980, Ch. 4). Our strategy was to first identify those occupational variables with significant effects on each psychological dimension of interest. We did this by including a number of probable candidates in a regression equation, and identifying those variables with significant net effects. In the second stage of the analysis, these occupational experiences, the lagged psychological variable (measured in the senior year of college) and one marriage related variable (either marital status or the wife's support) were regressed on the dependent variable. In this second phase, the additive net effect of each occupational variable on the criterion, net of the effects of the other occupational dimensions, the earlier psychological dimension, and the marriage variable, could be determined. In addition, the additive net effect of the marriage variable could be identified. That is, does marital status (or the wife's support) have any independent net effect on the psychological dimensions when these other important predictors are controlled?

These preliminary analyses laid the groundwork for testing the hypothesis of most crucial interest: the "buffering" or interactive model. In the third phase of analysis, interaction terms were created (the products of the marriage variables and the contemporary work experiences found to be significantly related to the criterion in the second stage). These were tested individually, by adding them, one at a time, as predictors to the previous regression equations. This third analytic procedure enables one to determine whether there are significant interaction effects between marriage and occupational experiences in influencing psychological change, over and above their additive influences. That is, does marriage moderate the effects of work experiences in producing psychological change?

Given the exploratory character of this part of the study, and our intent to investigate the moderating hypothesis as fully as possible, we extended the analysis beyond the work experience dimensions included in our previous, confirmatory model (the stability of the early career, work autonomy, income, and the social content of work). We explored the possibility that other occupational experiences and career features, beyond those considered in Chapters 2 and 3, might also influence the attitudes and values under consideration. These included some work experiences that might be considered unpleasant or distressing—the amount of time pressure at work, having responsibility for things that are outside one's control, and the lack of job protection (considered broadly, that is, by contract, seniority, unionization, tenure, civil service, or the organization's need for one's special knowledge or skills). These job pressures and uncertainties were found by Kohn and his colleagues to have important negative psychological consequences (Kohn and Schooler, 1973, 1981; Miller et al., 1979). We also included some additional variables reflecting the career pattern: the individual's location in his present career (just starting, or representing a second or subsequent job position), the number of work history entries, the number of major career changes since graduating from college, and the extent of mobility or advancement through the career (all derived from a detailed work history). In the first stage of analysis, all of the work-related variables were included in a single regression equation, predicting each of the five psychological outcomes. Those variables were then selected that had significant net effects on competence, work involvement and values.[6]

To repeat, in the second stage of analysis, the following variables were included in five predictive equations: (1) all occupational variables found to be significantly related to the dependent psychological variables in the first stage of analysis; (2) the lagged psychological variable (measured in the senior year of college; and (3) one marriage variable (either marital status or the wife's support, each of which was tested separately). All variables were either single indicators or factor-based additive indices.

Findings

Because of the exploratory character of the initial analyses, the many independent variables under consideration, and our central interest in the investigation of moderating influences, we only briefly summarize the results of the preliminary investigations. We then turn to the assessment of interaction effects.

The first series of regressions revealed that some work experiences that were not examined previously did have significant net effects on the psychological dimensions (Table 4-2 shows the effects of these work experiences and marital status on competence, intrinsic, and extrinsic values.) Thus, they may merit further consideration in future work. For example, there was evidence that mobility—movement, through the course of the career, from positions of lower to higher prestige or responsibility—strengthened the individual's sense of competence (beta = .140). And, as one might expect, the absence of job protection at work diminished both the sense of competence (-.136) and intrinsic occupational values (-.116). In contrast, time pressure stimulated an ex-

---

[6] Given the findings presented in Chapter 3, educational attainment was also included in the analyses of work involvement.

Table 4-2. Effects of Work Experiences and Marital Status on Psychological Variables (Married and Single Men)

Independent Variables	Competence	Intrinsic Values	Extrinsic Values
work autonomy	.232***	.245***	a
income	.067	a	.261***
lack of job protection	−.136***	−.116*	a
mobility pattern	.140***	a	a
career stability	a	−.141**	−.102*
time pressure	a	a	.139**
marital status	.032	.053	−.003
senior psychological dimension	.344***	.165***	.340***
N (listwise deletion)	418	415	407

a not included in regression equation
*$p < .05$
**$p < .01$
***$p < .001$

trinsic value orientation (.139). It should be noted that in the full panel (including all married and single men) the work dimensions continued to have significant effects on competence and values even when marriage, the lagged dependent variable, and the other salient occupational dimensions (identified earlier) were controlled.

Of greater pertinence to our present concerns is the fact that the two marriage-related variables rarely influenced the psychological dimensions under consideration. (Table 4-3 shows the effects of work experiences and the wife's support on competence and work involvement.) As noted earlier, the second-stage regressions permit observation of the additive effects of marriage and the wife's support, net of the occupational variables and the lagged psychological attribute. As would be expected from the findings presented in the first section of this chapter, marital status had no significant direct effect on competence once the other relevant variables were included in the model. But marital status also bore no significant relationship to any of the other psychological constructs—work involvement, intrinsic, extrinsic, or people-oriented values. Though it is reasonable to suppose that the dependency of spouses (and children) would heighten the extrinsic values (Wilensky, 1960) and work involvement of married men, there was no evidence that the married, in comparison to those who remained single, have distinctive work-related psychological orientations.

Among the married, however, the level of support obtained from the wife was found to enhance the sense of competence (beta = .093) as well as work involvement (beta = .126, see Table 4-3). Having a spouse who

Table 4-3. Effects of Work Experiences and the Wife's Support on Psychological Variables (Married Men)

Independent Variables	Dependent Variables	
	Competence	Work Involvement
work autonomy	.183***	.236***
income	.074	a
lack of job protection	−.134**	a
mobility pattern	.112*	.079
number of work history entries	a	.096
number of major career shifts	a	−.079
career location	a	−.123*
career stability	a	.098
educational attainment	a	.l'04
wife's support	.093*	.126*
senior psychological dimension	.382***	.192***
N (listwise deletion)	333	329

ªnot included in regression equation
*$p < .05$
**$p < .01$
***$p < .001$

is highly supportive contributed to the competence dimension of the self-concept—the perception of self as strong, active, competent, and successful—and the level of involvement in work. Support from the wife was not, however, related to the men's occupational values. (Consequently, only the effects of the wife's support on competence and work involvement are presented in Table 4-3.)

These findings, while interesting, do not bear directly upon the central question at issue: does marriage or support from the spouse moderate the effects of work experiences on psychological change? To answer this question, we included one interaction term in each equation: the product of one family variable (either marital status or the wife's support) and one contemporary occupational experience variable (which in the previous analysis was found to have significant additive net effects on the criterion). Given the varying lengths of the men's marriages, it was not considered appropriate to examine the moderating effects of marriage with respect to prior career experiences and current psychological outcomes. In this way, all contemporary occupational experiences were examined for the possibility of moderating effects.

An example may serve to make this procedure clearer. In the initial Phase 2 regression analyses predicting intrinsic values, five independent variables were included: work autonomy, the lack of job protection, career stability, senior intrinsic values, and marital status. All three work-related variables were found to be significantly related to intrinsic values even with the lagged dependent variable and marital status controlled. However, only two interaction terms were created. As noted above, given the varying lengths of men's marriages, career-related variables based on earlier experiences, such as career stability, were not included in the analysis of interaction effects. These variables were included, however, as controls, in examining the net impacts of marriage and the marriage–work interaction terms.

Thus, in investigating the moderating effects of marital status, two interaction terms were constructed: the product of marital status and work autonomy, and marital status and job protection. They were added, one at a time, to the prior variable set, in two separate regressions. The same procedure was used in investigating the moderating effects of the wife's support.

In the event that the beta coefficient for the interaction term is statistically significant, it can be concluded that the occupational dimensions have different effects, depending on the level of the conditioner. This series of analyses, however, indicated virtually no moderating effects associated with either conditioning variable. Of 11 tests of the moderating effects of marriage, none were positive, and only one of 11 tests of the interaction effects of the wife's support was significant. The one significant coefficient suggested that work autonomy has a weaker effect on work involvement under conditions of high wife support. However, this sole positive finding could clearly be expected by chance. (House, 1980:93, mentions that these tests, though conducted individually, cannot be considered independent of one another because the same variables are included in each analysis. Therefore, the precise number of chance conditioning effects is not readily determined.)

From this pattern of results, it would appear that there is little support in these data for the moderating effects of marriage. That is, married and single men were found to respond very similarly to their work experiences, at least with respect to the five psychological dimensions of interest. Moreover, those married men who perceived their wives as "extremely supportive" of their occupations were no different from other married men in their psychological responses to work. In view of these analyses, one might conclude that the effects of work experiences are rather general—not conditioned by this important social role outside of work.

Though no evidence in support of the moderating hypothesis has been found, it should be remembered that only a limited number of psychological variables have been taken into account. It is possible that investigation of other psychological dimensions would confirm the thesis that support from the spouse "buffers" the effects of work experience. Most prior research on the moderating influence of social support has dealt with a quite different set of outcomes—stress and its consequences for mental and physical health. Therefore, we decided to enter an additional dependent variable into the analysis, one that might reflect this kind of outcome. Only one item in the questionnaire directly addressed the issue of work-related personal stress: "After a day's work, how often do you feel exhausted—mentally or physically?" (Answers were given separately for each.) Mental exhaustion was chosen for analysis because it was thought to be a reasonable proxy for feelings of stress resulting from problems in the work setting. Our first and second stage regressions, including the occupational variables, indicated some support for this assumption (see Table 4-4). Having responsibility for things that are outside one's control (beta = .157), work autonomy (.095), and work with high social content (.114)—all aspects of work experience that place high demands on workers and might generate feelings of strain—contributed to mental exhaustion. Time pressure was the strongest occupational source of mental exhaustion (.255).

In the second stage of analysis, marriage and the wife's support were added to these variables, in two separate regressions. (No lagged psychological variable was available for this analysis.) But neither marriage, nor the wife's support, had significant additive effects on mental exhaustion. Moreover, no significant interaction effects were discovered between the two marriage-related variables and the work variables in influencing this measure of stress.

Thus far our results have been quite consistent. Work experiences have been found to have the same psychological consequences irrespec-

Table 4-4.   Effects of Work Experience and Marital Status on Mental Exhaustion (Married and Single Men)

Independent Variables	Mental Exhaustion after Work
work autonomy	.095*
social content	.114*
time pressure	.255***
responsibility	.157***
marital status	−.039
N (listwise deletion)	440

*$p < .05$
***$p < .001$

tive of the marital status of the individual or the degree of support obtained from the wife. These findings may be viewed as confirming the generalization model. However, another plausible reason for these negative findings is that we are focusing on the wrong sources of support. Support from the spouse may not be an effective moderator of the effects of work experiences; other sources of support may be far more effective in this regard. As noted earlier, there is evidence (see especially House, 1980) that support from persons in the work environment (such as the supervisor) is more important than support from the family in moderating the deleterious psychological and health outcomes of work experience.

Therefore, to provide a more complete assessment of the moderating hypothesis, we extended the domain of support to include persons in the work setting. We had no questions on the respondent's relationship with his supervisor (which, in any event, would be inapplicable to many of these professional and managerial men). We did, however, have a question on friends in the work setting: "How many of the people you work with would you consider good friends?" Those who reported at least one friend at work, indicating the presence of social support in the workplace, were coded 1 on a dummy variable (23 percent). The rest were coded 0. The same analytic procedures were then repeated—with respect to all six dependent psychological constructs and their significant predictors. Having friends at work did contribute to the individual's sense of competence (the beta coefficient was .168 with the four work-related variables shown in Table 4-2 included in the equation). But no supportive evidence for the interactive or moderating hypothesis was forthcoming.

In a final test of the "buffering hypothesis," we considered the effects of support from the father. It is plausible that young men who feel close to their fathers are less vulnerable to the effects of negative experiences in their work environments. By extending the domain of possible sources of support event further—to include the family of orientation—the moderating hypothesis receives an even more comprehensive test. But there were no additive or interactive effects of paternal support on the six dependent psychological variables. Again, the results support the null hypothesis.

Thus, in spite of the plausibility of the moderating hypothesis, these numerous analyses produced no evidence supporting it. The men in this study appear to respond quite similarly to their work experiences—regardless of whether they are married or single, whether they have a great deal of support or less support from their wives, whether they have friends or no friends at work, or whether they have highly supportive or less supportive relationships with their fathers. It is possible that our conceptualization (or measurement) of social support is faulty. Perhaps we are not investigating the types of social support that do act as effective moderators of the impacts of work experience. However, it would seem that the support variables that have been included in our investigation, while limited, represent diverse sources of support and have good face validity.

These negative findings could also be due to the restricted ranges of the variables under consideration. Because of the relatively high socioeconomic level of the panel members, not all occupational experiences are represented. It is possible that social support moderates the effects of extremely negative work experiences—such as prolonged unemployment, very low income, and very monotonous occupational tasks—that are extremely rare among this group of young men. Moreover, the ranges of the moderating variables may also be attentuated. For example, as noted earlier, there was rather little difference between those indicating high or less support from the wife. Most of those coded 0 on this dummy variable claimed that their wives were "somewhat supportive." But in spite of these problems, both marriage and the wife's support were found to have positive psychological consequences elsewhere in our analyses. As shown in the previous section of this chapter, the married had important psychological advantages. But marital status, in the present analysis, had no significant moderating effects. And though the wife's support was found to be highly important for the husband's marital satisfaction (this analysis will be described in the following section of this chapter) this variable also has no moderating impacts. Clearly, this evidence comes down hard in favor of the generalization model.

Thus far in this chapter we have examined two hypotheses, highly relevant to the linkages of work, personality and the family of procreation. The first hypothesis, that marriage fosters achievement, was supported: marriage had important effects on occupational attainment in the early work career, which persisted even when possible selection processes and numerous relevant controls were taken into account. In contrast, the second hypothesis, that marriage and support from the spouse moderate the effects of work experience on psychological change, received absolutely no support from the data.

It is striking how much this overall pattern of findings parallels those presented earlier in this book. Just as the family of orientation influences early occupational attainment (largely through fostering attitudes and values that are conducive to later achievement), the family of procreation has been found to provide advantages in the competitive realm of early career achievement. But once men, as adults, encounter important experiences in the work environment, they appear to respond quite similarly to them, regardless of the occupational origins from which they came, or their marital circumstances. In Chapter 3 we reported that there were no differences in job satisfaction or in other work-related psychological dimensions between men who inherited their fathers' occupations, and those who moved to different occupational destinations. Similarly, income had uniform effects on persons from business and nonbusiness origins, despite the special salience of income as a criterion of success in fathers' business careers. It was therefore concluded that the family of origin influences placement in different occupations, thereby affecting the kinds of work experiences that men have in early adulthood (as shown in Chapter 2). But once in their jobs, the men's reactions to work were found to be quite uniform, irrespective of the different occupational origins from which they came.

Similarly, we now find that while marriage provides important advantages with respect to occupational attainments and rewards, it has no discernible impact on the individual's response to his work experiences, in moderating or buffering the effects of work. We conclude, on the basis of these findings, that the institution of the family can be quite instrumental to the occupational achievements of its members. This applies in different stages of life, first in the family of orientation, and later in the family of procreation. However, in spite of the early and pervasive psychological influence of the family of origin, and the great emphasis in the literature on the family of destination as a refuge and haven from the world of work (Kanter, 1977a; Parsons, 1955; Piotrkowski, 1978), family-related experiences appear to have little if any effect in moderating, or "buffering" the psychological impacts of work experiences. The generalization model has again been strongly upheld.

THE EFFECTS OF WORK ON THE FAMILY

In assessing the linkages of work, personality, and the family of procreation, we have thus far considered the family as a source of influence—first, as a determinant of occupational attainment, and second, as a moderator of the effects of work experiences on psychological change. We now turn the question around by asking, how do work experiences influence the family? In doing so, we extend the investigation of the effects of work on individual psychological change, to consider the impacts of work experiences on family life as well.

Unlike many blue collar families, who struggle making ends meet and face the frequent threat of layoff (Rubin, 1976), for many men in professional and managerial occupations an acceptable socio-economic status and standard of living can generally be assumed, with increasing income through midlife (see Oppenheimer, 1974). According to Scanzoni's (1970, 1972) traditional exchange model of family dynamics, this situation is beneficial for marital satisfaction and adjustment. High economic resources and social status, provided by the husband's work, tend to induce a positive reciprocal response from the wife, who will be motivated to support her husband in his occupational role. Earlier in this chapter we described the extensive participation of wives in their husbands' work, and suggested that this support contributes to the socioeconomic advantages of married men. It is also congruent with this exchange model to expect that such a satisfactory pattern of exchange would increase both partners' marital satisfaction. The effect of the wife's occupational support on the husband's marital satisfaction may be especially heightened for professional and managerial men, given the importance of wives' activities for advancement in their occupations (Fowlkes, 1980).

In support of Scanzoni's model, numerous studies (see Hicks and Platt, 1970; Scanzoni, 1970) have indicated a positive relationship between the socio-economic status of the husband's occupation and marital satisfaction (but see also Glenn and Weaver, 1978). However, the positive relationship has been found to level off or reverse in direction at the highest socio-economic levels (Aldous et al., 1979; Dizard, 1968; Scanzoni, 1970; Young and Willmott, 1973). This pattern suggests that the special features of work experience in the most highly advantaged strata may sometimes counteract the benefits of high income and prestige. Men in occupations of high socio-economic status and responsibility have themselves recognized the conflict between their work and family commitments (Young and Willmott, 1973).

It is in the professional and managerial occupations, especially in the early phases of the career, that excessively long hours and time pressure, overnight travel, and geographic mobility can severely disrupt the family, interfering with time that would otherwise be spent with wives and children (Cooper and Marshall, 1978). The heavy responsibilities attached to these occupations, and the great effort and productivity often necessary for career advancement, can generate numerous strains in the family. At the same time, the magnitude of the rewards to be obtained increases the family's stake in the husband's career (Greiff and Munter, 1980), and may exacerbate work-related family stress.

These structural features of the husband's job are typically compounded by a high level of occupational involvement stimulated by the challenges and rewards of professional and managerial work. When there is deep occupational commitment and intense interpersonal involvement at work, there may be a tendency for the husband to withdraw from the family (Fowlkes, 1980; Machlowitz, 1980). When work involvement is high, it may become difficult to remove oneself, psychologically, from the job upon returning home. Both Kanter (1977b) and Maccoby (1976) have observed considerable detachment from their families on the part of high-level corporate executives. They may have little time or energy for family participation or for the sharing of family work. Under these circumstances, the family often adopts a highly differentiated and unsatisfying role structure, even when the couple feels committed to a more egalitarian life style (Aldous et al., 1979; Pahl and Pahl, 1971; Young and Willmott, 1973).

In view of these patterns, several commentators have pointed to a basic incompatibility between male work and family roles, especially at high occupational levels (Bernard, 1975; Gronseth, 1972; Pleck, 1977). In this third section of this chapter, we examine the implications of work for the family in this panel of professional and managerial men. While the range of family variables that we have available is not large, they allow us to address some pertinent questions. To what extent does the husband's high level of achievement, and the temporal requirements of his occupation, generate strain in the family? Do these features of his occupational role influence the wife's tendency to be a supportive career partner? Do they affect the husband's marital satisfaction? We will also investigate whether the husband's work involvement, stimulated, as we have seen, by autonomous and challenging work, affects his family and his marital satisfaction.

Before turning to the data, there is a further issue that requires some consideration. Given the prevalence of dual worker families, there is increasingly not only one, but two occupational roles which impinge on family life. Family tensions may be expected to increase when the wife, along with her husband, experiences the same work role demands. There is some evidence that wives in an earlier, more traditional era perceived the partnership of the "two-person career" rather positively, as an integral aspect of their marital role and a valued means of contributing to their husbands' occupational advancement (Lopata, 1966, 1971). But it is reasonable to expect that this pattern will have more negative consequences for marriage in the future as women develop their own career aspirations and are themselves subject to demanding work expectations. Furthermore, the husband's own work features and his level of occupational involvement may have different implications for the family in the dual work and single provider contexts. In an attempt to explore these possibilities, we investigate whether the effects of the husband's work experiences on the family differ depending on the wife's employment status. That is, do these important features of the husband's work have different implications for dual worker and single provider families?

The Perceived Linkages of Work and Family

In view of the sheer amount of time the men in the panel spend working, one would think that their work would often interfere with their family lives. The respondents reported a weekly average of 48 hours spent at their places of work, and one out of five spent more than 55 hours each week on the job. Time pressure is also quite prevalent; 70 percent of the panel reported that they "usually" or "frequently" work under pressure of time.

To assess the degree of work-induced strain in the family, the men were asked, "Have any of the following requirements of your work caused disruption or strain in your family life?" They were given a list of such family strains, and checked as many as applied. As judged by their responses to this question, such strain is quite common. Not surprisingly, in view of the temporal requirements of their jobs, "long hours, the need to work at night or on weekends" were considered disruptive by the majority (59 percent). Moreover, the men had difficulty detaching themselves from their jobs even when they were not working. "My fatigue or irritability due to tensions or problems at work" was viewed as problematic by 51 percent; and 41 percent checked "my preoccupation with work-related problems or demands while at home." "The need to bring work home" was indicated by 22 percent. Some problems, though cited relatively rarely, suggest two additional ways in which work comes to interfere with, and disrupt, family life—"extensive travel" (12 percent) and "residential moves made to locate employment or for career advancement" (12 percent).[7] It is noteworthy that only 15 percent reported no strains in their families that might be attributable to their work.

But as shown earlier, despite these strains and disruptions, the men generally viewed their wives as quite supportive of their occupations and accepting of their work demands. As described in the first section of this chapter, their wives became involved in their work in numerous ways, by entertaining, helping with office work, and making contacts in the community. These patterns of both strain and support imply that work has diverse effects on the family. They also suggest that the linkages between work and the family may have both negative and positive consequences for family well-being. On the one hand, there is clear rec-

---

[7] While the entertaining requirements of managerial and other careers have been viewed by sociologists as quite demanding, often irritating, and deleterious to wives' pursuit of their own interests, it is noteworthy that only 1 percent of the sample reported that "excessive entertaining requirements" caused disruption or strain in their family lives. This is in spite of the fact that 63 percent reported that their wives became involved in their work through "social activities with my co-workers and their spouses." (Wives' perceptions of this situation, however, could be different.)

ognition of the problems at home generated by highly demanding work roles. As suggested by Dizard (1968), Aldous et al. (1979), and others, such strains can be quite deleterious to marriage, alienating the wife and producing marital dissatisfaction. On the other hand, the patterns of wives' supportiveness of their husbands' occupations suggest widespread involvement which could be both integrative to the couple and conducive to marital satisfaction (Lopata, 1966, 1971; Papanek, 1973). The analysis which follows examines more closely these implications of husbands' work dimensions and orientations for their family lives.

Analytic Strategy

While our previous chapters have investigated the processes of attainment, and the development of work involvement, we now consider the effects of achievement and psychological involvement in work for family life. The implications of work for the family were investigated by means of a path analysis. In the model shown in Figure 4-2, three variables are considered exogenous: the husband's socio-economic status, the temporal requirements of the husband's work, and his occupational involvement.

The socio-economic variable representing the husband's level of attainment was constructed by adding three standardized indicators: income, educational attainment, and occupational prestige (1970 NORC Prestige Scores, cf. Hauser and Featherman, 1977, Appendix B). The exogenous variable called "temporal requirements," is an index, again created by summing two standardized items, reflecting the hours spent at work and the extent to which the respondent works under pressure of time. The exogenous variable, occupational involvement, is based on the summation of two standardized items. The first indicates the importance of work—it is the same item we examined in Chapters 2 and 3 over the decade following college. (This was the only item reflecting work involvement obtained at both points in time.) The second indicator, included in the 1976 questionnaire, was adapted from Elder (1974:186). The respondents were asked to indicate the specific areas of life (out of a possible list of 12, including occupation) which gave them the most enjoyment, the greatest sense of accomplishment, and the ones which they would like to devote more time to. (The questions, item responses, and modes of index construction for all constructs in Figure 4-2 are described more fully in Appendix B.)

The family variables include the strains derived from the husband's work, the wife's degree of supportiveness of the husband's occupation, and the husband's marital satisfaction. These family-related variables follow the work-related variables in staged sequence. The question re-

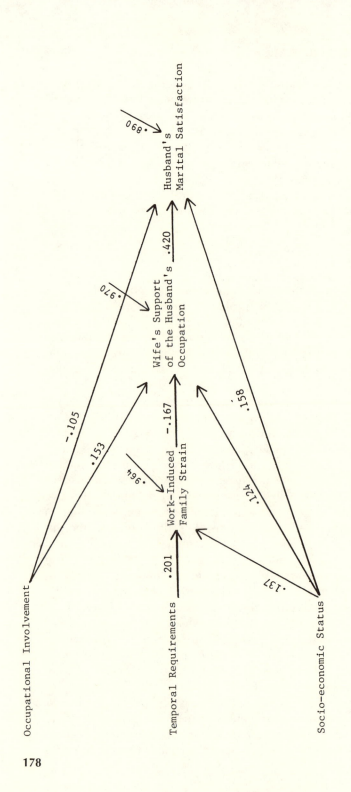

Figure 4-2. Path analysis of the effects of the husband's work attributes and orientation on family strain, the wife's supportiveness, and marital satisfaction

This figure is reprinted with permission from "Occupation-Family Linkages as Perceived by Men in the Early Stages of Professional and Managerial Careers," by Jeylan T. Mortimer. *Research in the Interweave of Social Roles*, edited by Helena Z. Lopata, JAI Press, 1980: p. 107.

garding work-induced family strain has already been described. The composite index—constructed by summing the interrelated item responses—indicates the level of strain in the family resulting from work requirements and demands—disruption that is caused by long hours, the need to bring work home, preoccupation with work-related problems while at home, and fatigue or irritability due to tensions at work.

The wife's supportiveness was gauged by simply asking, "Is your wife generally supportive of your occupation and accepting of its demands?" This single-item indicator was used since the variables describing the modes of wives' support (e.g., discussions, social activities, direct assistance, and contacts in the community) were only weakly intercorrelated, providing no justification for combining them in an additive index. Their weak interrelation may be attributable to the differences, by occupation, in opportunities for wives to engage in the four types of supportive activities. Moreover, it is reasonable to assume that the husband's perception of his wife's support would be a more important determinant of his marital satisfaction than the kinds or number of activities that she performs.

The husband's marital satisfaction was also registered by a single item, "All in all, how satisfied are you with your marriage?" This single-item measure of marital satisfaction could be unreliable and incorporate social desirability effects. While it would have been preferable to have additional indicators of marital satisfaction, one previous study (Orden and Bradburn, 1968) showed that a single item measure, very similar to the one used here, and a composite marital satisfaction scale had the same pattern of association with four marriage-related psychological dimensions.

It was expected that the three work-related variables—socio-economic attainment, the temporal requirements of work, and occupational involvement—would produce strain in the family. Moreover, we hypothesized that work-induced family strain would diminish the wife's supportiveness of her husband's occupation. The husband's long hours, need to work at night and on weekends, preoccupation with work, fatigue, irritability, and similar strains might initially induce a sympathetic response on the part of the wife. However, when these strains are compounded, and continue over long periods of time, the wife's supportiveness would likely decline. Moreover, given the premium on family time in the dual work family, and the tendency toward role overload, the negative effect of strain on the wife's support was expected to be exacerbated when the wife herself is employed full time.

Finally, we expected that the wife's supportiveness of the husband's occupation would have a strong salutary effect on his marital satisfaction. This hypothesis follows from Scanzoni's exchange model. For the wife's supportiveness would likely generate a strong reciprocal response from the husband, of gratitude and satisfaction. This positive relationship between support and marital satisfaction is also predictable from the literature on the dynamics and outcomes of the "two-person career" (see, for example, Fowlkes, 1980).

It should be noted at this point that the variables in the model were all measured contemporaneously, in 1976, though we are specifying a plausible causal ordering among them, consistent with the findings of previous research. A more definitive assessment of this hypothetical causal structure awaits collection of longitudinal data on these work and family processes. After examining the parameters of this model, we will speculate on possible alternative causal relationships among the variables.

Findings

The significant beta coefficients ($p<.05$), derived from a fully recursive path analysis (ordinary least squares regression) are shown in Figure 4-2. (Non-significant paths were deleted in the computation of these coefficients.) The analysis is based on the 368 married panel members (using pairwise deletion.) Generally, the results of this analysis support the proposition that both socio-economic and temporal dimensions of the husband's work, as well as his subjective response to his job, must be taken into account to fully understand the effects of work on family life.

First, the husband's socio-economic level was found to increase the wife's supportiveness of his occupation (beta = .124). This confirms Scanzoni's exchange model—high socio-economic rewards from the husband engender a favorable response to his work on the part of the wife. And, consistent with many prior studies, the husband's high socio-economic status directly enhanced his marital satisfaction (.158). It is, of course, likely that both spouses' satisfaction would be heightened when the family is operating in a favorable economic context, but since the data were obtained only from husbands, the effects of the husband's socio-economic achievement on the wife's marital satisfaction cannot be observed.

But in spite of these salutary effects, the husband's socio-economic attainment also induced strain in the family (.137). Turning to the second exogenous variable, the temporal requirements of work (including the hours spent on the job and time pressure) likewise contributed to strain in the family (.201). These more detrimental implications of professional and managerial careers are fully in accord with Aldous's "success constraint" formulation of marital dynamics (Aldous et al., 1979). At the higher levels of occupational achievement, work provides many benefits for the family, but also comes to interfere with, and disrupt, family functioning.

It is particularly interesting that a direct effect of work involvement is to reduce the husband's marital satisfaction. This negative coefficient (-.105), though small in magnitude, suggests that high occupational involvement can pull the husband away from the family psychologically, diminishing his marital satisfaction. Contrary to our expectations, work involvement had no significant effect on the men's perceptions of work-induced strain in their families; work involvement had a positive effect (.153) on the wife's support. There are a number of plausible interpretations of this latter finding. First, the husband's high level of interest in his work may be communicated to the wife, positively influencing her own attitudes and encouraging more tangible, supportive activities. Second, the husband's high work involvement could create a "positive set," generating an illusion of supportiveness from others. Third, while we have specified unidirectional causal influences, the wife's support of the husband's occupation could enhance his work involvement. But in the absence of data from the wives and longitudinal data relevant to the family, we cannot determine the relative merit of these likely interpretations.

Confirming our expectations, work-induced strain in the family was found to diminish the wife's support (-.167). It appears that, when disruptions caused by work cumulate, and perhaps when they are prolonged, the wife's supportiveness of her husband's occupation diminishes. The strains generated by work may thus interfere with the dynamics of marital reciprocity and support.

Finally, the husband's perception of the wife's support had a rather substantial positive effect (.420) on his marital satisfaction. Previous studies have emphasized the importance of the husband's support for the working wife. Several sociologists have stressed that the husband's attitude toward his wife's employment is of major importance for the marital satisfaction of the couple when faced with the constraints and overloads that are generally experienced by the dual career (and, to a lesser extent, the dual work) family (Bailyn, 1970; Rapoport and Rapoport, 1971; Rapoport et al., 1974). The findings of this study show that the marital satisfaction of the working husband is likewise contingent upon his perception that his wife supports his occupational role. The large magnitude of this effect is quite understandable given the great occupational demands on these individuals in this early stage of their careers, and the probable importance of the wife's support for professional and managerial advancement.

It remains to be seen whether the patterns of linkage between the husband's work characteristics and his perceptions of family dynamics differ in the dual work and the single provider family contexts. Previous studies (see Moen, 1982; Mortimer, 1978; Mortimer and London, 1984; Mortimer et al., 1978; and Mortimer and Sorensen, 1984 for reviews of relevant literature) have suggested that dual career families are subject to a high level of strain due to the demands of their two jobs, role overload, and the inability of either partner to enact the "two-person career" pattern. Furthermore, young dual career families may increasingly reject the traditional normative framework implied by Scanzoni's formulation.

Forty-eight percent of the wives of the respondents were employed at the time of the survey, rather evenly divided between full and part-time work. Among the working wives, 59 percent were concentrated in the female-dominated semi-professions (e.g., nursing, social work, teaching below the college level, and librarianship); the rest were distributed over a wide range of occupations. Since there were insufficient numbers of wives in male-dominated, vertically-structured careers (only 18 percent in the higher-level professional and managerial occupations), it was not feasible to repeat the analysis using data from the "dual career" husbands alone. Given this situation, it was decided to repeat the path analyses for husbands whose wives work full-time ($N = 90$) and for those whose wives are not currently employed ($N = 197$). It was assumed that the wife's full-time work would constitute a sufficient constraint on the wife's time that the pattern of relationships among the work and family variables would approach that found in the dual career family situation. Specifically, it was expected that family strains deriving from the husband's work would have a stronger negative effect on the wife's supportiveness when she was employed full-time. Full-time working wives would likely find it more difficult to accomodate to the demands and requirements of their husbands' work than would full-time homemakers. Moreover, it was anticipated that full-time working wives would be perceived as less supportive of their husbands' work, on the average, than full-time homemakers.

Rather surprisingly, however, these predictions did not materialize. The overall patterns of relationship among the work and family variables were essentially the same in the two subgroups, though, due to the small numbers involved, many of the path coefficients were not significant for the group of husbands whose wives work full-time. The effect of work-induced family strain on the wife's supportiveness was found to be the same, irrespective of her employment status. Moreover, the husband's perception of the wife's supportiveness, on the average, was virtually identical in the two sub-groups. Though somewhat unexpected, these findings are consistent with previous research on the dual career family. The literature indicates a surprising degree of adherence to traditional patterns in this family form, in spite of the demanding requirements of the wife's occupation, and often to the detriment of the wife's career (see Epstein, 1971; Hoffman and Nye, 1974; Holmstrom, 1973; Poloma, 1972; Poloma and Garland, 1971; Rapoport and Rapoport, 1971).

In a sense, this general pattern of findings parallels the central conclusion of the preceding section of this chapter: just as marriage failed to act as a significant moderator of the effects of work experience on psychological change, family circumstances (i.e., the wife's employment status) fail to moderate the relationships among work experiences and perceptions of strain in the family, the wife's support of the husband's occupation, and marital satisfaction. In both cases, the effects of work experiences appear to be quite independent of these broader life contexts in which they occur.

This last section of Chapter 4 carries us considerably beyond questions of psychological change in response to work, for we have extended the investigation to include attitudes and adjustment in an entirely different realm of life—that of the family. In view of this extension of the inquiry, the absence of data from wives is particularly unfortunate. It is probable that wives' views on the topics under consideration would differ from those of their husbands (Bernard, 1972). For example, the wife may perceive strains resulting from her husband's work when none are evident to her spouse. A fuller and more accurate understanding of the dynamics of these work and family linkages requires data from both members of the marital dyad. Moreover, because the data were obtained from men, there is no corroboration of the wife's actual level of supportiveness of her husband's work. Finally, this research does not allow assessment of the extent to which wives' work attributes engender the same family strains as do those of their husbands, nor their effects on husbands' tendencies to be supportive of their wives' occupations. Clearly, this problem requires more balanced and symmetric consideration.

A second major limitation is the cross-sectional character of the data upon which these last analyses are based. The only information we have about marriage is contained in the 1976 questionnaire. Longitudinal data on married couples would be highly preferable, in attempting to assess the causal ordering of the variables, as well as whether there are patterns of reciprocal effects. For example, it is possible that high marital satisfaction on the part of the husband, and the harmonious home environment which this implies, fosters, as well as results from, socio-economic achievement. We have already argued that wives' support of their husbands' occupations contributes to men's attainment. The wife's support of the husband's work could also reduce the extent to which his work induces strain and disruption in the family. Only longitudinal data can unravel the complex patterns of relations among these variables, to enable more adequate understanding of causal processes.

Data gathered over a long period would also permit assessment of whether the influences found in this study persist over time, or whether they are life-stage specific. It is likely that work-related strain in the family would diminish as the husband becomes more established in his career. It is also reasonable to suppose that the wife's support of the husband's work would have greater impact on his marital satisfaction when work role requirements and pressure for career advancement are greatest. In later stages of his work career, the importance of the wife's support for the husband's marital satisfaction could well decrease.

But in spite of these important limitations of the data, this analysis of the effects of work on family life has revealed some interesting trends and is suggestive of further research directions. This panel of professionals and managers has provided an opportunity to give preliminary test to the widespread hypothesis that men in the early stages of professional and managerial careers experience a high level of conflict between their work and family roles, with deleterious consequences for their family lives. The responses of panel members to the questions on family strain and the wife's support initially suggested that work has potentially positive as well as negative implications for family life. While work-induced strain in the family was widely recognized, the respondents also perceived their spouses as supportive of their occupations. For many of the couples, the husband's work provided a common focus for discussion, social life, and other activities.

Though previous research has focused rather exclusively on the socio-economic status of the husband's occupation as a factor influencing the wife's support and marital satisfaction (see Scanzoni, 1970, 1972), the results of these analyses suggest that both socio-economic attainment and the temporal aspects of work must be taken into account in studying the linkages between work and the family. Both were found to increase the perception of work-induced family strain. This study has also provided evidence that work-related strain in the family reduces the wife's supportiveness of the husband's career, and indirectly, through this effect, the husband's marital satisfaction. The husband's subjective response to his work also appears to be a significant influence on family dynamics. The husband's work involvement was found to increase his perception of his wife's supportiveness, while at the same time diminishing his marital satisfaction. The pattern of findings corroborates the growing concern that heavy time demands and pressures, high occupational involvement, and other concomitants of the husband's occupational succes may have negative implications for family well-being (see, for example, Bernard, 1975; Dizard, 1972; Kanter, 1977a; Pleck, 1977; Pleck et al., 1980; and Renshaw, 1976).

The substantial effect of the wife's support on the husband's marital satisfaction is especially noteworthy. Whereas considerable attention has been given to the importance of the husband's support of the wife's employment if marital satisfaction, under the conditions of dual labor force participation, is to be maintained (Bailyn, 1970; Rapoport and Rapoport, 1972; Rapoport et al., 1974), this relationship may be more symmetric than has been heretofore realized. The fact that the strain in the family, induced by the husband's work, had uniformly negative effects on his perceptions of his wife's supportiveness, regardless of her own employment status, also suggests a need for re-thinking the common assumption that having a career-oriented wife necessarily detracts from the husband's support at home and his pursuit of his career (Burke and Weir, 1976; Holmstrom, 1973; Hunt and Hunt, 1977; Mortimer et al., 1978).

CONCLUSION

This chapter has examined three different, but interrelated questions regarding the linkages of work experience, the family of procreation, and psychological change. In the first section, we investigated whether marriage fosters the occupational attainment of men. Though the "selection hypothesis" cannot be entirely ruled out, the data analyses provided evidence that the psychological and occupational advantages of married men are not attributable to processes of selection to marriage. In the second section, we investigated whether marriage acts as a "buffer," moderating the effects of work experiences on psychological change. But in this case there is no evidence that either marital status or the wife's support modifies the psychological consequences of work experience. Instead, all evidence was in favor of the "generalization model"—that men respond similarly to their work regardless of these important family-related life circumstances. Finally, in the third section, we studied the effects of work, including socio-economic attainment, its temporal requirements, and work involvement, on the family. This last analysis indicated that the work sphere can have important consequences for family life. Not only does the family of procreation promote occupational attainment, but attainment and other concomitants of professional and managerial careers—long work hours and high occupational involvement—may come to have both positive and negative implications for family well-being and marital satisfaction. Surely, the results of these analyses demonstrate that it is insufficient to ask how the family influences work, or how work affects the family; both processes must be studied in the context of a dynamic, reciprocal perspective.

In many respects the analyses described in this chapter are more exploratory than those presented in the preceding two. As noted earlier, this results partially from the fact that work and family linkages, as a subfield of study in sociology, is less fully developed than the research foundations of our previous chapters, the areas of status attainment and occupational social psychology. The tentative character of our conclusions also derives from the cross-sectional character and other limitations of the family-related data. Since the central focus of the study as conceived initially was the effect of work experiences on psychological change, relatively few family-related measures were included in the 1976 questionnaire.

But despite these admittedly important problems and limitations, we believe that the findings presented in the chapter enhance our understanding of the linkages of work, family, and personality during the transition to adulthood. Not only does the family of orientation influence attainment, but so too does the family of procreation. The substantial implications of work experience for psychological change have been found to be independent of family-related (and other) social supports to the individual. And, finally, the influence of work experience has been found to extend beyond the individual to include important facets of family life—to family strain, to the dynamics of supportiveness and reciprocity between spouses, and to marital satisfaction. This research has paved the way for more conclusive, longitudinal studies of the interrelations of work, personality, and the family of procreation in the future.

CHAPTER 5

Work, Family, and Personality: Summary and Concluding Note

What have we learned from this study of highly educated men? The research has examined the processes of psychological development and occupational attainment by following a panel of professional and managerial men from late adolescence to early adulthood. We have found that both the family of origin and the family of destination are of great importance in these processes. But we have also demonstrated that work experiences are both central to psychological development and consequential for family life during this early period of the life course. The findings thus enrich our understanding of the dynamics of individual stability and change over time, the interrelations of social structure and personality, and the linkages of work and family life.

Initially, we asked whether the family's linkage to the occupational structure, as indexed by social class background, affects the quality of the father-son relationship, and, through the father's level of support, the psychological development of sons. We examined the manner in which the family of origin influences occupational attainment through processes of socialization and attitude formation and through more direct forms of assistance. We also investigated whether attitudes and values, formed prior to labor force entry, affect subsequent occupational attainment. Each of these questions, as we have seen, has been subject to a long history of theoretical debate and empirical inquiry. But this project has several features which have enabled us to significantly extend prior work on the processes of psychological development and intergenerational attainment.

Most importantly, the availability of data on persons both prior to and ten years following college graduation allowed study of the implications of experience within the family of origin over a period of time encompassing crucial life transitions. The longitudinal character of this study thus represents a considerable advantage over cross-sectional research. Moreover, instead of focusing solely on achievement orientations, as has been typical in status attainment research, we have shifted the focus to salient values and attitudes—concerning self, work, and occupational rewards—that are also strongly implicated in the attainment process. Finally, we have broadened the range of occupational outcomes under consideration to include career stability, income, work autonomy, and the social content of work activities.

In Chapter 2, we tested the hypothesis that parental social class position and paternal support have important socializing effects which contribute to sons' attainment of rewarding occupational experiences in early adulthood. Kohn and Schooler's work (1969; Kohn, 1969) has been central to the development of an "occupational linkage" model. In this model, class-related paternal work characteristics are central independent variables, fostering change in the father's psychological states. The father's psychological attributes influence his socialization orientations and practices, which, in turn, affect important dimensions of the child's personality. As the last link in this causal chain, the child's psychological make-up is believed to have crucial implications for the attainment process (see Kohn, 1977; Lueptow et al., 1979; and Mortimer and Kumka, 1982, for further elaboration of this model). Kohn and his colleagues have not yet tested the entire sequence, as their research has been focused on the effects of the father's work experience for parental child-rearing values. They find that social class is important for parental values (as well as for the development of other psychological attributes), largely because it determines the conditions of occupational life to which the individual is exposed. Men who have self-directed work activities value self-direction in themselves as well as in their children. For Kohn and Schooler, the most psychologically crucial work condition is occupational self-direction.

Because we had no data on fathers' occupational conditions, the linkage model could not be fully examined in the present study. However, we have presented some compelling evidence confirming the last two linkages in the causal chain. First, we have found that the level of paternal support, a feature of the father–son relationship that is of central importance in the socialization process, had wide-ranging effects on the adolescent child's psychological development. Second, we have shown that the psychological outcomes under investigation—the self-image, work involvement, and the three occupational value dimensions—have major implications for adult occupational experiences and attainments. Thus, paternal support had extensive impacts on the men's psychological development, and these psychological outcomes, in turn, had major consequences for adult achievement.

But the findings of the study are also relevant to the initial linkages in the causal sequence. Kohn's model emphasizes the father's occupational conditions, as determined by social class, as sources of variation in parental orientations and practices. The father's work conditions thus constitute an intervening variable, mediating the relationship between social class and parental values. Due to the absence of data on fathers' occupational experiences, we considered the relationship between social class background and the quality of the parent–child relationship directly. We found a positive relationship between familial socio-economic status and paternal support and believe that this pattern is fully consistent with Kohn's hypothetical model. For if fathers of higher socio-economic position have greater occupational self-direction, as the research of Kohn and Schooler has demonstrated, and if this work experience generates parental values stressing self-direction in children, as they have also shown, then one would expect fathers of higher socio-economic level to be more supportive of sons, enabling the development of self-directed personality traits.

In interpreting our causal model, we placed primary emphasis on the socialization process, occurring within the family of origin, as a source of attitudes and values which contribute to subsequent achievement. But not all the effects of the family on attainment were mediated by sons' attitudes and values. The family's socio-economic status influenced sons' post-graduate educational attainment, even when relevant psychological variables were controlled. Moreover, paternal support fostered sons' early career stability. This evidence of direct assistance and support occurring after college graduation, coupled with the demonstrated processes of attitude and value socialization and achievement, illustrate the multifaceted dynamics of intergenerational attainment. For the family influences children's subsequent placement in the occupational structure not only through the development of achievement-related personality traits in adolescence, but also more directly, via assistance and support in early adulthood.

Through its development and confirmation of a modified version of "the occupational linkage model," the findings of Chapter 2 highlight the importance of occupational values, held prior to college graduation, for work experiences a decade later. Given the long history of research on occupational selection on the basis of prior attitudes and values (Davis, 1964, 1965; Rosenberg, 1957), this result may not seem very surprising. It must be remembered, however, that most prior research on the relationship between values and career decisions has been based on cross-sectional data, gathered while respondents are still in school. This study demonstrates the persistence of the process of occupational "self-selection." Adolescent work values not only influence initial occupational choices, but also the kinds of occupational experiences the men have several years following their entry to the work force. The fact that prior psychological characteristics, including the self-image and work involvement, as well as occupational values, influence subsequent life experiences demonstrates that the individual plays an important part in creating his future. Life experiences and events do not simply happen, but the person is an active creator of those later life conditions that will come to influence the further course of human development.

In Chapter 3, our attention turned to work experience as a source of adult development and psychological change. In extending our causal model to include psychological variables 10 years following college, a very interesting pattern of developmental influence was observed. While the level of paternal support was found to be important for the development of all five psychological outcomes in late adolescence, by this early stage of adulthood work experiences appeared to take precedence in determining the further course of psychological change. A decade following college graduation, the quality of the father–son relationship no longer had any significant effects on the psychological variables.

The findings of Chapter 3 point to the pervasive importance of work autonomy for psychological change. Experiences of autonomy—discretion in occupational decision-making, innovative thinking on the job, and a sense of challenge—had positive effects, either direct or indirect, on all five psychological dimensions under consideration. Work autonomy fostered a sense of personal competence, high work involvement and intrinsic occupational reward values. Our model specification suggested that work autonomy influences extrinsic and people-oriented occupational values indirectly through its positive impact on work involvement. Thus, autonomous occupational experiences build a sense of self-competence and positive attitudes toward work. Men with highly autonomous jobs become more involved in their work over time, and increasingly look to work as a source of gratification.

This study therefore provides strong support for Kohn's argument that self-directed occupational activities are of crucial importance for adult psychological functioning. Kohn, in studying a national representative panel of working men, initially showed that social class differences in values and orientation are largely attributable to systematic variations in opportunities for self-direction at work (Kohn, 1969: Ch. 10). In subsequent research, scrutinizing a wide range of occupational characteristics and psychological variables, Kohn and Schooler (1973, 1978, 1982) and their colleagues (1983; Slomczynski et al., 1981) have provided further evidence that occupational conditions indicative of self-direction have the most pervasive psychological effects.

Our findings encompass central work experiences and psychological variables that are very similar to those included in Kohn and Schooler's analyses. There is, to be sure, some discrepancy between the two studies in panel characteristics, terminology, operationalization, and emphasis. While they have studied a representative sample of employed men, our panel is quite restricted in terms of social class. We examine work autonomy, indexed by decision-making capacity, innovative thinking, and challenge; Kohn and Schooler focus on occupational self-direction, measured in terms of the substantive complexity of work with data, people and things, freedom from supervision, and the routenization of work activities. Our inclusion of challenge as an indicator of autonomy makes our measure of work experience somewhat more subjective than theirs. They call the competence or personal efficacy dimension of the self-concept "self-confidence"; our "work involvement" corresponds to their "occupational commitment." We examine three occupational value dimensions; they consider only the intrinsic and extrinsic components. They have emphasized intellectual flexibility (Kohn and Schooler, 1978), while we had no measure of this important psychological dimension in our study.

But in spite of these differences, the central conclusions of the two studies are essentiallly very similar. It is striking that even in our well educated and occupationally rather homogeneous group of men, whose work is generally highly autonomous, occupational characteristics indicating the opportunity for self-directed thought and behavior are still found to have significant implications for enhancing the self-concept, heightening work involvement, and fostering occupational values through time. These findings lead us to conclude, along with Kohn and Schooler, that the autonomy of work is the occupational feature with the most crucial psychological importance. Taken together, the two bodies of research convincingly affirm that work experience exerts a continuing effect on the personality long after childhood and adolescence, the stages of life that socialization theorists have heretofore given almost exclusive attention.

The other work-related variables that we examined as sources of attitude and value change had decidedly more limited psychological effects. We considered the stability of the early work career, income attainment, and the social content of work activities. While the social content of work was found to have no significant effects on the psychological outcomes, career stability and income did have some noteworthy impacts.

The attainment of high income was found to reinforce the respondent's evaluation of extrinsic occupational rewards—of income, social status, and advancement—whereas it diminished the perceived importance of people-oriented occupational values. The positive effect of income on extrinsic values, coupled with the finding that work autonomy enhances intrinsic values, suggests that the particular experiences encountered at work influence evaluations of corresponding occupational rewards. Thus, persons with highly autonomous work experiences come to value intrinsic rewards more highly—work allowing opportunities to be creative and to express individual interests and abilities. Persons receiving high income as a reward for their productive efforts come to value income and the related extrinsic components of reward. As a result, the rewards that are actually obtained in work increase in salience and value over time. Values change in response to reinforcing occupational experiences. The findings offer no support to the prevalent assumption that high levels of extrinsic reward lead to a decline in extrinsic concerns as attention turns toward "higher", more intrinsic or people-oriented satisfactions (Maslow, 1954). Again, Kohn and Schooler's psychological model—that people change in response to simple processes of generalization or reinforcement—is confirmed.

The stability of the career pattern affected the psychological orientations mainly indirectly, through the occupationally-related features of work autonomy and income, that were fostered by stable careers. This indirect effect, of course, was positive. However, the direct effects of career stability on values were negative. That is, those respondents with more unstable careers were found to have higher intrinsic and extrinsic values once the work experiences were controlled. An unstable career, perhaps because of the uncertainties and trauma which occupational change and employment problems can entail, heightened the perceived importance of extrinsic and intrinsic occupational rewards over time.

The findings described thus far, presented in Chapters 2 and 3, indicate that work experience and psychological development influence one another through the life course. Adolescent attitudes and values significantly determine the kinds of occupational experiences which men will have in their early work lives. But work experiences come to influence these psychological constructs at a later point in time, as men pursue their adult occupational careers. The psychological variables that we have studied, though quite stable over time, are certainly not fixed, but responsive to crucial adult experiences. We have focused on those encountered in the work environment. Though our adult work experience and psychological measures were obtained at the same time, the reciprocal effects models suggest that work takes precedence as the central causal variable in early adulthood. The psychological attributes tended to have lagged, not contemporaneous, effects on the occupational experiences. Earlier attitudes and values influence subsequent work experiences, which, in turn, become significant determinants of psychological development at a later point in the life course.

This complex and dynamic process of interchange between person and environment has considerable relevance for an understanding of individual stability over time. Is personal stability a "static" phenomenon, seemingly independent of external forces, at least after the most crucial early developmental period? Or is stability "dynamic," dependent on continual reinforcement and support from the environment? If stability is largely dynamic in character, individuals could maintain their attitudes and values over time by creating experiences that foster constancy of their original orientations. We find evidence of both kinds of stability processes, at least with respect to the kinds of environmental forces and psychological variables examined in this study. Self-competence was the most highly stable of the five psychological attributes, consistent with Erikson's (1959) claim that self-perception is quite well established by late adolescence. But the stability of this self-concept construct was seemingly the least affected by subsequent life experiences in the educational and work spheres. (That is, there was relatively little difference in the zero-order stability, or the simple correlation of constructs over time, and the stability manifested net of environmental influences.) Extrinsic values similarly manifested a pattern of relatively "static stability" over time. However, persistence in the other three psychological dimensions—work involvement, intrinsic values, and people-oriented reward values—was substantially dependent on adult experiences, particularly the level of autonomy at work. To promote constancy in these psychological dimensions, the individual may actively construct the circumstances that maintain psychological stability over time.

Social scientists have recently been giving increasing attention to the dynamics of stability and change over the life course (Brim and Kagan, 1980; Costa and McCrae, 1980a; Mortimer, et al., 1982; Sears, 1981). Longitudinal data are particularly important in the study of life span development, for the individual's active contribution to life experience—as well as his reactions to it—can be observed. A major implication of the findings reported here is that the individual actively creates the environmental context, which, at a later date, contributes to subsequent psychological development. (For further evidence supporting this conclusion, see Mortimer et al., 1982). Thus, the stability of personality is at least partially fostered by the construction of social contexts that are consistent with prior psychological states. The impact of earlier upon later life experiences occurs through the influence of relatively stable personality attributes, developed in adolescence, that foster the acquisition of consonant roles and experiences. This process also may engender stability of life circumstances, such as achievement over the life cycle (Featherman, 1980). What is indicated is a truly dynamic, active, and reciprocal relationship between the person and the environment—a pattern wholly consistent with major theoretical formulations in social psychology (Gecas, 1981; House, 1981; Howard, 1979; Looft, 1973; Mischel, 1973, 1977; Overton and Reese, 1973; Snyder, 1981a).

Chapter 4 turned our attention to the family of procreation, to the reciprocal interrelations of work and family life during the early years of marriage. As we observed in the introduction to this book, there has been a tendency to overlook or even discount the effects of the family on work behavior, and the effects of work on family life. As Kanter (1977a) points out, this "myth of separate worlds" has been fostered by our cultural emphasis on individualistic achievement, the organization's interest in treating the worker as if the family did not exist, and the sociologist's own tendency to specialize in the study of particular institutional areas.

However, a growing body of scholarly research and inquiry has led us to seek connections between these two areas, challenging this myth of separation (Mortimer and London, 1984). In chapter 4, we observed the socio-economic and psychological advantages of the married over the single men, a pattern that has been consistently demonstrated in prior studies. The longitudinal feature of the present research is again particularly beneficial in helping us to understand the causal dynamics of this relationship. For with cross-sectional data it is not possible to determine whether the advantages of married men are attributable to processes of selection to marriage, on the basis of prior attitudes and achievements, or to the fact that marriage fosters occupational attainment.

Our analyses indicate that selection processes play little part in producing the married men's higher objective achievements and their more positive subjective evaluations of their degree of success. The men who would later marry, in their senior year of college, manifested a higher level of competence and stronger extrinsic values than did those who would remain single. But examination of a series of additional achievement-related psychological variables indicated no other significant differences. We found, too, that most of the respondents—fully two-thirds—either married prior to entering their work careers, or they undertook these two life transitions simultaneously. Therefore, for most respondents it could not be reasonably argued that occupational achievement preceded, and thereby fostered, marriage.

Given this failure of the "selection hypothesis" we then turned to the "marital influence hypothesis." Estimating a comprehensive, though simplified model of attainment, including most of the variables in our prior causal model, showed that marriage continued to have positive effects on attainment and subjective indicators of success even when relevant prior variables were controlled. Moreover, there was evidence that the wife's support of the husband's career was implicated in the married men's higher level of achievement. Wives' support and tangible assistance fostered their husbands' careers.

Selection processes accounting for the differences in attainment between married and single men cannot, of course, be entirely ruled out. For there may be formative experiences or personality dimensions existing prior to marriage, that predict both marriage and achievement, that we have not taken into account. And even the psychological variables that we have studied in the senior year of college, as antecedents to marriage, may have shifted in the period intervening between this earlier wave of data collection and the time of marriage. Paralleling the reciprocal interrelations of work experience and personality, there may be a pattern of "dynamic stability" with respect to marriage and achievement as well. But, within the limits of our data, there was little justification for the "marriage selection hypothesis." Instead, the "two-person career pattern" (Papanek, 1973) appeared to foster married men's careers. We conclude that marriage may be an important "career contingency" in the lives of men. In Chapter 2 we saw that the family of orientation can foster (or detract from) the achievement of the next generation. In Chapter 4 we find that the family of procreation likewise plays a crucial part in the achievement of men.

Later in Chapter 4, we turned the question around. Instead of assessing the implications of the family for work, we considered the effects of work on the family. We examined the extent to which men's occupational experiences and orientation contribute to strain in the family, the wife's support of the husband's occupation, and the husband's marital satisfaction. Again we find evidence for important linkages between work and family life. The respondents generally viewed their spouses as highly supportive of their occupations. But, at the same time, they recognized that their work generated problems in their families. Strain in the family was heightened under conditions of high socioeconomic achievement and demanding temporal requirements—long hours and time pressure. The findings support Aldous's (Aldous et al., 1979) "success constraint" hypothesis, that occupational success, at the highest levels, has important costs, as well as benefits, for the family. Moreover, there was evidence that work-related strain in the family reduced the wife's level of support of her husband's occupation, which, in turn, was a substantial determinant of the husband's marital satisfaction. Though the findings of this part of the analysis might be questioned on grounds of methodological adequacy (a longitudinal study of marriage and work, with multiple measures of the marital variables, would more convincingly demonstrate the effects of work experience on the family), our findings indicate that work behavior and family life are closely interconnected, and that the wife's support of the husband's career is highly relevant to his satisfaction in the family sphere.

We have seen that marriage influences work, by fostering occupational attainment, and that work influences the family, through its impacts on family strain, the wife's support and marital satisfaction. Yet a third linkage of work and family life is assessed in Chapter 4. We investigate whether marriage "buffers" the effects of work experiences on the individual. Do married and single men differ in their responses to their work experiences? We also examine whether men who perceive their wives as highly supportive of their careers react differently to their work experiences than those who view their spouses as less supportive. These questions presume a potential interactive linkage between work and family. That is, the psychological impacts of occupational experiences may differ depending on one's family status, or the quality of family relations.

But our extensive analyses of this possible dynamic of work and family linkage yielded entirely negative findings. There was no evidence that marriage or the wife's support made any real difference in the men's reactions to their jobs, to their work autonomy or income, or to stressors in the workplace, such as time pressure or responsibility for things that are outside one's personal control. The analyses included all five psychological dimensions encompassed in our earlier model, as well as an additional indicator of work-related stress. Given these negative findings, we then expanded the investigation to include other sources of support—from friends in the workplace and from the father. But this extension of our investigation again failed to support the buffering hypothesis.

These negative findings are subject to several plausible interpretations. They could be attributable to the limited range of work experiences and psychological dimensions under consideration, to the highly skewed support variables, or to the failure to tap those sources of support that do act as effective buffers. Because of these possibilities, this set of analyses should be considered highly tentative. It is interesting, however, that while the evidence does not support an interactive linkage between work and family life in inducing psychological change, it is extremely consistent with the patterns reported earlier in this book. In Chapter 3, we showed that the men responded quite similarly to their work experiences, irrespective of their occupational origins. In Chapter 4, we find that work experiences appear to have similar effects regardless of the individual's present family situation or his level of social support—insofar as we have been able to measure these phenomena. Thus, once in their jobs, men's reactions to their work experiences appear to be quite uniform, unaffected by their family backgrounds or their current family circumstances.

A central question in the area of social structure and personality has been considered—do environmental conditions, associated with positions in the social structure, generally have the same impacts on the individual, or do their effects differ, depending on particular features of the person? At least with respect to the interrelations of work, family, and personality, our findings support simple additive models, not more complex interactive processes. Again, the findings come down squarely in favor of Kohn's "generalization model"; work experiences are of such significance that people will tend to respond similarly to them regardless of important individual differences between them.

We have frequently commented on the problem of generalizability. We have studied a panel of young men which is in many respects unique, coming from one college, from a highly advantaged socio-economic stratum of the population, and from a single cohort, which entered the labor market at a time when the demand for college graduates was quite high. Because of the selective character of the panel, we cannot purport to generalize the findings to women, to persons who come from different socio-economic backgrounds or who experience different occupational conditions, or even to young college-educated men entering professional and managerial occupations in less favorable, more competitive periods.

But, as we pointed out in Chapter 1, in some respects the particular features of this panel can be considered advantageous. We have been able to examine the linkages of work, family, and personality without having to control for numerous variables that would considerably complicate the analysis. Even without these complications, our analyses have sometimes been exceedingly complex. For more definitive and generalizable conclusions regarding the transition to adulthood, we must await more comprehensive longitudinal studies, including both men and women, persons from diverse socio-economic and racial backgrounds, and occupants of positions throughout the occupational structure. Differences in the effects of work experiences on the personality, depending on age and career phase, also require further consideration. Given the importance of historical conditions in the processes of psychological development and attainment, a cohort sequential design would be highly advantageous.

However, within the context of this particular panel, our analyses have provided some compelling illustrations of the manner in which work, family, and personality are interrelated over time. In the course of presenting these findings, we have often noted that they are similar to those of other investigators, using quite different samples and methodologies. This pattern lends credibility to our results and interpretations. But the longitudinal character of this study, and the special period of the life course encompassed by the research, have allowed us to extend the findings of earlier work, piecing together the several discrete linkages of work, personality, and family life, and viewing them within a broad life course framework.

In adolescence, we have seen that the family of orientation influences the development of important attitudes and values which come to have major consequences for occupational attainment. And in spite of the considerable stability of these psychological orientations over time, we find that work experiences, particulary work autonomy, are of central importance for psychological change in adulthood. To the early insights of Marx, Weber, and Durkheim, linking work experience and personality development, and the contemporary research of Kohn and Schooler, Rosenberg, and Elder, our study adds important corroborative evidence. Moreover, just as the family of orientation influences the attainment process, so too does the family of procreation. But once in the labor force, work experience and attainments feed back on the family—influencing the character of socialization processes as well as the quality of family life. To understand the generalizability of these linkages of work, family, and personality, we await further research.

APPENDIX A

Procedures Used to Locate the Respondents and Induce a High Response to the Survey

The importance of longitudinal data for understanding causal processes is well recognized by sociologists, and long term panel studies are becoming increasingly prevalent (Davidson, 1972; Duncan and Morgan, 1975; Elder, 1974; Kohn and Schooler, 1978, 1983; Sewell and Hauser, 1975; Spitze and Spaeth, 1976). Investigators attempting to conduct such studies are beset with two major problems: (1) locating the original participants in the study, and (2) obtaining a sufficiently high rate of response from them to assure adequate representation of the initial group. This appendix reports on the procedures used to cope with these difficulties in this panel study of 694 men who graduated from the University of Michigan in 1966 and 1967. Most of these individuals had been studied initially when they were freshmen, and were monitored throughout their four years in college (for a description of the Michigan Student Study sample, see Gurin, 1971).

Several papers have described the techniques that have been successfully utilized to locate respondents in panel studies (Clarridge et al., 1978; Crider et al., 1971/1972; Eckland, 1968; McAllister et al., 1973a,b). These articles demonstrate that with ample resources and enough effort, ingenuity, and perseverence, practically anyone can be located. However, each retrieval process must utilize somewhat different procedures depending on the characteristics of the sample to be located and the resources available to the investigator. It is, therefore, important to disseminate knowledge regarding efficient techniques and the usefulness of different methods with samples of varying demographic characteristics and other distinguishing features. Hopefully, the resulting accumulation of knowledge will lessen the resources necessary for searches in future longitudinal studies.

In the present search effort, the Alumni Office of the University of Michigan was a considerable asset, since it provided current addresses or sufficient information to allow us to find almost 68 percent of the sample rather efficiently. Another 15 percent were found through parents whose addresses were obtained from the same office or from 1965–67 student directories. These sources are available to most investigators embarking on longitudinal studies of previous college students.

Attempts to locate the remaining individuals, those who could not be found using Alumni and parental sources, are of greater pertinence for investigators who are attempting to locate more heterogeneous groups. At this stage of the tracking process, persons with the same name as the respondent, found through occupational and phone directories, were contacted and asked to provide information concerning the whereabouts of the study participant on a stamped and pre-addressed post card. Though only 5 percent of the total target sample was located by this means, it is noteworthy that 54 percent of those who were sought by this method were eventually located. In total, 88 percent of the target group was successfully located.

Once the persons were found, there remained the problem of inducing them to respond to the mail survey. A very extensive literature has developed describing the procedures which have proven useful in obtaining high response rates in longitudinal and cross-sectional surveys (see U.S. Bureau of the Census, 1974). In spite of this rather highly developed "state of the field," response rates of 50 percent or less are still quite common, and often investigators use only one or no follow-up procedure. The second section of this appendix provides further evidence of the effectiveness of several previously recommended survey procedures. Eighty-four percent of the located respondents eventually returned completed questionnaires.

LOCATING THE RESPONDENTS

The procedures used to locate the respondents took many forms and the better part of 5 months for two of the authors of this book and three additional part-time workers. Figure A-1 summarizes the steps in the search process and gives the percentage of the sample found through each source.

Use of "pre-letters" as the initial search procedure

Using addresses obtained from the Alumni Office, we sent each study participant an "advance' or "pre-letter" explaining the purposes of the

Figure A-1. Basic Search Procedures

Send initial mailings to address provided by the Alumni Office
64.1%* → Search telephone directories and operators of community of R's last address
3.9% → Search for parents' addresses through old student directories, telephone directories, and operators → Contact parents by phone or by letter
14.8% →

Search occupational directories (respondent's choice and father's occupation) → Check phone directories for persons with same last name as R in phone directories of vicinity surrounding R's last address or old home address → Send letters and post cards to persons with same last name
4.6% → Send certified letter to R's last address if previous mailings to it were not returned by Post Office
1.0%

*Numbers below the procedures indicate the percent of the target sample located (Total = 88.4% or 614 persons).

study and alerting him to the forthcoming mail questionnaire. In the initial phases of the study, it was decided to search only for the persons whose pre-letters were returned by the Post Office stamped "Not Forwardable" or "Addressee Unknown". We assumed that those letters not returned to us would be correctly addressed or forwarded to the respondent. Thus, while the pre-letter was used partly as an inducement to response (Heaton, 1965; Robin, 1965), it was also used as the initial step in the search procedure. Hopefully, it would eliminate those individuals who would not need to be searched, reducing the scope of this task.

While about 10 percent of the pre-letters were returned within a 3-week period, the Post Office did not return many letters which we later found were never received. Throughout the study, we continued to receive letters and questionnaires back from the Post Office (indicating the addressees were unknown), even after several previous mailings to the respondent at the same address. While this problem complicated the tracking procedures, we nevertheless consider this first step using the mail service highly useful, since it eliminated the necessity to search for more than half the target group. Other studies (Crider et al., 1971/1972; Eckland, 1965) have similarly reported considerable success with the use of the mail as a first step in the search process.

Use of Telephone Directories and Long Distance Operators

If the pre-letter or subsequent mailings to the respondent were returned by the Post Office, a "tracing form" was immediately established (following Clarridge et al., 1978) to record all information that might be helpful later in the search.[1] We then attempted to find the respondent in telephone directories of the communities to which the initial mailing(s) had been sent. When the respondent's name could not be found in the appropriate directories, or if those directories could not be easily located, we called long distance information and attempted to find the respondents through sometimes resistant operators.[2] An additional 4 percent of the sample was found rather quickly in this manner.[3]

---

[1] As the search proceeded, we recorded the respondent's Alumni address, the old home address located through student directories, the father's occupation and the son's occupational choice(s), persons with the same last name listed in telephone directories, and any other pertinent information that we had.

[2] Though telephone operators are not permitted to give addresses, it was often possible to confirm an individual's address or ascertain the new address by asking, "Please give me the number of John Doe on 25 Central Street." Many operators would reply, "I have a John Doe, but he is on 6 Oaks Drive." If no street number were given, we could proceed to the telephone book for the information. We found that, if one operator could not be persuaded to give the address, calling again later in the day often produced the desired result.

Often, the respondents could not be located in the directories but other persons were listed with the same last name. Their names, addresses, and phone numbers were copied on the tracing forms for later use. When the last names were very common and there were many persons listed, only those were copied whom we considered likely to be related to the respondent, e.g., persons with the same first names or initials as the respondent, or those living on the same street as the respondent's last known address. The page number of the phone directory where more persons were listed was indicated on the tracing form for later referral.

Parent Contacts

When initial attempts to locate the respondent in the community of previous residence proved unsuccessful, we tried to locate the *parent* by consulting 10-year-old U. of M. student directories.[4] These directories listed the home addresses of the respondents when they were seniors in college. If the home address were found (almost all the students were listed), we proceeded to conduct a similar search to ascertain whether the parents were still at the old home address—by consulting telephone books, calling long distance operators to find out whether they might have unlisted numbers, and so on. At this stage we discovered that many addresses initially given to us by the Alumni Office were the old home addresses of the students and that the parents had since moved.

An obstacle in this part of the search was our inability to obtain the parents' first names. Attempts to get this information through university offices were futile, since we were informed that such information could only be given legally with the student's consent. Because of this problem, we were unable to determine efficiently whether someone with the same *last* name as the respondent, but living at an address different from the one found through the student directory, was indeed the parent. Nevertheless, this phase of the search was highly effective. Since the majority of the respondents were from the state of Michigan, and quite concentrated around the Detroit area, parents within the state were contacted rather inexpensively from Ann Arbor by phone. Out-of-state parents were contacted by letter. The parents were generally quite coopera-

---

[3] When there was any doubt about the identity of the respondent, e.g., when the first and last names were both quite common, we confirmed that he was a student at Michigan in 1966–67 by telephone or by mail. In some cases, when the respondent was not reachable by phone, we sent the questionnaire to him directly with a note requesting its return, left blank, if he was not a student at Michigan in 1966–67.

[4] For a few respondents not listed in the Alumni Office records, the first step was to locate the parent through the student directory.

tive—87 percent of those contacted provided the information we sought. Altogether, 103 respondents, or 15 percent of the target sample, were located through their parents. The high socio-economic origins of this sample and the legitimacy of a college follow-up study of this kind may have contributed to the high degree of cooperation.

Our experience in contacting parents, however, confirms that of other investigators (Clarridge et al., 1978; McAllister et al., 1973a) who have cautioned that a refusal on the part of the parent does not necessarily. mean that the respondent will also refuse to participate. In several instances, the parents did refuse, but the respondent was subsequently located through another source and returned the questionnaire.[5]

Use of Occupational Directories

Because the respondents' occupational choices and the occupations of their fathers were obtained while the students were seniors in college, it was possible to locate some respondents or their relatives through professional directories. The medical and college faculty directories were particularly useful in this regard, since they are organized alphabetically for the entire nation.[6] Respondents were also found through directories of pharmacists, newspaper publishers, certified public accountants, and engineers. When searching these directories, persons with the same last (and sometimes first) names as the respondents were added to the tracing forms. These persons, who were likely to be the respondents, fathers, or other relatives, were then sent letters and return post cards (to be described below).

Use of Phone Directories for the Vicinity Surrounding the Last Known Address. When the respondents (or persons with the same last name) could not be located in occupational directories, the tracing forms were consulted for names previously copied from phone books of the community of the outdated alumni address. If there were no such names indicated, we returned to the phone books, making a more extensive search of all communities surrounding this address and the old home

---

[5] For example, in one case the mother would not give us her son's address, but mentioned during the conversation that he was in a large city. We then found him listed in the telephone directory, confirmed his identity using the post card technique (to be described below), and then sent out a questionnaire which was completed and returned within a week.

[6] Since the law directory is organized by community, one needs to have the geographical location of the respondent to avoid checking each town or city within a state. Though some respondents were searched by checking all communities in their home state, no one was found through this source.

address. This procedure was sometimes rather time-consuming, since the major metropolitan areas where the respondents were concentrated, such as Detroit, New York, and Los Angeles, have numerous phone directories.

Use of the "Post Card Technique". Some previous investigators (Clarridge et al., 1978; Eckland, 1968) have been quite successful in locating study participants by calling all persons with the same last name as the person sought who were previously found through directories and other sources similar to the ones used in the present study. This procedure, while very thorough, is quite expensive when the target group is dispersed throughout the country, unless the investigator has access to rented telephone lines. This resource was not available to the project. Another problem is the annoyance and suspicion which may be aroused in persons when contacted by phone. In such circumstances, it may be difficult to establish the legitimacy of the study in the first minute or two of a telephone encounter.

To avoid these problems, letters were sent to each of the individuals on the tracing forms, explaining the nature of the study, and asking their cooperation in helping us find the respondent. A stamped and preaddressed post card was enclosed. The persons were asked to check the card and return it if they had no knowledge of the individual we were seeking, or to give us his current address, if known. (Both the letter and enclosed post card are shown in Figure A-2.) When there were many individuals with the same last name as the respondent listed on the tracing form, letters and cards were sent first to those whom we believed were more likely to be the respondent or persons related to him. Thus, letters were sent first to those located through occupational directories, then to persons in the same community, and finally to those in the same vicinity of the respondent's previous addresses. If there were many persons found in the phone books, letters were sent first to those with the same first or middle names or initials as the respondents, or those living closest to the respondent's last known address.[7] After initial letters were sent, we would wait for a response and send letters to more persons as necessary.

Fifty-seven respondents were searched using this method, and 120 letters were sent. Of these, 31 were returned with the current address of the respondent, 54 percent of the total searched by this technique. This success rate is quite good, considering that these respondents were the hardest to locate, and many of the letters sent seemed at the time to be "shots in the dark." Forty-three letters, or 36 percent of the total

---

[7] See footnote 3.

Figure A-2.   Search Letter and Enclosed Post Card

SEARCH LETTER

MICHIGAN STUDENT FOLLOW-UP STUDY
1114 Social Sciences Building
University of Minnesota
Minneapolis, Minnesota 55455

I and my colleagues at the University of Michigan are doing a follow-up study of students who participated in the Michigan Student Study, an extensive research project on the impacts of college. We are attempting to gain a better understanding of the experiences and problems which Michigan graduates confront after they leave Ann Arbor.

We have been unable to locate   and are writing to persons with the same name in the community of the student's last known address.

If you are the person we are looking for, we would appreciate very much your giving us that information on the stamped and pre-addressed card which is enclosed. We will then send you a letter, describing the study more fully, along with the questionnaire. If you are related to this person, or know him, we would be very grateful if you would provide his current address.

Please let us know, by checking the last sentence on the card, if you have no knowledge of this individual, so that we will not bother you with any further correspondence or telephone calls.

Thank you very much for your help,

Sincerely yours,

Jeylan T. Mortimer, Ph.D.
University of Michigan, 1972
Director, Michigan Student Follow-up Study

RETURN POST CARD

MICHIGAN STUDENT FOLLOW-UP STUDY

I was at the University of Michigan in 1966 or 1967 and the address below is correct.

The correct address of the person you are trying to locate is:

I have no knowledge of this individual.

Thank you very much.

---

sent, were returned with "no knowledge" checked, and 13 (11 percent) were returned by the Post Office, indicating "addressee unknown." Only 33, or 28 percent of the total sent, were not returned to us. (See Table A-1.)

Though this method was not as efficient as the previous techniques utilized, the return rate does suggest its utility when parental addresses are unavailable. In addition to being relatively inexpensive, the readiness of the public to respond to such requests is encouraging. When resources are limited, this method could be used to eliminate many of the names of persons to be contacted (those who return the card with the current address of the respondent or with "no knowledge" checked), leaving only the remaining individuals to be telephoned.

Checking all Addresses of Non-respondents After the Fourth Mailing. In the course of the survey, after sending out four mailings (a pre-letter, questionnaire, reminder post card, and reminder letter) and getting only about a 50 percent response, we began to suspect that some of the questionnaires might not have reached the respondents. (To this point, we were assuming that mailings had been received by the respondents if they were not returned to us.) Moreover, by this time several persons had written to the study director saying that they had received the pre-letter or other letters, but not the questionnaire. We therefore began checking the addresses of all persons who had not yet responded to the survey and on whom we had received nothing from the Post Office marked undeliverable. This was accomplished by consulting phone boks and telephone operators to see whether the respondent was listed at the address to which we had been sending the survey materials. In addition, when the address was verified, we recorded the respondent's phone number for later use in making phone calls in the final stage of the

Table A-1. Response to the "Post Card Locating Technique" Used to Search 57 Respondents

	Percent of Letters Sent	N
Letters returned with address of respondent	25.8	31
Letters returned with "no knowledge" checked	35.8	43
Letters returned by Post Office (addressee unknown)	10.8	13
Letters not returned	27.5	33
Letters sent	99.9%*	120

*Percentages do not add to 100 due to rounding.

survey procedure or indicated on the tracing form that he had an unlisted phone number.

At this time, we discovered that many of the questionnaires had been sent to parents' addresses. Upon contacting the parents by phone or by letter, we attempted to get the current address and phone number of the respondent. As noted earlier, most parents were very cooperative. (New addresses obtained from parents during this phase of the search are included in Figure A-1 under Parent Contacts.) In these cases, the respondent was usually called to ascertain whether he had received earlier mailings.

The checking of each address of the nonrespondents up to that point in the survey proved to be of great importance, since many persons were found to have moved from the address to which materials were originally sent. When we went through the search procedures for these individuals and successfully located them, we sent questionnaires out immediately. (Persons found through the various procedures in this phase of the study are incorporated in the percentages given in Figure A-1.) Though we had no way of knowing exactly how many of the previous mailings had been forwarded by the Post Office, parents, or other persons at the original residence, in the course of our conversations with respondents we discovered that many had not. Moreover, the fact that many of the mailings to newly located participants who were *not* contacted by phone yielded responses within a very short period (1–2 weeks) suggested that they had received nothing from us before.

Use of Certified Mail. We could not locate 51 respondents through any of the previous methods, but had received none of the previous four mailings from the Post Office indicating "Addressee Unknown". In these cases, we had no way of knowing if the letters and questionnaires had been received. In an attempt to get this information, we sent questionnaires by certified mail to the respondents at the addresses given by the Alumni Office. Receipts were requested showing the name of the recipient and the address where delivered. The cost for this service was $1.31 per questionnaire ($0.85 plus the $0.46 first class postage). Much to our disappointment, only 11 receipts were returned with all information requested and 6 were returned unclaimed. In 13 cases, no addresses were given. The fact that 11 of the 51 questionnaires were returned, marked "undeliverable," serves as a warning to other researchers not to assume that mailings have been received just because first class letters are not returned to sender. We never received receipts for four certified questionnaires. Only 7 new addresses (1 percent of the target sample) were located through the use of certified mail.

OBTAINING A HIGH RESPONSE RATE

A review of mail survey methodology literature indicates that good questionnaire design and multiple follow-up procedures yield high response rates even when very long questionnaires are utilized (Bachrach and Scoble, 1967; Dillman et al., 1974; Pace, 1939). The questionnaire in this study was 28 pages. Numerous design features that have been recommended previously may have contributed to the high response rate obtained (84 percent of those located). For example, the questionnaire was attractively printed on both sides of each page and designed to facilitate response through simply worded questions and avoidance of arrows and complicated contingency directions. Items with similar content were grouped under boldface headings such as "Work," "Family," "Organization and Friendships," and so forth. Simple, factual, and nonthreatening items dealing with education and work experience were placed at the beginning of the instrument.[8] A summary report of the findings of the study was offered as an incentive to reply (Bachrach and Scoble, 1967; Sofer, 1970).

The letters to the respondent were printed on stationery with a Michigan Student Follow-Up Study letterhead. Though they were not individually typed, considerable effort was made to personalize them by the handwritten signature of the principal investigator and by typing the respondent's name and address in the letter heading. In the later phases of the study, hand-written notes were placed at the letter's end. Moreover, stamped (not machine cancelled) envelopes and first class mail were always utilized.[9]

The results of several studies indicate the value of three (Hochstim and Athanasopoulos, 1970; Mayer and Pratt, 1966; Phillips, 1951; Robin, 1965) or more (Dillman et al., 1974; Sewell and Hauser, 1975) followups to induce a high rate of response. Our survey procedures, summarized in Figure A-2 and described more fully below, involved from two to six contacts with each respondent. (The questionnaire and post card were sent to everyone and most respondents also received a preletter; the last three procedures were only applied to those who had not yet responded.) Altogether, 512 questionnaires were returned by 84 percent of the located, still living respondents ($n = 610$).

---

[8] Recommendations we followed concerning questionnaire design format are given in Robin (1965) and Levine and Gordon (1959).

[9] For discussions of these letter format and mailing procedures, see Kephart and Bressler (1958), Levine and Gordon (1959), Gullahorn and Gullahorn (1963), Robin (1965), Heaton (1965), Linsky (1965), and Bachrach and Scoble (1967).

Due to the concurrence of the search and survey procedures, it is not possible to isolate the increment to the response rate gained by each follow-up technique. The search procedures themselves may have contributed to the high response rate that was obtained. We believe that the thoroughness of the search process may have impressed the respondents with the importance of the study since we had gone to so much trouble to find them (by sending letters, making phone calls to the parent and/or the respondent, etc.). Several respondents even wrote to us, asking how in the world we were able to find them!

Moreover, in many cases after locating the respondent, it was not possible to ascertain with any certainty whether the letters and questionnaires sent previously were forwarded. After each respondent was located, we immediately sent out an initial questionnaire and cover letter. Respondents who sent back these questionnaires were recorded as responding to the first questionnaire mailing, when actually they may have received one previously, in addition to other communications. Because of these uncertainties, no attempt is made to attribute increments in the response rate to specific mailings (the pre-letter, questionnaire, post card, and three week follow-up letter) in the early phases of the study. Percentage increments to the response rate yielded by later procedures should be considered only as rough estimates of their effectiveness.

Survey Procedures

1. A *pre-letter* constituted the first contact with respondents for whom no search was necessary. (Pre-letters were *not* sent to respondents whose current addresses were found later, after the survey had begun.) A pre-letter has been recommended to reduce the likelihood that questionnaires will be discarded as "junk mail" and to lessen irritation with long questionnaires (Levine and Gordon, 1959). They also provide the opportunity to send important persuasive messages, to be repeated in later communications, concerning the worth of the study and the importance of each individual's participation (Heaton, 1965). In addition to these messages, the pre-letter assured the respondent that the data would be considered confidential, notified him that the questionnaire would arrive in two weeks, and pointed out the integral connection of the survey with the earlier study that he had participated in during college.[10]

2. A *questionnaire and cover letter* were sent 2 weeks after the pre-letter with a stamped and pre-addressed envelope enclosed. (For newly found

---

[10] For further discussions of letter content in mail surveys see Linsky (1965), Robin (1965), and Bachrach and Scoble (1967).

respondents who were searched, the questionnaire and cover letter constituted the initial survey contact.) In addition to repeating the content of the pre-letter, it encouraged comments on the margins of the questionnaires and requested a response within two weeks (Bachrach and Scoble, 1967; Deutscher, 1956; Levine and Gordon, 1959).

3. A *post card*, sent 1 week later, reminded the respondent to return the questionnaire and thanked them if they had already done so (Nichols and Meyer, 1966).

4. A *follow-up letter*, sent 3 weeks after the questionnaire, repeated much of the content of previous letters, mentioned the questionnaire and stamped envelope that were sent earlier, and invited communication with the study director for additional information (Bachrach and Scoble, 1967). These three or four mailings, in conjunction with the contacts involved in the location procedures, yielded a response from 73 percent of the located study participants. Eight questionnaires (adding 1 percent to the response rate) were received as a result of the certified questionnaire mailing in the final phase of the search.

5. A *second questionnaire and cover letter*, sent 7 weeks after the first to those respondents whose addresses could be verified, yielded an increment of 4 percent to the response rate. The second cover letter, while not identical to the first, repeated much of the same information, and was mailed with a stamped envelope.

6. A *phone call* or *"final letter"* was the last contact with the respondent.[11] One month following the second questionnaire, we called 95 persons whose phone number could be located. About one out of four persons expressed some annoyance, perhaps because of the numerous previous contacts. Most, however, said that they had simply not gotten around to filling out the questionnaire, but would do so shortly. We also found at this point that some had never received their questionnaires. Of the persons called, 36 actually did return their questionnaires, adding 6 percent to the response rate. The use of "final letters," sent to several persons with unlisted phone numbers, yielded no additional returns.

CONCLUSION

This appendix has described our attempts to surmount the two major problems confronting researchers in collecting data for panel studies:

---

[11] Levine and Gordon (1959), Eckland (1965), and Mayer and Pratt (1966) recommend telephone calls as an inducement to response.

locating the study participants, and inducing high response. Although there is considerable recognition of the need for longitudinal data to understand the nature of causal processes, such research may be increasingly difficult to conduct in the future. Already, the proliferation of legal safeguards is decreasing social scientists' access to records that were available previously for scrutiny during searches. For example, in a longitudinal study conducted more than a decade ago, McAllister et al. (1973a) report use of school records, public utility companies, voter registration lists, county welfare and probation departments, and a state department of motor vehicles. Information was also obtained by contacting previous employers and neighbors. Concerns about infringement of privacy have largely closed off sources such as these to researchers.

In the future, persons who wish to conduct longitudinal studies may, therefore, have to exert greater effort and invent new ways of making use of what little public information is still available to them. Given the increasingly formidable constraints, the use of letters and return post cards in the present study to contact individuals with the same last name as the study participant may be a useful, nonintrusive, and inexpensive method of search in future studies. A letter may arouse less suspicion than a request for information from an unknown caller. The high level of response to the post card, even when the individual had no knowledge of the person sought, is certainly encouraging.

Because, however, this method requires knowledge of the respondent's area of residence, occupation, or other information through which he or a relative could be traced, it is exceedingly important to have as much identifying information as possible to start with. For this reason, several researchers have recommended that every survey proceed as if a longitudinal study were planned, by getting extensive information that could be useful in tracking later (Crider et al., 1972; McAllister et al., 1973b). In the present study, our access to two addresses (an outdated one for the respondent, and the old home address), as well as identifying occupational information for the father and son, were of tremendous benefit in the search.

Our experience likewise suggests that when conducting follow-up surveys by *mail*, it may be useful to conduct the search and survey procedures simultaneously instead of trying to locate all study participants first, before conducting the survey. Such concurrence will lead to a significant saving of time and other resources if it is likely that a substantial proportion of subjects would still be reached at their previous addresses, or, if they had moved, that their mail would be forwarded. Proceeding as if our subjects were still at the addresses given to us by the Alumni Office, we sent out our initial mailings. More than half the respondents returned their questionnaires without our having to search for them.

While we do not know how many of the respondents who returned their questionnaires early in the study received them directly, and how many had them forwarded by parents, the Post Office, or others, confirming all their addresses initially would have added months of effort to the present study. Moreover, it is likely that substantial numbers of parents (or others) who would promptly forward letters to the respondents would not have given their current addresses if requested prior to the initial mailings. (About 13 percent of the parents refused to give us their sons' addresses when contacted in the present study.)

Finally, we wish to corroborate the oft-repeated message that persistence in tracking and follow-ups is rewarded in studies of this kind. We believe that the high response rate obtained is largely attributable to the numerous contacts with the respondent in the course of both search and survey procedures.

APPENDIX B

MEASURES AND MEASUREMENT PARAMETERS

CHAPTERS 2 AND 3

Socio-economic Status

x_1 father's occupational prestige (.9499[a])

Siegel Prestige Scores (Siegel, 1971: Ch. 2)

M[b] $= 58.0$ SD[c] $= 14.5$

range $= 19–82$

(Prestige scores were divided by ten for computation of variances and covariances)

x_2 family income (.5943): About how much total income do your parents earn yearly at the present time?

%[d]	Income
1.2	1. Less than $3,999
6.6	2. $4,000 to $7,499
9.0	3. $7,500 to $9,999
24.6	4. $10,000 to $14,999
19.3	5. $15,000 to $19,999
31.8	6. $20,000 and over
7.4	Missing data

$$M = 4.62 \qquad SD = 1.31$$

x_3 father's education (.6844): How far did your parents go in school?

%	Father's Education
3.9	1. Less than high school
4.1	2. Some high school (9–11 years)

---

[a]The lambda coefficient, expressing the relationship between the indicator and the construct, is given after each observed variable.

[b]Mean

[c]Standard Deviation

[d]The percent distributions for the variables, unless otherwise indicated, are based on all 512 panel members.

14.8	3. Completed high school (12 years)
19.9	4. Some college
21.9	5. Completed college
29.1	6. Advanced or professional degree
6.3	Missing data

$M = 4.48$ $SD = 1.40$

Paternal Support—Senior Year

y_1 Father's empathy (.6332): How well do you feel your parents understand you and what you want out of life?

%	Father
4.7	1. Not at all
20.3	2. Not too well
43.0	3. Fairly well
21.9	4. Very well
10.1	Missing data (includes parent deceased)

$M = 2.91$ $SD = .82$

y_2 Close to father (.8845): How close do you feel to your mother and to your father?

%	Father
16.2	1. Not very close
27.5	2. Fairly close
30.9	3. Quite close
15.2	4. Extremely close
10.2	Missing data (includes parent deceased)

$M = 2.50$ $SD = .98$

Paternal Support—1976

y_{26} Father's empathy (.6736): How well do you feel your parents understand you and what you want out of life?

%	Father
15.6	1. Not at all
43.9	2. Not too well
20.1	3. Fairly well
4.1	4. Very well
16.2	Missing data

$M = 2.90$ $SD = .77$

y_{27} Close to father (.8834): How close do you feel to your mother and to your father?

%	Father
15.6	1. Not very close
28.7	2. Fairly close
25.6	3. Quite close
13.7	4. Extremely close
16.4	Missing data

$M = 2.66$ $SD = .97$

Self-competence—Senior Year: Myself as a Person

	7	6	5	4	3	2	1		missing data
				Percent Distribution					
y_3 strong	8.8	40.4	31.4	4.3	7.0	2.0	.2	weak	5.9
.5869		$M = 5.35$		$SD = 1.11$					
y_4 active	17.4	35.9	20.9	3.3	12.3	3.9	.4	quiet	5.9
.5056		$M = 5.31$		$SD = 1.42$					
y_5 competent	17.4	50.6	20.5	2.7	2.1	.6	.2	not too competent	5.9
.4387		$M = 5.80$		$SD = .92$					
y_6 successful	8.8	45.7	29.7	4.1	3.3	1.8	.8	not too successful	5.9
.2632		$M = 5.47$		$SD = 1.06$					

$e_5 e_6 = .3643^c$

Self-competence—1976: Myself as a Person

	7	6	5	4	3	2	1		missing data
y_{29} strong	11.5	47.9	28.3	6.3	4.1	1.0	.2	weak	.8
.7846		$M = 5.53$		$SD = 1.01$					
y_{30} active	18.4	36.9	19.3	5.9	10.0	7.6	.8	quiet	1.2
.4964		$M = 5.22$		$SD = 1.53$					
y_{31} competent	31.8	57.8	8.2	.4	.8	0	0	not too competent	1.0
.4409		$M = 6.21$		$SD = .67$					
y_{32} successful	13.1	58.2	19.5	4.5	2.7	1.2	0	not too successful	.8
.3533		$M = 5.71$		$SD = .93$					

$e_{30} e_{31} = .0942 \qquad e_{31} e_{32} = .2702$

---

^{c}correlated error variances of indicators.

Work involvement—Senior Year

y_7 (.6172) : When you think of your life after college, how important do you expect each of the following areas will be to you?

%	Career or occupation
.6	0. Little or no importance
6.8	1. Important
48.0	2. Very important
38.3	3. Crucially important
6.3	Missing data

$M = 2.32 \quad SD = .63$

Work involvement—1976

y_{28} (.6519) : People differ in the importance they attach to different areas of life. How important are each of the following areas to you?

%	Career or occupation
1.4	0. Little or no importance
8.4	1. Important
53.9	2. Very important
35.9	3. Crucially important
.4	Missing data

$M = 2.24 \quad SD = .66$

Occupational Reward Values—Senior Year
The measures of occupational reward values directly followed a question concerning the respondent's occupational choice.
How important would you say the following things are in your decision about whether to go into this kind of work?

1. Not too important	2. Fairly important	3. Very important	4. Crucially important	Missing data

Percent Distribution

Extrinsic Orientation—Senior

y_{13} Prestige (.5102): This occupation is a very respected one in our society

31.4	43.9	16.4	1.6	6.6

$M = 1.87$ $SD = .75$

y_{14} Advancement (.6601): This occupation provides many opportunities for advancement

27.1	30.5	27.9	7.6	6.8

$M = 2.17$ $SD = .94$

y_{15} High income (.8993): This occupation brings a good salary—the income is high

24.0	30.1	30.1	9.4	6.4

$M = 2.26$ $SD = .95$

Intrinsic Orientation—Senior

y_{10} Abilities (.4957): This occupation is a unique fit with my abilities and skills—lets me do the things I can do best

8.4	24.2	40.0	21.1	6.3

$M = 2.79$ $SD = .89$

y_{11} Interests (.5089): This occupation is a unique expression of my interests, something I really like

5.3	15.8	35.2	37.7	6.1

$M = 3.12$ $SD = .88$

y_{12} Creative (.4555): In this occupation I can be creative and original

13.9	30.5	32.8	16.6	6.3

$M = 2.56$ $SD = .95$

$e_{10}e_{11} = .3807$

	1. Not too important	2. Fairly important	3. Very important	4. Crucially important	Missing data

Percent Distribution

People-orientation—Senior

y_8 Service to Others (.7882): This occupation gives me a chance to be helpful to others and/or useful to society in general

	13.1	26.2	29.3	25.2	6.3

$M = 2.71$ $SD = 1.01$

y_9 Work with People (.6818): This occupation gives me a chance to work with people rather than things

	18.2	19.1	31.6	24.4	6.6

$M = 2.67$ $SD = 1.07$

Occupational Reward Values—1976

If you were offered another occupational position, how important would you consider each of the following work characteristics in deciding whether to accept it?

Extrinsic Values 1976

y_{36} Prestige (.4144): How highly people regard the job

	28.7	39.8	24.6	5.3	1.6

$M = 2.07$ $SD = .87$

y_{37} Advancement (.4462): Opportunities for advancement

	10.4	26.0	36.1	25.6	2.0

$M = 2.78$ $SD = .95$

y_{38} High income (.6416): High income

	12.7	35.2	36.5	14.3	1.4

$M = 2.53$ $SD = .89$

$e_{36}e_{37} = .2009$ $e_{37}e_{38} = .1629$

	1. Not too important	2. Fairly important	3. Very important	4. Crucially important	Missing data

Percent Distribution

Intrinsic Values 1976

y_{33} Abilities (.7119): Opportunities to exercise my abilities and skills

	.4	5.1	39.3	53.7	1.6

$M = 3.49$ $SD = .61$

y_{34} Interests (.7901): Opportunities to express my interests

	2.3	12.7	42.6	41.0	1.4

$M = 3.24$ $SD = .76$

y_{35} Creative (.6401): Opportunity to be creative and original

	6.8	24.6	41.2	25.8	1.6

$M = 2.87$ $SD = .88$

People-Oriented Values 1976

y_{39} Service to Others (.9080): The chance to be helpful to others or useful to the society

	12.1	32.0	35.4	18.8	1.8

$M = 2.62$ $SD = .93$

y_{40} Work with People (.5133): A chance to work with people rather than things

	17.0	26.8	35.4	18.4	2.6

$M = 2.57$ $SD = .99$

Educational Attainment

y_{16} (1.000): Have you taken any college courses, or been enrolled in any educational program (e.g., a company or vocational training program, military education, etc.), since you graduated from the University of Michigan?

%		
5.3	5.	B.A. only
16.4	6.	Some education beyond B.A.
26.2	7.	Master's degree
52.0	8.	Ph.D. or professional degree
.2		Missing data

$M = 7.25$ $SD = .91$

Career Stability

y_{17} Employment Problems (.4451): Because of the unavailability of work in your field since you graduated from Michigan, have you ever had to take a job that could be done by someone with less training or education? Since you obtained your bachelor's degree, have you ever been *involuntarily unemployed and looking for work* for more than a month? Since you obtained your bachelor's degree, have you ever involuntarily worked part-time due to an inability to find full-time work?

%		
25.0	0.	Respondent has experienced underemployment, unemployment, or involuntary part-time employment
73.4	1.	Respondent has not experienced any one of these problems
1.6		Missing Data

$M = 0.75$ $SD = .19$

y_{18} Occupational Change (.7058): Is your present occupation the one that you planned to enter when you left Michigan?

%		
26.4	1.	No
16.6	2.	I didn't have specific plans when I graduated
55.3	3.	Yes
1.8		Missing Data (includes "Don't remember")

$M = 2.29$ $SD = .75$

Job Search

y_{19} (1.000): How exactly did you find out about your present job?

%		
29.9	1.	Only formal methods (U of M placement office; an employment agency or personnel consultants; an advertisement in a newspaper, magazine, trade, or technical journal; I applied directly to the organization)
11.3	2.	Offical and "informal" methods listed
49.0	3.	Only informal methods (a faculty member, college or post graduate program; a fellow undergraduate or post-graduate student; another friend or acquaintance; I worked for the organization while I was still in school; a relative; I was transferred or promoted from within my organization; someone I didn't know from another organization contacted me about the job; I became self-employed; I entered the family firm)
9.8		Missing data

$M = 2.21$ $SD = .91$

Income

$\dot{y}_{20}$ (1.000): What is the gross annual income that you earn in wages or salary from your *main* job?

%		
1.2	1.	Under $3,000
1.8	2.	$3,000–$4,999
4.1	3.	$5,000–$9,999
13.7	4.	$10,000–$14,999
22.5	5.	$15,000–$19,999
18.4	6.	$20,000–$24,999
14.5	7.	$25,000–$29,999
6.3	8.	$30,000–$34,999
4.9	9.	$35,000–$39,999
10.4	10.	$40,000 and over
2.5		Missing data

$M = 6.08 \qquad SD = 2.08$

Work Autonomy

y_{21} Decision-making ability (.5231): Overall, how much autonomy do you have in making important decisions about *what* you do at work and *how* you do it?

%		
.6	1.	Almost none at all
5.3	2.	Some, but not much autonomy
22.7	3.	A fair amount of autonomy
46.1	4.	A great deal of autonomy
23.6	5.	Complete autonomy
1.8		Missing data

$M = 3.88 \qquad SD = .85$

y_{22} Innovative thinking (.6075): How much *innovative thinking* does your job require? (Do you have to think of new ways of doing things, solving problems, presenting ideas, etc.?)

%		
.4	1.	Almost none at all
6.6	2.	Some, but not much
29.7	3.	A fair amount
37.3	4.	A great deal
24.6	5.	A tremendous amount
1.4		Missing data

$M = 3.80 \qquad SD = .90$

y_{23} Challenge (.6589): Overall, how *challenging* would you consider your present job?

%		
1.2	1.	Not at all challenging
9.6	2.	Only a little bit challenging
34.6	3.	Somewhat challenging
53.1	4.	Very challenging
1.6		Missing data

$M = 3.42 \qquad SD = .71$

Social Content

y_{24} People-oriented work activities (.5127): (Preceding question: how many hours per week do you spend dealing with people? Do not include passing the time of day, but *only* conversations necessary for carrying out your work activities; for example, giving and receiving directions, organizing groups of people, selling, and teaching.) What kind of activities are they?

%
- .4   2.   None
- 36.5   4.   Administering and supervising other workers; receiving instructions from my supervisor(s); selling or promoting my organization's products or services; working jointly with co-workers to solve problems, formulate policies and programs, or arrive at decisions.
- 60.7   6.   Teaching and advising students; providing services to clients (as in medical or legal work, counseling, social work, the ministry, etc.)
- 2.3   Missing data

$M = 5.24$ $SD = 1.59$

y_{25} Person-oriented occupation (.7287)

%
- 20.3   2.   Technical, data-oriented, blue collar occupations
- 27.0   4.   Managerial and other people-oriented occupations, excluding those in category 6
- 50.6   6.   Client-oriented or teaching professions (e.g., doctors, dentists, lawyers, teachers, college professors)
- 2.1   Missing data

$M = 4.62$ $SD = 1.18$

Correlated error terms of indicators of different endogenous constructs:

$e_1 e_{26} = .1708$	$e_{13} e_{36} = .1521$
$e_1 e_{30} = .2830$	$e_{14} e_{37} = .1160$
$e_6 e_{32} = .1347$	$e_{22} e_{35} = .1561$
$e_8 e_{12} = .0992$	$e_{23} e_{33} = -.1079$
$e_8 e_{13} = .1226$	$e_{23} e_{31} = -.1074$
$e_9 e_{13} = .0775$	$e_{33} e_{37} = .1833$
$e_9 e_{40} = .2325$	$e_{34} e_{37} = .0995$
$e_{10} e_{23} = .0853$	$e_{35} e_{37} = .1642$
$e_{12} e_{35} = .1716$	

Standardized Construct Residuals for Causal Model (Figure 3-1)

4	Paternal Support—Senior Year	.963
5	Competence—Senior Year	.918
6	Work Involvement—Senior Year	.884
7	Intrinsic Values—Senior Year	.582
8	Extrinsic Values—Senior Year	.925
9	People-oriented Values—Senior Year	.865
10	Educational Attainment	.897
11	Career Stability	.624
12	Work Autonomy	.752
13	Income	.699

14	Social Content of Work	.164
15	Job Search	.978
16	Paternal Support—1976	.643
17	Work Involvement—1976	.287
18	Competence—1976	.370
19	Intrinsic Values—1976	.772[a]
20	Extrinsic Values—1976	.349
21	People-oriented Values—1976	.755

[a]The correlation of the construct residuals for intrinsic and people-oriented values is .382.

CHAPTER 4

The analyses in Chapter 4 were performed using ordinary least squares regression, unlike the analyses in Chapters 2 and 3 which were based on structural equation models incorporating measurement error. Consequently, in Chapter 4 multiple-item indices were constructed by standardizing and then summing the responses to each question in the scale. In addition to the indicators included in the analyses for Chapters 2 and 3, the following measures were used in the analyses featured in Chapter 4.

Career Progress
How would you evaluate your own work performance?

%		
.0	1.	Inadequate
.0	2.	Just barely adequate
2.1	3.	Adequate
13.9	4.	Good
53.1	5.	Very good
29.5	6.	Extremely good
1.4		Missing data

$M = 5.12 \qquad SD = .72$

How would you compare yourself to the people who started out in your line of work at about the same time you did? Have you done . . .

%		
.6	1.	Much less well than average
2.7	2.	Less well than average
23.8	3.	About average
44.7	4.	Better than average
21.5	5.	Much better than average
6.7		Missing data (includes don't know)

$M = 3.90 \qquad SD = .81$

How would you rate your chances for future advancement in your occupation?

%		
2.1	1.	Poor
4.5	2.	Not so good
21.7	3.	Good
26.7	4.	Very good
27.9	5.	Excellent
17.8		Missing data (includes inapplicable and don't know)

$M = 3.89 \qquad SD = 1.02$

Facets of Job Satisfaction

The measures of the three facets of job satisfaction directly followed a question concerning the respondent's overall satisfaction with his job.

How satisfied are you with each of these aspects of your present job?

	M	SD	Very Dissatisfied 1	Dissatisfied 2	Satisfied 3	Very Satisfied 4	Missing Data
				Percent Distribution			
Extrinsic Satisfaction							
How highly people regard the job	3.09	.68	2.3	11.1	59.6	24.8	2.2
Opportunities for advancement	2.95	.81	4.9	19.1	47.5	24.0	4.5
High income	2.73	.85	9.0	24.4	47.5	16.0	3.1
Intrinsic Satisfaction							
Opportunities to exercise my abilities and skills	3.21	.81	3.9	12.3	41.6	40.2	2.0
Opportunities to express my interests	3.10	.74	1.8	16.6	49.2	30.3	2.2
Opportunity to be creative and original	3.05	.76	3.5	15.4	51.6	27.1	2.4
People Satisfaction							
A chance to work with people rather than things	3.27	.56	.2	5.1	60.0	32.0	2.8
The chance to be helpful to others or useful to the society	3.14	.64	2.0	8.2	60.9	25.8	3.1

Life Satisfaction Consider how your life is going now. Would you like it to continue in much the same way, or would you like it to change?

%		
7.0	1.	I would like to change many parts of it
62.1	2.	I would like to change some parts of it
30.1	3.	I would like it to continue in much the same way as it's going now
.8		Missing data

$M = 2.23$ $SD = .57$

Time Pressure
How often do you have to work under the pressure of time?

%	
1.8	1. Hardly ever
5.7	2. Rarely
24.8	3. Sometimes
35.4	4. Frequently
30.9	5. Usually
1.6	Missing data

$M = 3.89$ $SD = .97$

Responsibility for Things Outside One's Control
How often are you held responsible for things that are really outside your control?

%	
25.6	1. Hardly ever
34.2	2. Rarely
29.1	3. Sometimes
7.2	4. Frequently
2.3	5. Usually
1.6	Missing Data

$M = 2.25$ $SD = 1.00$

Job Protection
Which of the following forms of job protection do you *now* have? (Check all that apply.)

% with each job protection	
10.2	Seniority rights
12.9	Contract guarantees
5.1	Union support
7.0	Guarantee of permanency or tenure
5.3	Civil service
48.2	My organization's need for my knowledge and skills

Note: 20.7 percent indicated that they had no job protection.

Mental Exhaustion
After a day's work, how often do you feel exhausted-mentally or physically?

%	Mentally Exhausted
2.9	1. Hardly ever
9.4	2. Rarely
42.2	3. Sometimes
34.4	4. Frequently
9.4	5. Usually

$M = 3.38$ $SD = .89$

Note: Percentage distributions for the following variables, used in analyses of the effects of work on family life (Fig. 4-2), were computed for married respondents only (N = 368).

Occupational Involvement

How important are each of the following areas to you? The respondents evaluated the importance of twelve life areas, including career or occupation, religious activities, marriage, parenthood, and friendship.

Career or Occupation

	%
0. Little or no importance	.8
1. Important	8.4
2. Very Important	56.0
3. Crucially Important	34.8
Missing Data	0

$M = 2.25$ $SD = .64$

Percent Distribution

	First Choice Career or Occupation 2	Second Choice Career or Occupation 1	Career or Occupation Not Chosen 0
Given a choice among the same twelve areas, the respondents were asked: Which two activities do you enjoy the most?	23.7	16.2	60.1
Which two activities would you like to devote more time to?	5.3	5.5	89.2
Which two activities provide you with the greatest sense of accomplishment?	55.6	21.2	23.2

For each item, a code value of 2 was given if "career or occupation" was the "first preference"; a 1, if this were the "second preference"; and a 0, if "career or occupation" were not indicated. The responses to these three questions were then summed.

After transforming the responses to the single item evaluation and the index into standardized scores, the two measures were summed to create the index of occupational involvement.

227

Temporal Requirements

These three items were summed to form an index of hours spent working:

How many hours do you, in fact, put in at your place of work during a typical week?

How many hours do you work at home during a typical week?

Apart from your main job, have you earned any income in the past year from other work? (If yes) Roughly how many hours do you put in on this job during an average week?

$M = 48.28$ $SD = 11.86$

	M	SD	Usually 5	Frequently 4	Sometimes 3	Rarely 2	Hardly Ever 1	Missing Data
					Percent Distribution			
How often do you have to work under the pressure of time?	3.95	.97	33.4	36.4	22.0	6.3	1.4	.6

The index of temporal requirements was created by standardizing and then summing the measures of hours spent working and time pressure.

Socio-economic Status

Income

What is the gross annual income that you earn in wages or salary from your main job?

$M = 24,443$ $SD = 10,351$

Educational Attainment

The measure of educational attainment was derived from an educational history provided by the respondent.

	%
5. BA only	4.6
6. Some education beyond BA	15.5
7. Master's Degree	26.9
8. Ph.D. or Professional degree	53.0
Missing Data	0.0
	100.0

$M = 7.28$ $SD = .89$

Occupational Prestige

Occupational prestige was based on the respondent's current occupational title. (1970 NORC Prestige Scores, Hauser and Featherman, 1977: Appendix B)

$M = 67.08$ $SD = 12.13$

Occupationally-induced Family Strain

Have any of the following requirements of your work caused disruption or strain in your family life? (Check all that apply.)

	Yes	No	Missing Data
	1	0	
	Percent Distribution		
Long hours, the need to work at night or on weekends.	59.2	40.5	.3
The need to bring work home.	22.0	77.7	.3
My preoccupation with work-related problems and demands while at home.	41.0	58.7	.3
My fatigue or irritability due to tensions or problems at work.	51.1	48.6	.3

229

Wife's Supportiveness
Is your wife generally supportive of your occupation and accepting of its demands?

Percent Distribution

	M	SD	4 Extremely Supportive	3 Usually Supportive	2 Sometimes Supportive	1 Not Supportive	Missing Data
	3.37	.68	47.0	43.8	7.9	1.1	.3

Husband's marital satisfaction. All in all, how satisfied are you with your marriage?

Percent Distribution

	M	SD	6 Very Satisfied	5 Satisfied	4 Somewhat Satisfied	3 Somewhat Dissatisfied	2 Dissatisfied	1 Very Dissatisfied	Missing Data
	5.47	.88	63.6	26.6	4.3	3.0	1.6	.3	.5

References

Abeles, Ronald P.; Steel, Lauri; and Wise, Lauress L. "Patterns and Implications of Life-Course Organization: Studies from Project TALENT." Pp. 307-37 in *Life-Span Development and Behavior*, Vol. 3, edited by Paul B. Baltes and Orville G. Brim, Jr. New York: Academic Press, 1980.

Aberle, David F., and Naegele, Kaspar D. "Middle Class Fathers' Occupational Role and Attitudes Toward Children." *American Journal of Orthopsychiatry* 22(April 1952): 366-78.

Adorno, Theodor W.; Frenkel-Brunswik, Else; Levinson, Daniel J.; and Sanford, R. Nevitt. *The Authoritarian Personality*. New York: Harper, 1950.

Agnew, Robert S. "Success and Anomie: A Study of the Effects of Goals on Anomie." *Sociological Quarterly*, 21(Winter 1980): 53-64.

Aldous, Joan. *Family Careers: Developmental Change in Families*. New York: Wiley, 1978.

Aldous, Joan; Osmond, Marie W.; and Hicks, Mary W. "Men's Work and Men's Families." Pp. 227-256 in *Contemporary Theories about the Family*, Vol. 1, *Research-Based Theories*, edited by Wesley R. Burr, Reuben Hill, F. Ivan Nye, and Ira L. Reiss. New York: Free Press, 1979.

Andrews, Frank M., and Withey, Stephen B. *Social Indicators of Well-Being: Americans' Perceptions of Life Quality*. New York: Plenum, 1976.

Andrisani, Paul J. "Internal-External Attitudes, Personal Initiative, and Labor Market Experience." Pp. 101-34 in *Work Attitudes and Labor Market Experience*, edited by Paul J. Andrisani with the assistance of Eileen Applebaum, Ross Koppel, and Robert C. Miljus. New York: Praeger, 1978.

———, and Abeles, Ronald P. "Locus of Control and Work Experience: Cohort and Race Differences." Paper presented at the American Psychological Association Meetings, 1976.

———, and Miljus, Robert C. "A Multivariate Analysis of Individual Differences in Preferences for Intrinsic versus Extrinsic Aspects of Work among National Samples of Young and Middle-Aged Male Workers." Paper presented at the American Sociological Association Meetings, 1976.

———, and Nestel, Gilbert. "Internal-External Control as Contributor to and Outcome of Work Experience." *Journal of Applied Psychology* 61 (April 1976): 156-65.

Antonovsky, Aaron. *Health, Stress, and Coping.* San Francisco: Jossey-Bass, 1979.

Astin, Alexander W., and Panos, Robert J. *The Educational and Vocational Development of College Students.* Washington, D.C.: American Council on Education, 1969.

Atkinson, John W.; Lens, Willy; and O'Malley, Patrick M. "Motivation and Ability: Interactive Psychological Determinants of Intellective Performance, Educational Achievement, and Each Other." Pp. 29-60 in *Schooling and Achievement in American Society,* edited by William H. Sewell, Robert M. Hauser, and David L. Featherman. New York: Academic Press, 1976.

Bachman, Jerald G. *Youth in Transition,* Vol. II, *The Impact of Family Background and Intelligence on Tenth-Grade Boys.* Ann Arbor: Survey Research Center, Institute for Social Research, 1970.

————, and O'Malley, Patrick M. "Self-esteem in Young Men: A Longitudinal Analysis of the Impact of Educational and Occupational Attainments." *Journal of Personality and Social Psychology* 35(June 1977): 365-80.

————; O'Malley, Patrick M.; and Johnston, Jerome. *Adolescence to Adulthood—Change and Stability in the Lives of Young Men. Youth in Transition,* Vol. VI. Ann Arbor: Survey Research Center, Institute for Social Research, 1978.

Bachrach, Stanley D., and Scoble, Harry M. "Mail Questionnaire Efficiency: Controlled Reduction of Non-Response." *Public Opinion Quarterly* 31(Summer 1967): 265-71.

Bailyn, Lotte. "Career and Family Orientations of Husbands and Wives in Relation to Marital Happiness." *Human Relations* 23 (April 1970):97-113.

Bakke, Edward Wright. *Citizens without Work.* New Haven: Yale University Press, 1940.

Baltes, Paul B., and Nesselroade, John R. "The Developmental Analysis of Individual Differences on Multiple Measures." Pp. 219-251 in *Life-Span Developmental Psychology. Methodological Issues,* edited by John R. Nesselroade and Hayne W. Reese. New York: Academic, 1973.

————, Reese, Hayne W.; and Lipsitt, Lewis P. "Life-Span Developmental Psychology." *Annual Review of Psychology,* 31(1980): 65-110.

Bandura, Albert. "Self-Efficacy: Toward a Unifying Theory of Behavioral Change." *Psychological Review* 84 (March 1977): 191-215.

Becker, Henry Jay. "The Search for a Job Early in the Career: A Research Agenda." Paper presented at the American Sociological Association Meetings, 1979.

Becker, Howard S. "Notes on the Concept of Commitment." *American Journal of Sociology* 66 (July 1960): 32-40.

————, and Carper, James. "The Elements of Identification and Occupation." *American Sociological Review* 21 (June 1956): 341-8.

————; Geer, Blanche; Hughes, Everett C.; and Strauss, Anselm. *Boys in White: Student Culture in Medical School.* Chicago: University of Chicago Press, 1961.

Bedeian, Arthur G. "The Role of Self-Esteem and N Achievement in Aspiring to Prestigious Vocations." *Journal of Vocational Behavior* 11 (August 1977): 109-19.

Belcher, David W., and Atchison, Thomas J. "Compensation for Work." Pp. 567-611 in *Handbook of Work, Organization, and Society,* edited by Robert Dubin. Chicago: Rand McNally, 1976.

Bengtson, Vern L.; Kasschau, Patricia L., and Ragan, Pauline K. "The Impact of Social Structure on Aging Individuals." Pp. 327-353 in *Handbook of the Psychology of Aging,* edited by James E. Birren and K. Warner Schaie. New York: Van Nostrand Reinhold, 1977.

Benham, Lee. "Benefits of Women's Education within Marriage." Pp. 375-89 in *Economics of the Family, Marriage, Children and Human Capital.* Chicago: University of Chicago Press, 1974.

———. "Nonmarket Returns to Women's Investment in Education." Pp. 292-309 in *Sex, Discrimination, and the Division of Labor,* edited by Cynthia B. Lloyd. New York: Columbia University Press, 1975.

Berdie, Ralph F. "Factors Associated with Vocational Interests." *Journal of Educational Psychology* 34 (May 1943): 257-77.

Bernard, Jessie. *The Future of Marriage.* New York: World, 1972.

———. *Women, Wives, and Mothers: Values and Options.* Chicago: Aldine, 1975.

Beynon, Huw, and Blackburn, Robin M. *Perceptions of Work: Variations within a Factory.* Cambridge: Cambridge University Press, 1972.

Biller, Henry B. *Paternal Deprivation: Family, School, Sexuality, and Society.* Lexington, Mass.: Heath Lexington, 1974.

———. "The Father and Personality Development: Paternal Deprivation and Sex-Role Development." Pp. 89-156 in *The Role of the Father in Child Development,* edited by Michael E. Lamb. New York: Wiley, 1976.

Blau, Peter M., and Duncan, Otis Dudley. *The American Occupational Structure.* New York: Wiley, 1967.

———; Gustad, John W.; Jessor, Richard; and Wilcox, Richard C. "Occupational Choice: A Conceptual Framework." *Industrial and Labor Relations Review* 9 (July 1956): 531-43.

Blauner, Robert. *Alienation and Freedom: The Factory Worker and His Industry.* Chicago: University of Chicago Press, 1964.

Block, Jack, and Haan, Norma. *Lives Through Time.* Berkeley: Bancroft, 1971.

Bloom, Benjamin S. *Stability and Change in Human Characteristics.* New York: Wiley, 1964.

Bowles, Samuel, and Gintis, Herbert. *Schooling in Capitalist America.* New York: Basic Books, 1976.

Brim, Orville G., Jr. "Personality Development as Role-Learning." Pp. 158-69 in *Social Processes and Social Structures,* edited by W. Richard Scott. New York: Holt, 1970.

———. "Types of Life Events." *Journal of Social Issues* 36 (1980a): 148-57.

———. "Socialization in an Unpredictable Society." Paper presented at the American Sociological Association Meetings, 1980b.

———, and Kagan, Jerome. "Constancy and Change: A View of the Issues." Pp. 1-25 in *Constancy and Change in Human Development,* edited by Orville G. Brim, Jr. and Jerome Kagan. Cambridge: Harvard University Press, 1980.

———, and Ryff, Carol D. "On the Properties of Life Events." Pp. 367-88 in

Life-span Development and Behavior, Vol. 11, edited by Paul B. Baltes and Orville G. Brim, Jr. New York: Academic Press, 1980.

Bronfenbrenner, Urie. "Socialization and Social Class through Time and Space." Pp. 400-25 in *Readings in Social Psychology,* edited by Eleanor E. Maccoby, Theodore M. Newcomb, and Eugene Hartley. New York: Holt, Rinehart, and Winston, 1958.

————, and Crouter, Ann C. "Work and Family Through Time and Space." Report prepared for the Panel on Work, Family, and Community, Committee on Child Development Research and Public Policy. National Academy of Sciences, National Research Council, 1981.

Buben, Judith. "Adolescent and Young Adult Rorschach Responses." Pp. 127-49 in *From Teenage to Young Manhood,* edited by Daniel Offer and Judith B. Offer. New York: Basic Books, 1975.

Burke, Ronald J., and Weir, Tamara. "Relationship of Wives' Employment Status to Husband, Wife, and Pair Satisfaction and Performance." *Journal of Marriage and the Family* 38 (May 1976): 279-87.

————, and Weir, Tamara. "Marital Helping Relationships: The Moderators between Stress and Well-Being." *Journal of Psychology* 95 (January 1977): 121-30.

Campbell, Angus. *The Sense of Well-Being in America: Recent Patterns and Trends.* New York: McGraw-Hill, 1981.

————; Converse, Philip E.; and Rodgers, Willard J. *The Quality of American Life: Perceptions, Evaluations, and Satisfactions.* New York: Russell Sage, 1976.

Campbell, John D. "The Child in the Sick Role: Contributions of Age, Sex, Parental Status, and Parental Values." *Journal of Health and Social Behavior* 19 (March 1978): 35-51.

Card, Josefina J.; Steel, Lauri; and Abeles, Ronald P. "Sex Differences in Realization of Individual Potential for Achievement." *Journal of Vocational Behavior* 17 (August 1980): 1-21.

Carlson, Rae. "Identification and Personality Structure in Preadolescents." *Journal of Abnormal and Social Psychology* 67 (December 1963): 566-73.

Centers, Richard. "Motivational Aspects of Occupational Stratification." *Journal of Social Psychology* 28 (November 1948): 187-217.

————, and Bugental, D. E. "Intrinsic and Extrinsic Job Motivations among Different Segments of the Working Population." *Journal of Applied Psychology* 50 (June 1966): 193-97.

Clark, Burton R., and Trow, Martin. "The Organizational Context." Pp. 17-70 in *College Peer Groups: Problems and Prospects for Research,* edited by Theodore M. Newcomb and Everett K. Wilson. Chicago: Aldine, 1966.

Clark, Robert A.; Nye, F. Ivan; and Gecas, Viktor. "Husband's Work Involvement and Marital Role Performance." *Journal of Marriage and the Family* 40 (February 1978): 9-21.

Clarridge, Brian R.; Sheehy, Linda L.; and Hauser, Taissa S. "Tracing Members of a Panel: A 17-Year Follow-Up." Pp. 185-203 in *Sociological Methodology 1977,* edited by Karl F. Schuessler. San Francisco: Jossey-Bass, 1978.

Clausen, John A. "The Life Course of Individuals." Pp. 457-514 in *Aging and*

Society, Vol. III, edited by Matilda White Riley, M. Johnson, and Anne Foner. New York: Russell Sage, 1972.

————. "Glimpses into the Social World of Middle Age." *International Journal of Aging and Human Development* 7 (1976), No. 2: 99-106.

Cobb, Sidney, and Kasl, Stanislav V. *Termination: The Consequences of Job Loss.* U.S. Department of Health, Education, and Welfare, HEW (NIOSH) Publication No. 77-224. Washington, D.C.: U.S. Government Printing Office, 1977.

Cohen, Gaynor. "Absentee Husbands in Spiralist Families." *Journal of Marriage and the Family* 39 (August 1977): 595-604.

Cohen, Jacob, and Cohen, Patricia. *Applied Multiple Regression/Correlation Analysis for the Behavioral Sciences.* Hillsdale, New Jersey: Lawrence Erlbaum, 1975.

Cohn, Richard M. "The Effect of Employment Status Change on Self-Attitudes." *Social Psychology* 41 (June 1978): 81-93.

Cooper, Cary L., and Marshall, Judi. "Sources of Managerial and White Collar Stress." Pp. 81-105 in *Stress at Work*, edited by Cary L. Cooper and Roy Payne. New York: Wiley, 1978.

Coopersmith, Stanley. *The Antecedents of Self-Esteem.* San Francisco: W. H. Freeman & Co., 1967.

Costa, Paul T., Jr., and McCrae, Robert R. "Age Differences in Personality Structure Revisited: Studies in Validity, Stability, and Change." *International Journal of Aging and Human Development* 8(1977-78): 261-75.

————, and McCrae, Robert R. "Still Stable After All These Years: Personality as a Key to Some Issues in Aging." Pp. 65-102 in *Lifespan Development and Behavior*, Vol. 3, edited by Paul Baltes and Orville G. Brim. New York: Academic, 1980a.

————, and McCrae, Robert R. "Influence of Extraversion and Neuroticism on Subjective Well-Being: Happy and Unhappy People." *Journal of Personality and Social Psychology* 38(April 1980b): 66-78.

————; McCrae, Robert R.; and Arenberg, David. "Enduring Dispositions in Adult Males." *Journal of Personality and Social Psychology* 38 (May 1980): 793-800.

Cottrell, Leonard S. "Interpersonal Interaction and the Development of the Self." Pp. 543-70 in *Handbook of Socialization Theory and Research*, edited by David A. Goslin. Chicago: Rand McNally, 1969.

Cox, Rachel D. *Youth into Maturity.* New York: Mental Health Materials Center, 1970.

Crandall, Virginia C. "The Fels Study: Some Contributions to Personality Development and Achievement in Childhood and Adulthood." *Seminars in Psychiatry* 4 (November, 1972): 383-98.

Crider, Donald M.; Willits, Fern K.; and Bealer, Robert C. "Tracking Respondents in Longitudinal Surveys" *Public Opinion Quarterly* 35 (Winter 1971/1972): 613-20.

Crites, John O. "Parental Identification in Relation to Vocational Interest Development." *Journal of Educational Psychology* 53 (December 1962): 262-70.

Crockett, Harry J., Jr. "The Achievement Motive and Differential Occupational Mobility in the U.S." *American Sociological Review* 27 (April 1962): 191-204.

Dannefer, Dale. "Adult Development and Social Theory." *American Sociological Review* 49 (February, 1984): 100-116.

Davidson, Terrence N. *Youth in Transition, Vol. IV, Evolution of a Strategy for Longitudinal Analysis of Survey Panel Data.* Ann Arbor: Institute for Social Research, University of Michigan, 1972.

Davis, James A. *Great Aspirations: The Graduate School Plans of America's College Seniors.* Chicago: Aldine, 1964.

———. *Undergraduate Career Decisions: Correlates of Occupational Choice.* Chicago: Aldine, 1965.

Della Fave, Richard. "Success Values: Are They Universal or Class-Differentiated?" *American Journal of Sociology* 80 (July 1974): 153-69.

———, and Klobus, Patricia. "Success Values and the Value Stretch: A Biracial Comparison." *Sociological Quarterly* 17 (Autumn 1976): 491-502.

Deutscher, Irwin. "Physicians' Reactions to a Mailed Questionnaire: A Study in 'Resistentialism.' " *Public Opinion Quarterly* 20 (Fall 1956): 599-604.

Dillman, Don A.; Christenson, James A.; Carpenter, Edwin H.; and Brooks, Ralph M. "Increasing Mail Questionnaire Response: A Four State Comparison." *American Sociological Review* 39 (October 1974): 744-56.

Dizard, Jan. *Social Change in the Family.* Chicago: Community and Family Center, University of Chicago, 1968.

Douvan, Elizabeth, and Adelson, Joseph. *The Adolescent Experience.* New York: Wiley, 1966.

Douglas, William. *Ministers' Wives.* New York: Harper and Row, 1965.

Douglass, Gordon K. "Economic Returns on Investments in Higher Education." Pp. 359-87 in *Investment in Learning. The Individual and Social Value of American Higher Education,* edited by Howard R. Bowen. San Francisco: Jossey-Bass, 1977.

Dubin, Robert. "Industrial Workers' Worlds: A Study of the Central Life Interests of Industrial Workers." *Social Problems* 3 (January 1956): 131-42.

——— and Champoux, Joseph E. "Workers' Central Life Interests and Job Performance." *Sociology of Work and Occupations* 1 (August 1974): 313-26.

———; Hedley, R. Alan; and Taveggia, Thomas C. "Attachment to Work." Pp. 281-341 in *Handbook of Work, Organization, and Society,* edited by Robert Dubin. Chicago: Rand McNalley, 1976.

———, and Porter, Lyman W. "Central Life Interests and Organizational Commitment of Blue-Collar and Clerical Workers." *Administrative Science Quarterly* 20 (September, 1975): 411-421.

Duncan, Greg J., and Morgan, James N. *Five Thousand American Families: Patterns of Economic Progress.* Ann Arbor: Institute for Social Research, University of Michigan, 1975.

Duncan, Otis Dudley; Featherman, David L.; and Duncan, Beverly. *Socioeconomic Background and Achievement.* New York: Seminar Press, 1972.

Durkheim, Emile. *Suicide.* New York: Free Press, 1951.

———. *The Division of Labor in Society.* Translated by George Simpson. New York: Free Press, 1964. First published, 1893.

Eckland, Bruce K. "Effects of Prodding to Increase Mail-Back Returns." *Journal of Applied Psychology* 49 (June 1965): 165-69.

———. "Retrieving Mobile Cases in Longitudinal Surveys." *Public Opinion Quarterly* 32 (Spring 1968): 51-64.

Elder, Glen H., Jr. "Structural Variations in the Child-Rearing Relationship." *Sociometry* 25 (September 1962): 241-62.

———. "Parental Power Legitimation and its Effects on the Adolescent." *Sociometry* 26 (1963): 50-65.

———. *Adolescent Socialization and Personality Development.* Chicago: Rand McNally, 1968.

———. "Occupational Mobility, Life Patterns, and Personality." *Journal of Health and Social Behavior* 10 (December 1969): 308-23.

———. *Children of the Great Depression.* Chicago: University of Chicago Press, 1974.

———. "Approaches to Social Change and the Family." *American Journal of Sociology* 84 (supplement, 1978): S1-S38.

———, and Rockwell, Richard C. "Marital Timing in Women's Life Patterns." *Journal of Family History* 1 (Autumn 1976): 34-53.

———, and Rockwell, Richard C. "The Life Course and Human Development: An Ecological Perspective." International Journal of Behavioral Development 2 (1979a): 1-21.

———, and Rockwell, Richard C. "Economic Depression and Postwar Opportunity in Men's Lives: A Study of Life Patterns and Health." Pp. 249-303 in *Research in Community and Mental Health,* Vol. 1, edited by Roberta G. Simmons. Greenwich, Conn.: JAI Press, 1979b.

Epstein, Cynthia F. "Law Partners and Marital Partners." *Human Relations* 24 (December 1971): 549-64.

Epstein, Seymour. "The Self-Concept Revisited: Or a Theory of a Theory." *American Psychologist* 28 (May 1973): 404-16.

Erikson, Erik H. "The Problem of Ego Identity." *Psychological Issues,* 1 (1959): 101-164.

———. *Identity, Youth, and Crisis.* New York: W. W. Norton, 1968.

Faunce, William A., and Dubin, Robert. "Individual Investment in Working and Living." Pp. 299-316 in *The Quality of Working Life, Vol. I., Problems, Prospects, and the State of the Art,* edited by Louis E. Davis and Albert B. Cherns. New York: Free Press, 1975.

Featherman, David L. "The Socioeconomic Achievement of White Religio-Ethnic Subgroups: Social and Psychological Explanations." *American Sociological Review* 36 (April 1971): 207-22.

———. "Schooling and Occupational Careers: Constancy and Change in Worldly Success." Pp. 675-738 in *Constancy and Change in Human Development,* edited by Orville G. Brim, Jr. and Jerome Kagan. Cambridge: Harvard University Press, 1980.

Feldberg, Roslyn, and Glenn, Evelyn. "Male and Female: Job vs. Gender Models in the Sociology of Work." *Social Problems,* 26 (June 1979): 524-538.

Feldman, Kenneth A., and Newcomb, Theodore M. *The Impact of College on Students, Vol. 1, An Analysis of Four Decades of Research.* San Francisco: Jossey-Bass, 1969.

———, and Weiler, John. "Changes in Initial Differences among Major-Field

Groups: An Exploration of the 'Accentuation Effect.' " Pp. 373-407 in *Schooling and Achievement in American Society*, edited by William M. Sewell, Robert M. Hauser, and David L. Featherman. New York: Academic Press, 1976.

Finlayson, Elizabeth M. "A Study of the Wife of the Army Officer: Her Academic and Career Preparations, Her Current Employment and Volunteer Services." Pp. 19-41 in *Families in the Military System*, edited by Hamilton I. McCubbin, Barbara B. Dahl, and Edna G. Hunter. Beverly Hills: Sage, 1976.

Fischer, Anita Kassen; Marton, James; Millman, E. Joel; and Srole, Leo. "Long-Range Influences on Adult Mental Health: The Midtown Manhattan Longitudinal Study, 1954-1974." Pp. 305-33 in *Research in Community and Mental Health*, Vol. 1, edited by Roberta G. Simmons. Greenwich, Conn.: JAI Press, 1979.

Flanagan, Robert J.; Strauss, George; and Ulman, Lloyd. "Worker Discontent and Workplace Behavior." *Industrial Relations* 13 (May 1974): 101-23.

Fowlkes, Martha R. *Behind Every Successful Man: Wives of Medicine and Academe.* New York: Columbia University Press, 1980.

Franks, David D., and Marolla, Joseph. "Efficacious Action and Social Approval as Interacting Dimensions of Self-Esteem: A Tentative Formulation through Construct Validation." *Sociometry* 39 (December 1976): 324-41.

French, John R. P., Jr. "The Conceptualization and Measurement of Mental Health in Terms of Self-Identity Theory." Pp. 135-59 in *The Definition and Measurement of Mental Health*, edited by S. B. Sells. Washington, D.C.: Department of Health, Education, and Welfare, 1968.

———, and Caplan, Robert D. "Organizational Stress and Individual Strain." Pp. 30-66 in *The Failure of Success*, edited by Alfred J. Marrow. New York: Amacom, 1972.

Furstenberg, Frank F., Jr. "The Transmission of Mobility Orientation in the Family." *Social Forces* 49 (June 1971): 595-603.

Gecas, Viktor. "Parental Behavior and Dimensions of Adolescent Self-Evaluation." *Sociometry* 34 (December 1971): 466-82.

———. "The Influence of Social Class on Socialization." Pp. 365-404 in *Contemporary Theories about the Family*, Vol. 1, Research-Based Theories, edited by Wesley R. Burr, Reuben Hill, F. Ivan Nye, and Ira L. Reiss. New York: Free Press, 1979.

———. "Contexts of Socialization." Pp. 165-99 in *Social Psychology: Sociological Perspectives*, edited by Morris Rosenberg and Ralph H. Turner. New York: Basic Books, 1981.

——— and Mortimer, Jeylan T. "Stability and Change in the Self-Concept from Adolescence to Adulthood." In *Self and Identity: Individual Change and Development*, edited by Terry M. Honess and Krysia M. Yardley. London: Routledge and Kegan Paul, Forthcoming.

———, and Nye, F. Ivan. "Sex and Class Differences in Parent-Child Interaction: A Test of Kohn's Hypothesis." *Journal of Marriage and the Family* 36 (November 1974): 742-49.

Gergen, Kenneth J. "Stability, Change, and Chance in Understanding Human Development." Pp. 135-58 in *Life-Span Developmental Psychology: Dialectical Perspectives on Experimental Research,* edited by Nancy Datan and Hayne W. Reese. New York: Academic, 1977.

Ghez, Gilbert, and Becker, Gary S. *The Allocation of Time and Goods over the Life Cycle.* New York: National Bureau of Economic Research, 1975.

Girod, Robert; Fricher, Yves; and Korffy, Andras. "Counter-Mobility." Pp. 17-27 in *Social Stratification and Career Mobility,* edited by Walter Muller and Karl Ulrich. Paris: Mouton, 1973.

Glenn, Norval D. "Values, Attitudes, and Beliefs." Pp. 596-640 in *Constancy and Change in Human Development,* edited by Orville G. Brim, Jr. and Jerome Kagen. Cambridge: Harvard University Press, 1980.

———, and Weaver, Charles N. "A Multivariate, Multisurvey Study of Marital Happiness." *Journal of Marriage and the Family* 40 (May 1978): 269-82.

Golden, Jules; Mandel, Nathan; Glueck, Bernard C., Jr.; and Feder, Zetta F. "A Summary Description of Fifty 'Normal' White Males." *American Journal of Psychiatry* 119 (July 1962): 48-56.

Goldman, Daniel R. "Managerial Mobility Motivations and Central Life Interests." *American Sociological Review* 38 (February 1973): 119-26.

Goldman, Nancy. "Women in the Armed Forces." *American Journal of Sociology* 78 (January 1973): 892-911.

Goodwin, Leonard. *The Work Incentive (WIN) Program and Related Experiences.* Washington, D.C.: U.S. Government Printing Office, 1977.

Gordon, Chad. *Looking Ahead: Self-Conceptions, Race and Family as Determinants of Adolescent Orientation to Achievement.* Rose Monograph Series. Washington, D.C.: American Sociological Association, 1972.

Granovetter, Mark S. *Getting a Job.* Cambridge, Mass.: Harvard University Press, 1974.

Greiff, Barrie S., and Munter, Preston K. *Tradeoffs: Executive, Family and Organizational Life.* New York: New American Library, 1980.

Grinker, Roy R., Sr.; Grinker, Roy R., Jr.; and Timberlake, John. "Mentally Healthy Young Males (Homoclites)." *Archives of General Psychiatry* 6 (June 1962): 405-53.

Gronseth, Erick. "The Breadwinner Trap." Pp. 175-91 in *The Future of the Family,* edited by Louise Kapp Howe. New York: Simon and Schuster, 1972.

Gullahorn, Jeanne E., and Gullahorn, John T. "An Investigation of the Effects of Three Factors on Response to Mail Questionnaires." *Public Opinion Quarterly* 27 (Summer 1963): 294-96.

Gurin, Gerald. *A Study of Students in a Multiversity.* Ann Arbor, Michigan: Survey Research Center, Institute for Social Research, 1971.

———, and Gurin, Patricia. "Personal Efficacy and the Ideology of Individual Responsibility." Pp. 131-57 in *Economic Means for Human Needs,* edited by Burkhard Strumpel. Ann Arbor, Michigan: Survey Research Center, Institute for Social Research, 1976.

———; Veroff, Joseph; and Feld, Sheila. *Americans View Their Mental Health.* New York: Basic Books, 1960.

Haan, Norma, and Day, David. "A Longitudinal Study of Change and Sameness in Personality Development: Adolescence to Later Adulthood." *International Journal of Aging and Human Development* 5 (Winter, 1974): 11-39.

Hall, Douglas, T. "A Theoretical Model of Career Subidentity Development in Organizational Settings." *Organizational Behavior and Human Performance* 6 (January 1971): 50-76.

————, and Nougaim, Khalil E. "An Examination of Maslow's Need Hierarchy in an Organizational Setting." *Organizational Behavior and Human Performance* 3 (February 1968): 12-35.

Handy, Charles. "The Family: Help or Hindrance?" Pp. 107-23 in *Stress at Work*, edited by Cary L. Cooper and Roy Payne. New York: Wiley, 1978.

Hanushek, Eric A., and Jackson, John E. *Statistical Methods for Social Scientists.* New York: Academic Press, 1977.

Hauser, Robert Mason. *Socioeconomic Background and Educational Performance.* Washington, D.C.: ASA Rose Monograph Series, 1971.

————, and Featherman, David L. *The Process of Stratification: Trends and Analyses.* New York: Academic Press, 1977.

Havens, Elizabeth M. "Women, Work and Wedlock: A Note on Female Marital Patterns in the United States." *American Journal of Sociology* 78 (January 1973): 975-81.

Heath, Douglas H. *Growing up in College.* San Francisco: Jossey-Bass, 1968.

Heaton, Eugene E. "Increasing Mail Questionnaire Returns with a Preliminary Letter." *Journal of Advertising Research* 5 (Decemer 1965): 36-39.

Heilbrun, Alfred B., Jr. "Parental Identification and the Patterning of Vocational Interests in College Males and Females." *Journal of Counseling Psychology* 16 (July 1969): 342-47.

Heise, David R. "Causal Inference from Panel Data." Pp. 3-27 in *Sociological Methodology 1970*, edited by Edgar F. Borgatta and George W. Bohrnstedt. San Francisco: Jossey-Bass, 1970.

Helfrich, Margaret L. *The Social Role of the Executive's Wife.* Columbus, Ohio: Ohio State University, Bureau of Business Research, 1965.

Herzberg, Frederick. *Work and the Nature of Man.* New York: World, 1966.

————; Mausner, Bernard; and Snyderman, Barbara B. *The Motivation of Work* (2nd edition). New York: Wiley, 1959.

Hicks, Mary W., and Platt, Marilyn. "Marital Happiness and Stability: A Review of the Research in the Sixties." *Journal of Marriage and the Family* 32 (November 1970): 553-74.

Hill, Reuben, and Mattessich, Paul. "Family Development Theory and Life-Span Development." Pp. 161-204 in *Life Span Development and Behavior,* Vol. 2 edited by Paul B. Baltes and Orville G. Brim, Jr. New York: Academic Press, 1979.

Hochschild, Arlie R. "The Role of the Ambassador's Wife: An Exploratory Study." *Journal of Marriage and the Family* 31 (February 1969): 73-87.

————. "Inside the Clockwork of Male Careers." Pp. 47-79 in *Women and the Power to Change,* edited by Florence Howe. New York: McGraw-Hill, 1975.

Hochstim, Joseph R., and Athanosopoulos, Demetrios A. "Personal Follow-up in a Mail Survey: Its Contribution and its Cost. *Public Opinion Quarterly* 34 (Spring 1970): 69-81.

Hoffman, Lois Wladis, and Nye, Ivan F. *Working Mothers*. San Francisco: Jossey-Bass, 1974.

Hogan, Dennis P. "The Transition to Adulthood As a Career Contingency." *American Sociological Review* 45 (April 1980): 261-76.

Holland, John L. "Vocational Preferences." Pp. 521-70 in *Handbook of Industrial and Organizational Psychology*, edited by Marvin D. Dunnette. Chicago: Rand McNally, 1976.

Holmstrom, Lynda Lytle. *The Two-Career Family*. Cambridge, Mass.: Schenkman, 1973.

House, James S. *Occupational Stress and the Mental and Physical Health of Factory Workers*. Ann Arbor: Survey Research Center, Institute for Social Research, University of Michigan, 1980.

———. "Social Structure and Personality." Pp. 525-61 in *Social Psychology: Sociological Perspectives*, edited by Morris Rosenberg and Ralph H. Turner. New York: Basic Books, 1981.

Howard, Judith A. "Person-Situation Interaction Models." *Personality and Social Psychology Bulletin* 5 (April 1979): 191-95.

Hughes, Everett C. *Men and Their Work*. Glencoe, Ill.: Free Press, 1958.

Hunt, Jane V., and Eichorn, Dorothy H. "Maternal and Child Behaviors: A Review of Data from the Berkeley Growth Study." *Seminars in Psychiatry* 4 (November 1972): 367-81.

Hunt, Janet G., and Hunt, Larry L. "Dilemmas and Contradictions of Status: The Case of the Dual-Career Family." *Social Problems* 24 (April 1977): 407-16.

Inkeles, Alex, and Smith D. *Becoming Modern: Individual Change in Six Developing Countries*. Cambridge, Mass.: Harvard University Press, 1974.

International Educational Services. *Analysis of Linear Structural Relationships by the Method of Maximum Likelihood*. Chicago: National Educational Resources, 1972.

Jacques, Jeffrey M., and Chason, Karen J. "Self-Esteem and Low Status Groups: A Changing Scene?" *Sociological Quarterly* 18 (Summer 1977): 399-412.

Jennings, M. Kent, and Niemi, Richard G. "The Persistence of Political Orientations: An Over-Time Analysis of Two Generations." *British Journal of Political Science*, 8 (July 1978): 333-63.

Jones, Mary C.; Bayley, Nancy; Macfarlane, Jean W.; and Honzik, Marjorie P. *The Course of Human Development*. Waltham, Mass.: Xerox, 1971.

Jones, Russell A. *Self-Fulfilling Prophecies: Social, Psychological, and Physiological Effects of Expectancies*. Hillsdale, N.J.: Erlbaum, 1977.

Jordaan, Jean Pierre, and Super, Donald E. "The Prediction of Early Adult Vocational Behavior." Pp. 108-30 in *Life History Research in Psychopathology* Vol. 3, edited by David F. Ricks, Alexander Thomas, and Merrill Roff. Minneapolis: University of Minnesota Press, 1974.

Joreskog, Karl G. "A General Method for Estimating a Linear Structural Equation System." Pp. 85-112 in *Structural Equation Models in the Social Sciences*, edited by Arthur S. Goldberger and Otis Dudley Duncan. New York: Seminar Press, 1973.

———, and Sorbom, Dag. "Statistical Models and Methods for Analysis of Longitudinal Data." Pp. 285-325 in *Latent Variables in Socio-economic Models*, edited by Dennis J. Aigner and Arthur S. Goldberger. Amsterdam: North-Holland Publishing Co., 1977.

————, and Sorbom, Dag. *Advances in Factor Analysis and Structural Equation Models*. Cambridge, Mass.:, Abt Associates, 1979.

————, and Van Thillo, Marielle. *LISREL: A General Computer Program for Estimating a Linear Structural Equation System Involving Multiple Indicators of Unmeasured Variables*. Research Bulletin 72-56. Princeton, N.J.: Educational Testing Service, 1972.

Kagan, Jerome. "Perspectives on Continuity." Pp. 26-74 in *Constancy and Change in Human Development*, edited by Orville G. Brim, Jr. and Jerome Kagan. Cambridge: Harvard University Press, 1980.

————, and Moss, Howard A. *Birth to Maturity*. New York: Wiley, 1962.

Kahn, E. M. *Sociometric Variables, Parental Identification, and Sons' Interests*. Ph.D. Dissertation. Columbia University, 1968.

Kahn, Robert L. "The Meaning of Work: Interpretation and Proposal for Measurement." Pp. 159-204 in *The Human Meaning of Social Change*, edited by Angus Campbell and Philip Converse. New York: Russell Sage, 1972.

————, and Antonucci, Toni C. "Convoys over the Life Course: Attachment, Roles, and Social Support." Pp. 253-86 in *Life-Span Development and Behavior*, Vol. 3, edited by Paul B. Baltes and Orville G. Brim, Jr. New York: Academic, 1980.

————, and Antonucci, Toni C. "Convoys of Social Support: A Life-Course Approach." Pp. 383-405 in *Aging: Social Change*, edited by Sara B. Kiesler, James N. Morgan, and Valerie Kincade Oppenheimer. New York: Academic Press, 1981.

Kalleberg, Arne L. "Work Values and Job Rewards: A Theory of Job Satisfaction." *American Sociological Review* 42 (February 1977): 124-43.

Kanter, Rosabeth M. *Work and Family in the United States: A Critical Review and Agenda for Research and Policy*. New York: Russell Sage, 1977a.

————. *Men and Women of the Corporation*. New York: Basic Books, 1977b.

Kasl, Stanislav V.; Gore, Susan; and Cobb, Sidney. "The Experience of Losing a Job: Reported Changes in Health, Symptoms and Illness Behavior." *Psychosomatic Medicine* 37 (March-April 1975): 106-21.

Katz, Joseph. "Four Years of Growth, Conflict and Compliance." Pp. 3-73 in *No Time for Youth*, edited by Joseph Katz, Harold A. Korn, Viny Ellis, Peter Madison, Susan Singer, Marjorie M. Lozoff, Max M. Levin, and Nevitt Sanford. San Francisco: Jossey-Bass, 1968.

Kelley, Jonathan. "Causal Chain Models for the Socioeconomic Career." *American Sociological Review* 38 (August 1973): 481-93.

Kelly, E. Lowell. "Consistency of the Adult Personality." *American Psychologist* 10 (November 1955): 659-81.

Kephart, William M., and Bressler, Marvin. "Increasing the Responses to Mail Questionnaires: A Research Study." *Public Opinion Quarterly* 22 (Summer 1958): 123-32.

Kerckhoff, Alan C. *Socialization and Social Class*. Englewood Cliffs, N.J.: Prentice Hall, 1972.

————. *Ambition and Attainment. A Study of Four Samples of American Boys.* Washington, D.C.: ASA Rose Monograph Series, 1974.

Kilpatrick, Franklin; Cummings, Milton C.; and Jennings, M. Kent. *The Image of the Federal Service.* Washington, D.C.: Brookings Institution, 1964.

King, Stanley H. *Five Lives at Harvard: Personality Change During College.* Cambridge: Harvard University Press, 1973.

Kohn, Melvin L. *Class and Conformity: A Study in Values.* Homewood, Ill.: Dorsey, 1969.

————. "Bureaucratic Man: A Portrait and an Interpretation." *American Sociological Review* 36 (June 1971): 461-74.

————. "Looking Back—a 25-Year Review and Appraisal of Social Problems Research." *Social Problems* 24 (October, 1976): 94-112.

————. *Class and Conformity: A Study in Values.* 2nd edition. Chicago: University of Chicago Press, 1977.

————. "Job Complexity and Adult Personality." Pp. 193-210 in *Themes of Love and Work in Adulthood,* edited by Neil J. Smelser and Erik H. Erikson. Cambridge, Massachusetts: Harvard University Press, 1980.

————. "Personality, Occupation, and Social Stratification: A Frame of Reference." Pp. 267-97 in *Research in Social Stratification and Mobility,* Vol. 1, edited by Donald J. Treiman and Robert V. Robinson. Greenwich, Conn.: JAI Pres, 1981.

————, and Carroll, Eleanor E. "Social Class and the Allocation of Parental Responsibilities." *Sociometry* 23 (1960): 372-92.

————, and Schooler, Carmi. "Class, Occupation, and Orientation." *American Sociological Review* 34 (October, 1969): 659-678.

————, and Schooler, Carmi. "Occupational Experience and Psychological Functioning: An Assessment of Reciprocal Effects." *American Sociological Review* 38 (February 1973): 97-118.

————, and Schooler, Carmi. "Follow-up Survey on Occupational Conditions and Psychological Functioning." National Institute of Mental Health, 1974.

————, and Schooler, Carmi. "The Reciprocal Effects of the Substantive Complexity of Work and Intellectual Flexibility: A Longitudinal Assessment." *American Journal of Sociology* 84 (July 1978): 24-52.

————, and Schooler, Carmi. "Job Conditions and Intellectual Flexibility: A Longitudinal Assessment of their Reciprocal Effects." Pp. 281-313 in *Factor Analysis and Measurement in Sociological Research: A Multi-Dimensional Perspective,* edited by David J. Jackson and Edgar F. Borgatta. Beverly Hills: Sage, 1981.

————, and Schooler, Carmi. "Job Conditions and Personality: A Longitudinal Assessment of their Reciprocal Effects." *American Journal of Sociology* 87 (May 1982): 1257-86.

————, and Schooler, Carmi, with the collaboration of Joanne Miller, Karen A. Miller, Carrie Schoenbach, and Ronald Schoenberg. *Work and Personality: An Inquiry into the Impact of Social Stratification.* Norwood, New Jersey: Ablex Publishing Corporation, 1983.

Kolb, David A., and Plovnick, Mark S. "The Experimental Learning Theory of

Career Development." Pp. 65-87 in *Organizational Careers: Some New Perspectives,* edited by John Van Maanen. New York: Wiley, 1977.

Komarovsky, Mirra. *Dilemmas of Masculinity.* New York: W. W. Norton & Co., 1976.

Korman, Abraham K. "Toward an Hypothesis of Work Behavior." *Journal of Applied Psychology* 54 (February 1970): 31-41.

Korn, Harold A. "Careers: Choice, Chance, or Inertia?" Pp. 207-38 in *No Time for Youth,* edited by Joseph Katz, Harold A. Korn, Viny Ellis, Peter Madison, Susan Singer, Marjorie M. Lozoff, Max M. Levin, and Nevitt Sanford. San Francisco: Jossey-Bass, 1968.

Kornhauser, Arthur. *Mental Health of the Industrial Worker: A Detroit Study.* New York: John Wiley and Sons, 1965.

Kuhlen, Raymond G. "Personality Change with Age." Pp. 524-55 in *Personality Change,* edited by Philip Worchel and Donn Byrne. New York: Wiley, 1964.

Lawler, Edward E., III. *Motivation in Work Organizations.* Monterey, Calif.: Brooks/Cole, 1973.

———, and Hall, Douglas. "Relationship of Job Characteristics to Job Involvement, Satisfaction, and Intrinsic Motivation." *Journal of Applied Psychology* 54 (August 1970): 305-12.

Lecky, Prescott. *Self-Consistency: A Theory of Personality.* New York: Island, 1945.

Leon, Gloria R.; Gillum, Brenda; Gillum, Richard; and Gouze, Marshall. "Personality Stability and Change over a 30-Year Period—Middle Age to Old Age." *Journal of Consulting and Clinical Psychology* 47 (June 1979): 517-24.

Levine, Sol, and Gordon, Gerald. "Maximizing Returns on Mail Questionnaires." *Public Opinion Quarterly* 22 (Winter 1959): 568-75.

Lidz, Theodore. *The Person.* New York: Basic Books, 1968.

Linsky, Arnold S. "A Factorial Experiment in Inducing Responses to a Mail Questionnaire." *Social Research* 49 (January 1965): 183-9.

Lipman-Blumen, Jean, and Tickamyer, Ann R. "Sex Roles in Transition: A Ten-Year Perspective." *Annual Review of Sociology* 1 (1975): 297-337.

Littig, Lawrence W., and Yeracaris, Constantine A. "Achievement Motivation and Intergenerational Occupational Mobility." *Journal of Personality and Social Psychology* 1 (April 1965): 386-9.

Locke, Edwin A. "Nature and Causes of Job Satisfaction." Pp. 1297-1349 in *Handbook of Industrial and Organizational Psychology,* edited by Marvin D. Dunnette. Chicago: Rand McNally, 1976.

Lodahl, Thomas M., and Kejner, Mathilde. "The Definition and Measurement of Job Involvement." *Journal of Applied Psychology* 49 (February 1965): 24-33.

Lofquist, Floyd H., and Dawis, Rene V. *Adjustment to Work.* New York: Meredith, 1969.

Long, J. Scott. "Estimation and Hypothesis Testing in Linear Models Containing Measurement Error." *Sociological Methods and Research* 2 (November 1976): 157-206.

Looft, William R. "Socialization and Personality throughout the Life Span: An Examination of Contemporary Psychological Approaches." Pp. 25-52 in

Life-Span Developmental Psychology. Personality and Socialization, edited by Paul B. Baltes and K. Warner Schaie. New York: Academic, 1973.

Lopata, Helena Z. "The Life Cycle of the Social Role of Housewife." *Sociology and Social Research* 51 (October 1966): 2-22.

———. *Occupation: Housewife.* London: Oxford University Press, 1971.

Lorence, Jon, and Mortimer, Jeylan T. "Work Experience and Political Orientation: A Panel Study." *Social Forces* 58 (December 1979): 651-676.

———, and Mortimer, Jeylan T. "Work Experience and Work Involvement." *Sociology of Work and Occupations* 8 (August 1981): 297-326.

———, and Mortimer, Jeylan T. "Job Involvement through the Life Course: A Panel Study of Three Age Groups." *American Sociological Review,* in press.

Luborsky, Lester, and Schimek, Jean. "Psychoanalytic Theories of Therapeutic and Developmental Change: Implications for Assessment." Pp. 73-99 in *Personality Change,* edited by Philip Worchel and Donn Byrne. New York: Wiley, 1964.

Luck, Patrick W., and Heiss, Jerold. "Social Determinants of Self-Esteem in Adult Males." *Sociology and Social Research* 57 (October, 1972): 69-84.

Lueptow, Floyd B. "Parental Status and Influence and the Achievement Orientations of High School Seniors." *Sociology of Education* 48 (Winter 1975): 91-110.

———; McKee, J. McClendon; and McKeon, John W. "Father's Occupation and Son's Personality: Findings and Questions for the Emerging Linkage Hypothesis." *Sociological Quarterly* 20 (Autumn 1979): 463-75.

Maas, Henry S., and Kuypers, Joseph A. *From Thirty to Seventy: A Forty-Year Study of Adult Life Styles and Personality.* San Francisco: Jossey-Bass, 1974.

Maccoby, Michael. *The Gamesman: The New Corporate Leaders.* New York: Simon and Schuster, 1976.

Machlowitz, Marilyn. *Workaholics: Living with Them, Working with Them.* New York: Mentor, 1980.

MacPherson, Myra. *The Power Lovers: An Intimate Look at Politicians and their Marriages.* New York: Putnam, 1975.

Mannheim, Bilha. "A Comparative Study of Work Centrality, Job Rewards and Satisfaction: Occupational Groups in Israel." *Sociology of Work and Occupations* 2 (February 1975): 79-102.

Marx, Karl. *Karl Marx. Selected Writings in Sociology and Social Philosophy.* Translated by Tom B. Bottomore. New York: McGraw-Hill, 1964.

Maslow, Abraham. *Motivation and Personality.* New York: Harper & Row, 1954.

Mayer, Charles S., and Pratt, Robert W., Jr. "A Note on Nonresponse in a Mail Survey." *Public Opinion Quarterly,* 30 (Winter 1966): 637-46.

McAllister, Ronald J.; Butler, Edgar W.; and Goe, Steven. "Evolution of a Strategy for the Retrieval of Cases in Longitudinal Survey Research." *Sociology and Social Research,* 58 (October 1973a): 37-47.

———; Goe, Steven; and Butler, Edgar W. "Tracking Respondents in Longitudinal Surveys: Some Preliminary Considerations." *Public Opinion Quarterly* 37 (Fall 1973b): 413-16.

McClelland, David C. "N Achievement and Entrepreneurship: A Longitudinal Study." *Journal of Personality and Social Psychology* 1 (April 1965): 389-92.

McKinley, Donald G. *Social Class and Family Life.* New York: Free Press, 1964.

McMichael, Anthony J. "Personality, Behavioral, and Situational Modifiers of Work Stressors." Pp. 127-48 in *Stress at Work,* edited by Cary J. Cooper and Roy Payne. New York: Wiley, 1978.

Mead, Margaret. *Coming of Age in Samoa.* New York: Morrow, 1928.

———. *Sex and Temperament in Three Primitive Societies.* New York: Morrow, 1935.

Miller, David R., and Swanson, Guy. *The Changing American Parent.* New York: Wiley, 1958.

Miller, Joanne. "Individual and Occupational Determinants of Job Satisfaction: A Focus on Gender Differences." *Sociology of Work and Occupations* 7 (August 1980): 337-66.

———; Schooler, Carmi; Kohn, Melvin L.; and Miller, Karen. "Women and Work: The Psychological Effects of Occupational Conditions." *American Journal of Sociology* 85 (July 1979): 66-94.

Miller, Karen A.; Kohn, Melvin L.; and Schooler, Carmi. "Educational Self-Direction and Psychological Functioning." Paper presented at the American Sociological Association Meetings, 1982.

Mischel, Walter. "Toward a Cognitive Social Learning Reconceptualization of Personality." *Psychological Review* 80 (July 1973): 252-83.

———. "On the Future of Personality Measurement." *American Psychologist* 32 (April, 1977): 246-54.

Moen, Phyllis. "The Two-Provider Family: Problems and Potentials." Pp. 13-43 in *Nontraditional Families: Parenting and Child Development,* edited by Michael E. Lamb. Hillsdale, NJ: Erlbaum, 1982a.

———. "Continuities and Discontinuities in Women's Labor Force Activity." Pp. 113-155 in *Life Course Dynamics: Trajectories and Transitions, 1968-1980,* edited by Glen H. Elder, Jr. Ithaca: Cornell University Press, 1985.

Moore, Wilbert E. "Occupational Socialization." Pp. 861-83 in *Handbook of Socialization Theory and Research,* edited by David A. Goslin. Chicago: Rand McNally, 1969.

Morgan, William R., Alwin, Duane F., and Griffin, Larry J. "Social Origins, Parental Values, and the Transmission of Inequality." *American Journal of Sociology* 85 (July 1979): 156-66.

Morrison, Robert F. "Career Adaptivity: The Effective Adaptation of Managers to Changing Role Demands." *Journal of Applied Psychology* 62 (October 1977): 549-58.

Mortimer, Jeylan T. *Family Background and College Influences upon Occupational Value Orientations and the Career Decision.* Unpublished doctoral dissertation. University of Michigan. Ann Arbor, 1972.

———. "Patterns of Intergenerational Occupational Movements: a Smallest-Space Analysis." *American Journal of Sociology* 79 (March 1974): 1278-99.

———. "Occupational Value Socialization in Business and Professional Families." *Sociology of Work and Occupations* (February 1975): 29-53.

———. "Social Class, Work, and the Family: Some Implications of the Father's Occupation for Familial Relationships and Sons' Career Decisions." *Journal of Marriage and the Family* 38 (May 1976): 241-56.

———. "Dual Career Families: A Sociological Perspective." Pp. 1-30 in *The Two-*

Career Family—Issues and Alternatives, edited by Samiha S. Petersen, Judy M. Richardson, and Gretchen V. Kreuter. Washington, D.C.: University Press of America, 1978.

————. *Changing Attitudes toward Work. Work in America Institute Studies in Productivity,* Vol. 11. Scarsdale, New York: Work in America Institute, 1979.

————. "Occupation-Family Linkages as Perceived by Men in the Early Stages of Professional and Managerial Careers." Pp. 99-117 in *Research in the Interweave of Social Roles,* edited by Helena Z. Lopata. Greenwich, CT: JAI Press, 1980.

————, and Finch, Michael D. "The Development of Self-Esteem in the Early Work Career." *Work and Occupations,* In press.

————; Finch, Michael D.; and Kumka, Donald. "Persistence and Change in Development: The Multidimensional Self-Concept." Pp. 263-313 in *Life-Span Development and Behavior,* Vol. 4, edited by Paul D. Baltes and Orville G. Brim, Jr. New York: Academic Press, 1982.

————; Finch, Michael D., and Maruyama, Geoffrey. "Work Experience and Job Satisfaction: Variation by Age and Gender." Paper presented at the 1985 Meeting of the American Association for the Advancement of Science, Los Angeles.

————; Hall, Richard; and Hill, Reuben. "Husbands' Occupational Attributes as Constraints on Wives' Employment." *Sociology of Work and Occupations* 7 (August 1978): 285-313.

————, and Kumka, Donald. "A Further Examination of the 'Occupational Linkage Hypothesis'." *Sociological Quarterly* 23 (Winter 1982): 3-16.

————, and London, Jayne. "The Varying Linkages of Work and Family." Pp. 20-35 in *Work and Family: Changing Roles of Men and Women,* edited by Patricia Voydanoff. Palo Alto: Mayfield Publishing Company, 1984.

————, and Lorence, Jon. "Work Experience and Occupational Value Socialization: A Longitudinal Study." *American Journal of Sociology* 84 (May 1979a): 1361-85.

————, and Lorence, Jon. "Occupational Experience and the Self-Concept: A Longitudinal Study." *Social Psychology Quarterly* 42 (December 1979b): 307-23.

————, and Lorence, Jon. "Self-concept Stability and Change from Late Adolescence to Early Adulthood." Pp. 5-42 in *Research in Community and Mental Health,* Vol. 2, edited by Roberta G. Simmons, JAI Press, 1981.

————; Lorence, Jon; and Kumka, Donald S. "Work and Family Linkages in the Transition to Adulthood: A Panel Study of Highly Educated Men." *Western Sociological Review* 13 (1, 1982): 50-68.

————, and Simmons, Roberta G. "Adult Socialization." *Annual Review of Sociology* 4 (1978): 421-54.

————, and Sorensen, Glorian. "Men, Women, Work, and Family." Pp. 139-167 in *Women in the Workplace: The Effects on Families,* edited by Kathryn Borman, Daisy Quarm, and Sarah Gideonse. Norwood, NJ: Ablex Publishing Corporation, 1984.

Moss, Howard A., and Kagan, Jerome. "Report on Personality Consistency and

Change from the Fels Longitudinal Study." Pp. 21-28 in *Personality and Socialization*, edited by David R. Heise. Chicago: Rand McNally, 1972.

————, and Susman, Elizabeth J. "Longitudinal Study of Personality Development." Pp. 530-95 in *Constancy and Change in Human Development*, edited by Orville G. Brim, Jr. and Jerome Kagan. Cambridge, Mass.: Harvard University Press, 1980.

Murphy, Patrick P., and Burck, Harman. "Career Development of Men at Mid-Life." *Journal of Vocational Behavior* 9 (December 1976): 337-43.

Neugarten, Bernice L. "Personality and Aging." Pp. 626-49 in *Handbook of the Psychology of Aging*, edited by James E. Birren and K. Warner Schaie. New York: Van Nostrand, 1977.

Nichols, Robert C., and Meyer, Mary Alice. "Timing Postcard Follow-ups in Mail-Questionnaire Surveys." *Public Opinion Quarterly* 30 (Summer 1966): 306-7.

Nye, F. Ivan, and Hoffman, Lois Wladis, editors. *The Employed Mother in America*. Chicago: Rand McNally, 1963.

Oden, Melita H. "The Fulfillment of Promise: 40 Year Follow-up of the Terman Gifted Group." *Genetic Psychology Monographs* 77 (February 1968): 3-93.

Offer, Daniel, and Offer, Judith B. *From Teenage to Young Manhood*. New York: Basic Books, 1975.

Oppenheimer, Valerie K. "The Life Cycle Squeeze." *Demography* 11 (1974): 227-46.

————. "The Sociology of Women's Economic Role in the Family." *American Sociological Review* (June 1977): 386-406.

Orden, Susan R., and Bradburn, Norman M. "Dimensions of Marriage Happiness." *American Journal of Sociology* 73 (May, 1968): 715-731.

Ornstein, Michael D. *Entry into the American Labor Force*. New York: Academic, 1976.

Osgood, Charles E.; Suci, George J.; and Tannenbaum, Percy H. *The Measurement of Meaning*. Urbana: University of Illinois Press, 1957.

O'Toole, James. *Work in America*. Cambridge, Mass.: MIT Press, 1973.

Otto, Luther B. "Class and Status in Family Research." *Journal of Marriage and the Family* 37 (May 1975): 315-32.

Overton, Willis F., and Reese, Hayne W. "Models of Development: Methodological Implications." Pp. 65-86 in *Life-Span Developmental Psychology, Methodological Issues*, edited by John R. Nesselroade and Hayne W. Reese. New York: Academic, 1973.

Pace, C. Robert. "Factors Influencing Questionnaire Returns from Former University Students." *Journal of Applied Psychology* 23 (June 1939): 388-97.

Pahl, Jan M., and Pahl, Raymond E. *Managers and Their Wives*. London: Allen Lane, 1971.

Papanek, Hanna. "Men, Women, and Work: Reflections on the Two-Person Career." *American Journal of Sociology* 78 (January 1973): 852-72.

Park, Robert E.; Burgess, Ernest W.; and McKenzie, Roderick D. *The City*. Chicago: University of Chicago Press, 1925.

Parker, Stanley R., and Smith, Michael. "Work and Leisure." Pp. 37-62 in *Handbook of *Work, Organization, and Society,* edited by Robert Dubin. Chicago: Rand McNally, 1976.

Parsons, Talcott. *The Social System.* New York: Free Press, 1951.

————. "The American Family: Its Relation to Personality and the Social Structure." Pp. 3-33 in *Family, Socialization, and Interaction Process,* edited by Talcott Parsons and Robert F. Bales. New York: Free Press, 1955.

————, and Smelser, Neil J. *Economy and Society.* Glencoe: Free Press, 1956.

Patchen, Martin. *Participation, Achievement, and Involvement on the Job.* Englewood Cliffs, New Jersey: Prentice-Hall, 1970.

Pearliñ, Leonard I., and Lieberman, Morton A. "Social Sources of Emotional Distress." Pp. 217-48 in *Research in Community and Mental Health,* Vol. 1, edited by Roberta G. Simmons. Greenwich, CN: JAI Press, 1979.

————, and Schooler, Carmi. "The Structure of Coping." *Journal of Health and Social Behavior* 19 (March, 1978): 2-21.

Perrucci, Robert. "The Significance of Intra-Occupational Mobility: Some Methodological and Theoretical Notes, Together with a Case Study of Engineers." Pp. 494-502 in *Social Stratification: A Reader,* edited by Joseph Lopreato and Lionel S. Lewis. New York: Harper & Row, 1974.

Peskin, Harvey, and Livson, Norman. "Pre- and Postpubertal Personality and Adult Psychologic Functioning." *Seminars in Psychiatry* 4 (November 1972): 343-53.

Phillips, William M. "Weakness of the Mail Questionnaire." *Sociology and Social Research* 35 (April 1951): 260-67.

Piotrkowski, Chaya S. *Work and the Family System: A Naturalistic Study of Working-Class and Lower-Middle Class Families.* New York: Free Press, 1978.

Pleck, Joseph H. "The Work-Family Role System." *Social Problems* 24 (April 1977): 417-27.

————; Staines, Graham L.; and Lang, Linda. "Conflicts between Work and Family Life." *Monthly Labor Review* 103 (March 1980): 29-32.

Polacheck, Solomon W. "Discontinuous Labor Force Participation and Its Effects on Women's Market Earnings." Pp. 90-122 in *Sex, Discrimination, and the Division of Labor,* edited by Cynthia B. Lloyd. New York: Columbia University Press, 1975.

Poloma, Margaret. "Role Conflict and the Married Professional Woman." Pp. 187-98 in *Toward a Sociology of Women,* edited by Constantina Safilios-Rothschild. Lexington, Mass.: Xerox, 1972.

————, and Garland, T. Neal. "The Myth of the Egalitarian Family: Familial Roles and the Professional Employed Wife." Pp. 741-61 in *The Professional Woman,* edited by Athena Theodore. Cambridge, Mass.: Schenkman, 1971.

Powell, Douglas H., and Driscoll, Paul. "Middle Class Professionals Face Unemployment." *Society* 10 (January 1973): 18-26.

Pullum, Thomas W. *Measuring Occupational Inheritance.* New York: Elsevier Scientific Publishing Co., 1975.

Quinn, Robert, and Staines, Graham. *Quality of Employment Survey: 1977.* Ann Arbor: Inter-University Consortium for Political and Social Research, 1979.

————; Staines, Graham L.; and McCullough, Margaret R. "Job Satisfaction: Is

There a Trend?" U.S. Department of Labor Manpower Research Monograph No. 30. Washington D.C.: U.S. Government Printing Office, 1974.

Rapoport, Rhona, and Rapoport, Robert N. *Dual Career Families*. Great Britain: Chaucer Press, 1971.

————; Rapoport, Robert; and Thiessen, Victor. "Couple Symmetry and Enjoyment." *Journal of Marriage and the Family* 36 (August 1974): 588-91.

Rapoport, Robert, and Rapoport, Rhona. "The Working Woman and the Enabling Role of the Husband." Paper presented at the XIIth International Family Research Seminar. Moscow, 1972.

Renshaw, Jean. R. "An Exploration of the Overlapping Worlds of Work and Family." *Family Process* 15 (March 1976): 143-65.

Reubens, Beatrice G. *Bridges to Work. International Comparisons of Transition Services*. Montclair, N.J.: Allanheld, Osman, & Co., 1977.

Rice, David. *Dual Career Marriage: Conflict and Treatment*. New York: Free Press, 1979.

Riley, Matilda White; Foner, Anne; Hess, Beth; and Toby, Marcia L. "Socialization for Middle and Later Years." Pp. 951-82 in *Handbook of Socialization Theory and Research*, edited by D. A. Goslin. Chicago: Rand McNally, 1969.

Roberts, K. "The Entry into Employment: An Approach toward a General Theory." *Sociological Review* 16 (July 1968): 165-84.

Robin, Stanley S. "A Procedure for Securing Returns to Mail Questionnaires." *Sociology and Social Research* 50 (October 1965): 24-35.

Robinson, John P.; Athanasiou, Robert; and Head, Kendra B. *Measures of Occupational Attitudes and Occupational Characteristics*. Ann Arbor, Mich.: Survey Research Center, 1969.

Rogoff, Natalie. "Recent Trends in Urban Occupational Mobility." Pp. 442-54 in *Class, Status and Power*, edited by Reinhard Bendix and Seymour Martin Lipset. New York: Free Press, 1953.

Rosen, Bernard C. "The Achievement Syndrome: A Psychocultural Dimension of Social Stratification." *American Sociological Review* 21 (April, 1956): 203-211.

————. "Social Class and the Child's Perception of the Parent." *Child Development* 35 (December 1964): 1147-54.

————, and D'Andrade, Roy G. "The Psychosocial Origins of Achievement Motivation." *Sociometry* 22 (1959): 185-218.

Rosenberg, Morris. *Occupations and Values*. Glencoe, Ill.: Free Press, 1957.

————. *Society and the Adolescent Self-Image*. Princeton: Princeton University Press, 1965.

————. "Beyond Self-Esteem: Some Neglected Aspects of the Self-Concept." Paper presented at the American Sociological Association Meetings, 1976.

————. *Conceiving the Self*. New York: Basic Books, 1979.

————. "The Self-Concept: Social Product and Social Force." Pp. 593-624 in *Social Psychology: Sociological Perspectives*, edited by Morris Rosenberg and Ralph H. Turner. New York: Basic Books, 1981.

————, and Pearlin, Leonard I. "Social Class and Self-Esteem Among Children and Adults." *American Journal of Sociology* 84 (July 1978): 53-77.

Rotter, Julian B. "Generalized Expectancies for Internal versus External Control of Reinforcement." *Psychological Monographs* 80 (1966).

———, and Mulry, Ray C. "Internal versus External Control of Reinforcement and Decision Time." *Journal of Personality and Social Psychology* 2 (October 1965): 598-604.

Rubin, Lillian Breslow. *Worlds of Pain: Life in the Working-Class Family.* New York: Basic Books, 1976.

Safilios-Rothschild, Constantina. "Dual Linkages between the Occupational and Family Systems: A Macro-Sociological Analysis." *Signs* 1 (Spring 1976): 51-60.

Scanzoni, John. "Resolution of Occupational Conjugal Role Conflict in Clergy Marriages." *Journal of Marriage and the Family* 27 (August 1965): 396-402.

———. *Opportunity and the Family.* New York: Free Press, 1970.

———. *Sexual Bargaining.* Englewood Cliffs, N.J.: Prentice-Hall, 1972.

———. "Social Processes and Power in Families." Pp. 295-316 in *Contemporary Theories about the Family*, edited by Wesley R. Burr, Reuben Hill, F. Ivan Nye, and Ira L. Reiss. New York: Free Press, 1979.

Scheck, Dennis C.; Emerick, Robert; and El-Assal, Mohamed M. "Adolescents' Perceptions of Parent-Child Relations and the Development of Internal-External Control Orientation." *Journal of Marriage and the Family* 35 (November 1973): 643-54.

———, and Emerick, Robert. "The Young Male Adolescent's Perception of Early Child-Rearing Behavior: The Differential Effects of Socioeconomic Status and Family Size." *Sociometry* 39 (March 1976): 39-52.

Schein, Edgar H. "The Individual, the Organization, and the Career: A Conceptual Scheme." *Journal of Applied Behavioral Science* 7 (July/August 1971): 401-26.

Schooler, Carmi. "Social Antecedents of Adult Psychological Functioning." *American Journal of Sociology* 78 (September 1972): 299-322.

———. "Psychological and Social Perspectives on Status Attainment." Paper presented at the Social Science Research Council Japan-U.S. Conference on Social Stratification and Mobility, January 3-7, 1980.

———; Kohn, Melvin L.; Miller, Karen A.; and Miller, Joanne. "Housework as Work." Pp. 242-260 in *Work and Personality: An Inquiry into the Impact of Social Stratification*, by Melvin L. Kohn and Carmi Schooler with the collaboration of Joanne Miller, Karen A. Miller, Carrie Schoenbach, and Ronald Schoenberg. Norwood, NJ: Ablex Publishing Corporation, 1983.

Sears, David O. "Life-Stage Effects on Attitude Change, Especially among the Elderly." Pp. 183-204 in *Aging: Social Change*, edited by Sara B. Kiesler, James N. Morgan, and Valerie Kincade Oppenheimer. New York: Academic Press, 1981.

Sears, Robert R.; Maccoby, Eleanor E.; and Levin, Harry. *Patterns of Child Rearing.* Evanston, Ill.: Row, Peterson, 1957.

Seashore, Stanley E., and Taber, Thomas D. "Job Satisfaction Indicators and their Correlates." *American Behavioral Scientist* 18 (January/February 1975): 333-68.

Seeman, Melvin. "On the Personal Consequences of Alienation in Work." *American Sociological Review* 32 (April 1967): 273-85.

Sennett, Richard, and Cobb, Jonathan. *The Hidden Injuries of Class.* New York: Vintage Books, 1972.

Sewell, William H., and Hauser, Robert M. *Education, Occupation, and Earnings: Achievement in the Early Career.* New York: Academic Press, 1975.

————, and Hauser, Robert M. "Causes and Consequences of Higher Education: Models of the Status Attainment Process." Pp. 9-27 in *Schooling and Achievement in American Society,* edited by William H. Sewell, Robert M. Hauser, and David Featherman. New York: Academic Press, 1976.

————; Hauser, Robert M.; and Wolf, Wendy C. "Sex, Schooling, and Occupational Careers." Center for Demography and Ecology Working Paper 77-31. Madison: University of Wisconsin, October, 1977.

————; Hauser, Robert M.; and Wolf, Wendy C. "Sex, Schooling, and Occupational Status." *American Journal of Sociology* 86 (November 1980): 551-83.

Sharp, Laure. *Education and Employment: The Early Careers of College Graduates.* Baltimore: Johns Hopkins University Press, 1970.

Siegal, Alan L., and Ruh, Robert A. "Job Involvement, Participation in Decision Making, Personal Background, and Job Behavior." *Organizational Behavior and Human Performance,* 9 (April 1973): 318-27.

Siegel, Paul M. *Prestige in the American Occupational Structure.* Ph. D. Dissertation, University of Chicago, 1971.

Siegelman, Ellen; Block, Jack; Block, Jeanne; and von der Lippe, Anna. "Antecedents of Optimal Psychological Adjustment." *Journal of Consulting and Clinical Psychology* 35 (December 1970): 283-89.

Slomczynski, Kazimierz; Miller, Joanne; and Kohn, Melvin. "Stratification, Work, and Values: A Polish-United States Comparison." *American Sociological Review* 46 (December 1981): 720-44.

Smelser, Neil J. *Social Change in the Industrial Revolution.* Chicago: University of Chicago Press, 1959.

Smith, Adam. *An Inquiry into the Nature and Causes of the Wealth of Nations.* London: George Rutledge & Sons, 1913 (first published 1776).

Snyder, Mark. "On the Influence of Individuals on Situations." Pp. 309-29 in *Cognition, Social Interaction, and Personality,* edited by Nancy Cantor and John F. Kihlstrom. Hillsdale, N.J.: Erlbaum, 1981a.

————. "On the Self-Perpetuating Nature of Social Stereotypes." Pp. 183-212 in *Cognitive Processes in Stereotyping and Inter-Group Behavior,* edited by David L. Hamilton. Hillsdale, N.J.: Erlbaum, 1981b.

Sofer, Cyril. *Men in Mid-Career: A Study of British Managers and Technical Specialists.* Cambridge, England: Cambridge University Press, 1970.

Sorbom, Dag. "Detection of Correlated Errors in Longitudinal Data." *British Journal of Mathematical and Statistical Psychology* 28 (November 1975): 138-51.

Sorokin, Pitirim. *Society, Culture, and Personality.* New York: Harper, 1947.

Spaeth, Joe L. "Cognitive Complexity: A Dimension Underlying the Socioeconomic Achievement Process." Pp. 103-31 in *Schooling and Achievement in*

American Society, edited by William H. Sewell, Robert M. Hauser, and David L. Featherman. New York: Academic, 1976a.

———. "Characteristics of the Work Setting and the Job as Determinants of Income." Pp. 161-76 in *Schooling and Achievement in American Society,* edited by William H. Sewell, Robert M. Hauser, and David L. Featherman. New York: Academic, 1976b.

Spenner, Kenneth I. *From Generation to Generation: The Transmission of Occupation.* Ph.D. Dissertation. Madison: Univesity of Wisconsin, 1977.

———. "Occupational Role Characteristics and Intergenerational Transmission." *Sociology of Work and Occupations,* 8 (February 1981): 89-112.

———, and Featherman, David L. "Achievement Ambitions." *Annual Review of Sociology* 4 (1978): 373-420.

Spitze, Glenna D., and Spaeth, Joe L. "Labor Force Participation among 1961 Female College Graduates." Paper presented at the American Sociological Association Meetings, 1976.

Stone, Eugene F. "The Moderating Effect of Work-Related Values on the Job Scope-Job Satisfaction Relationship." *Organizational Behavior and Human Performance* 15 (April 1976): 147-67.

Strong, Edward K. *Vocational Interests Eighteen Years After College.* Minneapolis: University of Minnesota Press, 1955.

———. "Interests of Fathers and Sons." *Journal of Applied Psychology* 41 (October 1957): 284-92.

Strumpel, Burkhard. "Higher Education and Economic Behavior." Pp. 55-79 in *A Degree and What Else?,* edited by Stephen B. Withey. New York: McGraw-Hill, 1971.

Super, Donald E. "Career Development." Pp. 428-75 in *Psychology of the Educational Process,* edited by Joel R. Davitz and Samuel Ball. New York: McGraw-Hill, 1970.

———; Starishevsky, Reuben; Matlin, Norman; and Jordaan, Jean Pierre. *Career Development: Self-Concept Theory.* Princeton: College Entrance Examination Board, 1963.

———, and Bohn, Martin J., Jr. *Occupational Psychology.* Belmont, Calif.: Wadsworth, 1970.

Symonds, Percival M. *From Adolescent to Adult.* New York: Columbia University Press, 1961.

Tangri, Sandra S. "Effects of Background, Personality, College and Post-College Experiences on Women's Post-Graduate Employment." Final Report, Grant Number 91-34-71-02. Washington, D.C.: U.S. Department of Labor, Manpower Administration, 1974.

Taubman, Paul. *Sources of Inequality in Earnings.* Amsterdam: North-Holland, 1975.

Taylor, Mary G., and Hartley, Shirley F. "The Two-Person Career: A Classic Example." *Sociology of Work and Occupations* 2 (November 1975): 354-72.

Temme, Lloyd V. *Occupation: Meanings and Measures.* Washington, D.C.: Bureau of Social Science Research, 1975.

Thomas, Darwin L.; Gecas, Viktor; Weigert, Andrew; and Rooney, Elizabeth. *Family Socialization and the Adolescent.* Lexington, Mass.: D.C. Heath, 1974.

Tuddenham, Read D. "The Constancy of Personality Ratings over Two Decades." Pp. 395-403 in *The Course of Human Development,* edited by Mary C. Jones, Nancy Bayley, Jean W. MacFarlane, and Marjorie P. Honzik. Waltham, Mass.: Xerox, 1971.

Turner, Jonathan H. "Entrepreneurial Environments and the Emergence of Achievement Motivation in Adolescent Males." *Sociometry* 33 (June 1970): 147-65.

Turner, Ralph H. "Some Family Determinants of Ambition." *Sociology and Social Research* 46 (July 1962): 397-411.

———. "The Real Self: From Institution to Impulse." *American Journal of Sociology* 81 (March 1976): 989-1016.

Turner, R. Jay, and Noh, Samuel. "Social Support, Life Events, and Psychological Distress: A Three Wave Panel Analysis." Paper presented at the American Sociological Association Meetings, 1982.

U.S. Bureau of the Census. *Indexes to Survey Methodology Literature.* Technical Paper #34. Washington, D.C.: U.S. Government Printing Office, 1974.

U.S. Department of Labor, Bureau of Labor Statistics. *Jobseeking Methods Used by American Workers,* Bulletin 1886. Washington, D.C.: U.S. Government Printing Office, 1975a.

U.S. Department of Labor, Bureau of Labor Statistics. "U.S. Working Women: A Chartbook." Washington, D.C.: U.S. Government Printing Office, 1975b.

Vaillant, George E. "Natural History of Male Psychological Health II. Some Antecedents of Healthy Adult Adjustment." *Archives of General Psychiatry* 31 (July 1974): 15-22.

———. "Natural History of Male Psychological Health V. The Relation of Choice of Ego Mechanisms of Defense to Adult Adjustment." *Archives of General Psychiatry* 33 (April 1976): 535-45.

———. *Adaptation to Life.* Boston: Little, Brown, 1977.

———, and McArthur, Charles C. "Natural History of Male Psychologic Health, I. The Adult Life Cycle from 18-50." *Seminars in Psychiatry* 4 (November 1972): 415-27.

Van Maanen, John. "Breaking-in: Socialization to Work." Pp. 67-130 in *Handbook of Work, Organization, and Society,* edited by Robert Dubin. Chicago: Rand McNally, 1976.

———. "Experiencing Organization: Notes on the Meaning of Careers and Socialization.: Pp. 15-45 in *Organizational Careers: Some New Perspectives,* edited by John Van Maanen. New York: Wiley, 1977.

———, and Schein, Edgar H. "Toward a Theory of Organizational Socialization." Pp. 209-64 in *Research in Organizational Behavior,* 1, edited by B.M. Staw. Greenwich: JAI Press, 1979.

Veninga, Robert L., and Spradley, James P. *The Work/Stress Connection: How to Cope with Job Burnout.* Boston: Little, Brown, 1981.

Voydanoff, Patricia. *The Implications of Work-Family Relationships for Productivity. Work in America Institute Studies in Productivity.* Vol. 13. Scarsdale, N.Y.: Work in America Institute, 1980.

Wachtel, Paul L. "Psychodynamics, Behavior Therapy, and the Implacable Experimenter: An Inquiry into the Consistency of Personality." *Journal of Abnormal Psychology* 82 (October 1973): 324-34.

Walker, Charles, and Guest, Robert. *The Man on the Assembly Line.* Cambridge, Mass.: Harvard University Press, 1952.

Weidman, John C.; Phelan, William T.; and Sullivan, Mary A. "The Influence of Educational Attainment on Self-Evaluations of Competence." *Sociology of Education* 45 (Summer 1972): 303-12.

Weinstock, S. Alexander. "Role Elements: A Link between Acculturation and Occupational Status." *British Journal of Sociology* 14 (June 1963): 144-49.

Wells, L. Edward, and Marwell, Gerald. *Self-Esteem: Its Conceptualization and Measurement.* Beverly Hills: Sage, 1976.

Werts, Charles E. "Social Class and Initial Career Choice of College Freshmen." *Sociology of Education* 39 (Winter, 1966): 74-85.

————; Joreskog, Karl G.; and Linn, Robert L. "Identification and Estimation in Path Analysis with Unmeasured Variables." *American Journal of Sociology* 78 (May 1973): 1469-84.

Wheaton, Blair; Muthen, Bengt; Alwin, Duane F.; and Summers, Gene F. "Assessing Reliability and Stability in Panel Models." Pp. 84-136 in *Sociological Methodology 1977,* edited by David R. Heise. San Francisco: Jossey-Bass, 1977.

White, Robert W. *Lives in Progress: A Study in the Natural Growth of Personality.* New York: Dryden, 1952.

Whyte, William H. *The Organization Man.* New York: Doubleday Books, 1956.

Wilensky, Harold L. "Work, Careers, and Social Integration." *International Social Science Journal* 12 (Fall 1960): 543-60.

————. "Varieties of Work Experience." Pp. 125-154 in *Man in a World at Work,* edited by Henry Borow. Boston: Houghton Mifflin, 1964.

Wiley, David E., and Wiley, James A. "The Estimation of Measurement Error in Panel Data." *American Sociological Review* 35 (February 1970): 112-17.

Williams, Robin M., Jr. *American Society* (3rd Edition). New York: Alfred A. Knopf, 1970.

Winch, Robert F., and Campbell, Donald T. "Proof? No. Evidence? Yes. The Significance of Tests of Significance." *American Sociologist* 4 (May 1969): 140-43.

Winterbottom, Marian R. "The Relation of Need for Achievement to Learning Experiences in Independence and Mastery." Pp. 453-78 in *Motives in Fantasy, Action and Society,* edited by John W. Atkinson. Princeton: D. Van Nostrand, 1958.

Wylie, Ruth. *The Self-Concept* (Revised edition), Vol. 2. Lincoln: University of Nebraska Press, 1979.

Yarrow, Leon J., and Yarrow, Marion Radke. "Personality, Continuity and Change in the Family Context." Pp. 489-523 in *Personality Change,* edited by Philip Worchel and Donn Byrne. New York: John Wiley, 1964.

Young, Anne A. "Labor Market Experience of College Graduates." *Monthly Labor Review* 97 (October 1974): 33-40.

Young, Michael, and Willmott, Peter. *The Symmetrical Family.* New York: Pantheon, 1973.

Author Index

Italics indicate References entries

A

Abeles, R., 31, 97, 142, 145, 149, 150, *231, 234*
Aberle, D.F., 22, *231*
Adelson, J., 50, *236*
Adorno, T.W., 10, *231*
Agnew, R.S., 128, *231*
Aldous, J., 20, 23, 37, 43, 143, 174, 175, 177, 180, 195, *231*
Alwin, D.F., 45, 46, 96, *246, 255*
Andrews, F.M., 147, *231*
Andrisani, P.J., 50, 53, 93, 97, 98, 127, *231*
Antonovsky, A., 9, 162, *232*
Antonucci, T.C., 92, 162, 163, *242*
Arenberg, D., 5, *235*
Astin, A.W., 66, *232*
Atchison, T.J., 53, 93, *233*
Athanosopoulos, D.A., 210, *240*
Atkinson, J.W., 55, *232*

B

Bachman, J.G., 5, 45, 50, 97, 98, 108, 138, *232*
Bachrach, S.D., 209, 210, 211, *232*
Bailyn, L., 144, 147, 181, 185, *232*
Bakke, E.W., 99, *232*
Baltes, P.B., 4, 7, 8, *232*
Bandura, A., 55, *232*
Bayley, N., 5, *241*
Bealer, R.C., 199, 202, 213, *235*
Becker, G.S., 24, *239*
Becker, H.J., 48, 53, *232*
Becker, H.S., 51, 59, *232*
Bedeian, A.G., 50, *232*
Belcher, D.W., 53, 93, *233*
Bengtson, V.L., 163, *233*
Benham, L., 145, *233*
Berdie, R.F., 43, *233*
Bernard, J., 5, 175, 183, 185, *233*
Beynon, H., 51, *233*
Biller, H.B., 46, 47, *233*

B

Blackburn, R.M., 51, *233*
Blau, P.M., 38, 53, 54, 145, *233*
Blauner, R., 91, *233*
Block, J., 5, 6, 52, 64, 138, *233, 252*
Bloom, B.S., 4, 5, 96, 110, 138, *233*
Bohn, M.J., 48, 57, *253*
Bowles, S., 22, 37, 45, *233*
Bradburn, N.M., 179, *248*
Bressler, M., 210, *242*
Brim, O.G., 4, 7, 21, 95, 193, *233*
Bronfenbrenner, U., 25, 44, 114, *234*
Brooks, R.M., 209, 210, *236*
Buben, J., 5, *234*
Bugental, D.E., 92, *234*
Burck, H., 135, *248*
Burgess, E.W., *248*
Burke, R.J., 163, 185, *234*
Butler, E.W., 199, 204, 212, 213, *245*

C

Campbell, A., 148, 162, *234*
Campbell, D.T., 74, 147, *255*
Campbell, J.D., 45, *234*
Caplan, R.D., 161, *238*
Card, J.J., 31, *142, 234*
Carlson, R., 64, *234*
Carpenter, E.H., 209, 210, *236*
Carper, J., 51, *232*
Carroll, E.E., 45, *243*
Centers, R., 92, *234*
Champoux, J.E., 52, *236*
Chason, K.J., 50, 93, *241*
Christenson, J.A., 209, 210, *236*
Clark, B.R., 31, *234*
Clark, R.A., 144, *234*
Clarridge, B.R., 199, 202, 204, 205, *234*
Clausen, J.A., 8, 52, *234*
Cobb, J., 163, *252*
Cobb, S., 24, 25, 95, 142, *235, 242*
Cohen, G., *235*
Cohen, J., 156, *235*

256

Subject Index